WHITE COLLAR CRIME

IN A NUTSHELL

THIRD EDITION

By

ELLEN S. PODGOR
Professor of Law
Georgia State University College of Law

JEROLD H. ISRAEL
Ed Rood Eminent Scholar in Trial
Advocacy and Procedure,
University of Florida College of Law
Alene and Allan F. Smith Professor
of Law Emeritus,
University of Michigan Law School

THOMSON

Mat #40147042

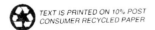

TEXT IS PRINTED ON 10% POST
CONSUMER RECYCLED PAPER

Dedicated to our parents:

Yetta & Benjamin Podgor

Florence & Harry Israel

PREFACE

White collar crime is a relatively new concept, having first achieved recognition in 1939. Despite its short life, white collar crime has quickly grown to its present status of being a major focus of the Department of Justice. This nutshell is intended to provide to students a general overview of this growing area. It is hoped that this book will assist in providing a structure to a basically unstructured body of law.

Because of the general focus of this book, it is not recommended as a source for deciding a specific legal issue. Cases were selected for this book to be illustrative, rather than comprehensive of each area being discussed. Specific crimes were selected to provide a sampling of the wide array of crimes encompassed within this enormous body of law. This book focuses on white collar crime in the federal criminal context, and does not delve into developments at the state and local level. References to one gender includes the other unless the context otherwise indicates.

The second edition added the expertise of Jerold Israel, resulting in its substantial expansion of the coverage of procedural issues that impact white collar crime. This third edition updates materials by adding new cases and statutory developments that occurred since the prior edition.

PREFACE

It is important to note that the study of white collar crime is a continuing study, with ever changing rules and precedent. Many of the issues within white collar crime, as noted throughout this book, have yet to be resolved.

Thanks go to those who assisted with the first edition, specifically Susan Rappa Bain, Sara Sun Beale, Mark E. Budnitz, Anne S. Emanuel, Marjorie L. Girth, Melissa Harrison, Marjorie Fine Knowles, Eli Lederman, Alfred R. Light, David J. Maleski, Ira Mickenberg, Patricia T. Morgan, Betty Turner, Steve Wermiel, Jack Williams, and Deborah Young. Thanks also go to those who assisted with the second edition, specifically Paul Borman, Victor Flatt, Marjorie Girth, Marjorie Fine Knowles, Eli Lederman, Patricia T. Morgan, and Myrtle Smith. Finally thanks go to those who assisted with this third edition, specifically Paul Borman, Peter Henning, Joyce Kenney, Christine Nwakamma, and Leslie Toran.

ELLEN S. PODGOR
JEROLD H. ISRAEL

March, 2004

OUTLINE

PART I - GENERAL PRINCIPLES

Chapter One - Scope of White Collar Crime ... 1

Chapter Two - Corporate Criminal Liability . 15

PART II - SPECIFIC OFFENSES

Chapter Three - Conspiracy 35

Chapter Four - Mail, Wire and Bank Fraud .. 53

PART IV - PUNISHMENT

TABLE OF CASES

References are to Pages

TABLE OF CASES

TABLE OF CASES

TABLE OF CASES

TABLE OF CASES

TABLE OF CASES

TABLE OF CASES

TABLE OF CASES

TABLE OF CASES

TABLE OF CASES

TABLE OF CASES

TABLE OF CASES

TABLE OF CASES

TABLE OF CASES

TABLE OF CASES

TABLE OF CASES

TABLE OF CASES

TABLE OF CASES

TABLE OF CASES

TABLE OF CASES

TABLE OF CASES

TABLE OF CASES

xliii

TABLE OF CASES

PART ONE
GENERAL PRINCIPLES

CHAPTER ONE
SCOPE OF WHITE COLLAR CRIME

§ 1.01 Introduction

Sociologist Edwin Sutherland is noted for having coined the phrase "White Collar Crime." The term appeared in a speech he gave to the American Sociological Society in 1939. In his speech, Sutherland openly attacked criminologists whose theories considered crime to be a result of poverty or psychopathic and sociopathic conditions. His criticism was in part based upon their failure to consider white collar criminals. Sutherland saw improper business practices of individuals in powerful positions as criminal offenses and not simply civil wrongs. He saw this as a significant issue for society's consideration.

In his book *White Collar Crime*, Sutherland defined the term white collar crime as "crime committed by a person of respectability and high social status in the course of his occupation." His definition concentrated on the offender's social status and occupation, although his focus tended to be more narrowly confined to crimes committed by large corporate enterprises.

Although white collar crime has been subject to varying definitions, a definition that focuses on the offense rather than the offender is prevalent today. In the 1983 Annual Report of the Attorney General, white collar crimes were defined as:

> ... illegal acts that use deceit and concealment—rather than the application or threat of physical force or violence—to obtain money, property, or service; to avoid the payment or loss of money; or to secure a business or professional advantage. White collar criminals occupy positions of responsibility and trust in government, industry, the professions and civic organizations.

Even when one adopts an offense approach in defining white collar crime, the scope of the term remains uncertain in that there is no list of included and excluded offenses.

Although there are no set categories of offenses that make up white collar crime, there are several federal statutes that continually appear in this context. Some of these federal offenses are not limited solely to white collar crime, but have been used to prosecute street and property crimes as well. These statutes are often used for white collar criminality due to the broad interpretation given to them by the courts. For example, many white collar offenses are prosecuted as mail fraud (18 U.S.C. § 1341), wire fraud (18 U.S.C. § 1343), conspiracy (18 U.S.C. § 371), racketeering (18 U.S.C. §§ 1961–1963), bribery (18 U.S.C. § 201), false statements (18 U.S.C. § 1001), obstruction of justice (18 U.S.C. §§ 1501–1520) and tax crimes (26 U.S.C. §§ 7201–7207). There are other statutes that are used almost exclusively for white collar offenses. For example, criminal acts involving bank fraud (18 U.S.C. § 1344) and false claims (18 U.S.C. § 287) usually fit the white collar crime category.

These lists of offenses are by no means exhaustive. White collar crime includes corporate offenses and most offenses involving public corruption. Many white collar crime prosecutions have employed statutes relating to securities fraud and antitrust violations. Encompassed by the term in recent years are criminal acts prohibited by environmental, health, and computer laws.

Although white collar crime is a relatively new concept, it has grown extensively during its short life. Key areas within white collar crime that the Department of Justice has recently focused on are financial institution fraud, defense procurement fraud, health care fraud, computer crime, international fraud, and telemarketing fraud. The Department of Justice has also continued its efforts in combating antitrust violations, public corruption, and money laundering.

§ 1.02 Scope of Federal Criminal Law

Clearly a prosecutor needs a statutory base for prosecuting white collar criminal conduct. In the realm of the federal criminal law system, this conduct can be based on a vast array of statutory offenses. In recent years there has been a growth of statutes added to the federal criminal code that specifically pertain to white collar criminal conduct.

This has been noticeable in provisions added to combat financial frauds.

It is necessary that Congress, in enacting these statutes, remain within the bounds of the Constitution. Article I, Section 8 of the United States Constitution sets forth the congressional powers, including provisions that grant Congress postal, taxing, and commerce powers.

Federal criminal law's use of Congress' postal power is best evidenced by the mail fraud statute. (18 U.S.C. § 1341). This pervasive statute has been extensively used in the realm of white collar crime.

The taxing power granted Congress serves as the jurisdictional base for many tax offenses. (26 U.S.C. §§ 7601–7607). Before 1970 it also served to criminalize many drug offenses. Drug statutes today usually employ the commerce powers.

The most widely used jurisdictional base for criminalizing federal offenses is the commerce power. The Constitution of the United States gives Congress the power "to regulate Commerce with Foreign Nations, and among the several States, and with the Indian Tribes." "Congress may regulate the use of the channels of interstate commerce," "regulate and protect the instrumentalities of interstate commerce, or persons or things in interstate commerce, even though the threat may come only from intrastate activities," and "regulate those activities having a substantial relation to interstate commerce, i.e., those activities that substantially affect interstate commerce." *United States v. Lopez* (S.Ct.1995).

Many federal statutes used in the prosecution of white collar crime employ the commerce clause as the jurisdictional basis. For example, wire fraud (18 U.S.C. § 1343) requires interstate commerce. A racketeering prosecution requires an "enterprise which is engaged in, or the activities of which affect, interstate or foreign commerce." (18 U.S.C. § 1962). Likewise, the Hobbs Act requires that the robbery or extortion affect commerce.

The conduct itself, under certain federal criminal statutes, can be purely local and yet be prosecuted as a federal offense. These local activities are part of a class of activities that Congress determines warrants congressional intervention because of their impact on commerce. In *Perez v. U.S.* the Supreme Court affirmed a conviction under the Consumer Credit Protection Act. (18 U.S.C. § 891 et seq.). The Court found that although petitioner's loan sharking may have been intrastate, he was a member of a class that engaged in "extortionate credit transactions" that affected commerce. The Court found that "loan sharking in its national setting is one way organized crime holds its guns to the heads of the poor and the rich alike and syphons funds from numerous localities to finance its national operations."

Most federal criminal statutes using the commerce clause as its jurisdictional base predicate the action on direct transportation in interstate commerce or conduct that actually affects interstate commerce. In *U.S. v. Lopez* the Supreme Court held that the Gun–Free School Zone Act, prohibiting possession of a weapon in the vicinity of a school, exceeded Congress' Commerce Clause authority in that it involved intrastate activity not involved in commerce and not economic activity.

§ 1.03 State and/or Federal Prosecution

Of the roughly 1.5 million felony prosecutions brought in the United States each year, less than 50,000 are brought in the federal system. Prosecutions against white collar crimes are, likewise, not limited to the federal system in that many state statutes focus on conduct that meets accepted definitions of white collar crime. The same white collar criminal offenses often can be prosecuted by both the federal and state systems. For example, the RICO statute uses nine state crimes as predicates for a racketeering charge. (18 U.S.C. § 1961). These predicate acts can be prosecuted as state crimes.

When criminal conduct fits the definition of both the federal and state jurisdictions a joint decision is often made as to which body will proceed with the prosecution. Factors considered in choosing the jurisdiction include the available investigative and prosecutorial resources, the jurisdiction with the law that best supports the government, the location with the maximum possible penalty and the place where the criminality best fits the policy priorities of that jurisdiction. Efficiency factors such as the jurisdiction with greater expertise and experience, the better ability to handle the case within their caseload and present location of the suspects can play a part in determining who will proceed with the action. In many instances the conduct is subject to state prosecution but has been ignored by the state prosecutor or local police for political reasons. The use of the federal system in these instances offers a neutral forum for proceeding.

Under the dual sovereignty rule, there is no restriction to both the state and federal jurisdiction prosecuting the defendant for what is basically the same conduct. Because the state and federal governments are separate entities each may determine its own offenses. *U.S. v. Lanza* (S.Ct.1922). Some states, however, by statute or case law prohibit a state prosecution following a federal trial. Additionally, some federal statutes prohibit a federal prosecution when the same act or acts previously resulted in a conviction or acquittal on the merits under state law. For example, the federal statute that criminalizes certain acts involving the interstate or foreign shipments by carrier, expressly prohibits a federal prosecution under the statute where there has been a conviction or acquittal on the merits under the laws of any state. (18 U.S.C. § 659).

Often the issue of dual prosecution is resolved by examination of the policies of the respective government prosecutors. For example, the Department of Justice has a policy against duplicative federal and state prosecutions. Known as the *Petite* policy, it "precludes the initiation or continuation of a federal prosecution, following a prior state or federal prosecution based on substantially the same act(s) or transaction(s), unless:" the matter involves a "substantial federal interest," the prior prosecution left the interest "demonstrably unvindicated," and the "defendant(s)' conduct constitutes a federal offense" with admissible evidence "sufficient to obtain and sustain a conviction." The prosecution must also "be approved by the appropriate Assistant Attorney General." Where the government fails to abide by the *Petite* policy, cases have found that there is no legal basis for overturning the defendant's conviction. *Haley v. U.S.* (W.D.Mo.1975).

Besides overlapping prosecutions within the federal and state system, white collar offenses often find themselves the subject of parallel proceedings in regulatory bodies and civil courts. Procedural questions related to collateral estoppel, staying of proceedings, effect upon fifth amendment rights, and use of grand jury materials are questions that have merited resolution in this context (see chap. 18).

§ 1.04 Federal Influence in International Prosecutions

Federal prosecutions may also be premised upon conduct occurring outside the United States. In some instances the federal statute will specifically contain a provision providing for extraterritoriality. (18 U.S.C. § 1512). Other instances require courts to ascertain whether an extraterritorial application should be permitted. *U.S. v. Bowman* (S.Ct.1922). Several courts have allowed white collar prosecutions where the conduct occurred outside the United States. For example, in *U.S. v. Nippon Paper Industries Co., Ltd.* (1st Cir. 1997), the First Circuit held that as with civil antitrust actions involving extraterritorial conduct, criminal antitrust actions could be predicated "on wholly foreign conduct which has an intended and substantial effect in the United States."

Some federal statutes are specifically focused on conduct occurring outside the United States. For example, the Foreign Corrupt Practices Act (FCPA) was implemented to combat bribery of foreign officials by United States companies (see § 7.01).

In *U.S. v. Castle* (5th Cir. 1991), the Fifth Circuit held that since "foreign officials" were excluded from prosecution under the FCPA, the United States government could not prosecute foreign officials "under 18 U.S.C. § 371, for conspiracy to violate the FCPA." The court noted the "legislative policy to leave unpunished a well-defined group of persons [foreign officials] who were necessary parties to the acts constituting a violation of the substantive law." "Most likely Congress made this choice because United States businesses were perceived to be the aggressors and the efforts expended in resolving the diplomatic, jurisdictional, and enforcement difficulties that would arise upon the prosecution of foreign officials was not worth the minimal deterrent value of such prosecutions." The court also noted that "many foreign nations already prohibited the receipt of a bribe by an official."

§ 1.05 Application of General Principles of Criminal Law

White collar crimes, like other crimes, are subject to general principles of criminal law. These principles emanate from the United States Constitution, federal and state statutes, and court interpretations. They are affected in some instances by the procedures provided by administrative regulations and rulings. Although there is no specific principle that is altered when applied in the white collar crime setting, there are certain statutory principles and criminal defenses that routinely appear and others that are seldom dominating forces. For example, one occasionally sees an entrapment defense in a white collar crime case. It is rare, however, to see an insanity defense.

General principles relative to actus reus, mens rea, and causation are placed in the perspective of the specific federal statute as it is examined within this book. Many of these statutes include attempts to commit the offense within the statutory terms. Additionally, conspiracy is discussed (18 U.S.C. § 371) as both a separate federal offense premised on a conspiracy to defraud the United States and as it relates to other statutes as a conspiracy to commit any offense against the United States. Punishment of white collar offenders, although now subject to the federal sentencing guidelines, provides unique considerations that merit separate examination.

In addition to the general adoption of criminal law principles relative to white collar offenses, it is also important to note that federal law includes general provisions regarding principals and accessories. In 18 U.S.C. § 2 a principal is defined as one who "commits an offense against the United States or aids, abets, counsels, commands, induces or procures its commission." A second provision of this same statute incorporates the agency theory that one is a principal if they willfully cause an act to be done that if performed by that person or another would be a criminal offense.

Accessories after the fact are the subject of a separate federal statute. 18 U.S.C. § 3 criminalizes and defines accessories after the fact and also provides a lesser penalty for the accessory then would be received by the principal. The application of these provisions appears to be no different in the context of white collar crimes then with other types of crime.

§ 1.06 Defenses

Defenses available to white collar defendants are,

likewise, no different from those available to the nonwhite collar defendants. Limitations to responsibility premised upon infancy, insanity, or intoxication have equal applicability in white collar crime cases as in other types of crime. Principles relating to duress and necessity remain unmodified when applied to white collar offenses. Defenses such as alibi, self defense, or defense of property, although available, seldom constitute an issue in the white collar case.

More prominent in white collar cases is the entrapment defense. Entrapment arises from individual instances of the government enticing a defendant to commit acts of criminality as well as elaborate government sting operations that attempt to net central figures and groups of individuals engaged in criminal activity.

For the last several decades, differing views have appeared in the law as to whether entrapment should be judged from an objective or subjective perspective. The objective view concentrated on the government conduct while the subjective view looked to the defendant's predisposition to commit the offense. The majority view today adopts a test that is predominantly a subjective approach. This view has been adhered to in federal courts.

"Where the Government has induced an individual to break the law and the defense of entrapment is at issue, ..., the prosecution must prove beyond reasonable doubt that the defendant was disposed to commit the criminal act prior to first being approached by Government agents." *Jacobson v. U.S.* (S.Ct.1992). Government officials may not originate a criminal design, "implant in the mind of an innocent person the disposition to commit the alleged offense and induce its commission in order that they may prosecute." *Sorrells v. U.S.* (S.Ct.1932).

Entrapment first requires a showing of government inducement. A private party, unrelated to the government, who induces the defendant does not provide a basis for invoking an entrapment defense. Where defendants were convicted of conspiracy for knowingly transporting stolen shirts in interstate commerce, an entrapment defense was properly denied where the alleged entrapment was by a shirt manufacturer who used private investigators to locate the individuals suspected of taking the shirts. The Fifth Circuit held that "entrapment does not extend to inducement by private citizens." *U.S. v. Maddox* (5th Cir.1974).

In addition to government inducement, entrapment requires a lack of predisposition by the defendant to engage in criminal conduct. Recently, in reversing a conviction for an alleged violation of the Child Protection Act (18 U.S.C. § 2252), the Supreme Court in *Jacobson v. U.S.* stated that "[w]hen the Government's quest for convictions leads to the apprehension of an otherwise law-abiding citizen who, if left to his own devices, likely would have never run afoul of the law, the courts should intervene."

There is no requirement in federal criminal law that a defendant admit all the elements of the crime in order to proceed with an entrapment defense. Where the facts support an entrapment defense, an instruction on entrapment should be submitted to the jury, despite inconsistent defenses being offered by the defendant. *Mathews v. U.S.* (S.Ct.1988).

In *Mathews*, an employee of the Small Business Administration (SBA) was convicted of accepting a gratuity in exchange for an official act. (18 U.S.C. § 201 (g)). The defendant was alleged to have accepted loans in return for cooperation in SBA matters. The district court refused defendant's request for an entrapment jury instruction finding that the instruction should not be given where the defendant failed to admit the elements of the offense. The Supreme Court reversed and remanded this case, noting the permissibility of inconsistent defenses but also finding it necessary for the lower court to consider whether there was sufficient evidence to support the giving of an entrapment instruction.

The use, although unsuccessfully, of the entrapment defense in the context of white collar crime prosecutions is seen in examining cases resulting from Operation Abscam. One such case is *U.S. v. Williams* (2d Cir.1983).

In *Williams*, Senator Harrison Williams was convicted of charges, including bribery, as part of Operation Abscam. His defense was based alternatively upon no crime being committed and entrapment. On appeal the Second Circuit rejected defendant's argument that there was insufficient evidence to support the jury's conclusion that the defendant was predisposed to commit the crime. The Senator had argued that he initially rejected the criminal conduct and that it was performed as a result of the government's persistence "in persuading [him] to commit the crimes that [he was] not ready and willing to commit." Although the court in *Williams* found strong evidence of government persuasion, it likewise found that the totality of the evidence provided a sufficient basis for the jury's finding that the defendant was " 'ready and willing' to commit the crimes charged as soon as the opportunity was first presented."

In *Williams* the defendant also argued that the "government's agents in developing the case against them exceeded an outer limit of fairness mandated by the Due Process Clause." Outrageous government conduct differs from an entrapment defense in that the focus of a claim is on the government's improper conduct as opposed to whether the defendant is predisposed to commit the offense. In examining a claim of outrageous government conduct one looks at the government conduct to decide whether there is a constitutional due process violation. In *Williams* the Second Circuit rejected this claim as it had in other Abscam cases. Despite the enormity of the inducement offered Senator Williams, the court did not consider it "unconstitutional when offered to a person with the experience and sophistication of a United States Senator."

CHAPTER TWO
CORPORATE CRIMINAL LIABILITY

§ 2.01 Overview of Corporate Criminal Liability

The initial common law view was that a corporation could not be held criminally liable, although the individual members of the corporation could. Lacking a mind, the corporation could not form the mens rea necessary for criminality. Not having physical attributes, there was no actus reus. Additionally, even if convicted of an offense, the corporation could not be imprisoned for the crime.

The development toward corporate criminal liability emerged in response to corporate violations involving acts of omission with respect to regulatory nuisance type offenses. Since these strict liability offenses did not require a mens rea, lacked an affirmative act, and had punishment in the form of fines, the acceptance of corporate criminal liability for these crimes was in keeping with accepted doctrine.

The barriers to corporate criminal liability further disintegrated by the extension of criminality to acts of misfeasance. Although still applicable only to the strict liability offenses, courts found no rationale for differentiating between acts of nonfeasance and those of misfeasance.

Eventually, corporate criminal liability expanded beyond the strict liability arena and grew to encompass crimes with an intent element. Pivotal in this development of corporate criminal liability was the Supreme Court's ruling in *New York Central & Hudson River Railroad Co. v. U.S.* (S.Ct.1909).

In *New York Central*, the railroad company and its assistant traffic manager were convicted for violations of the Elkins Act. The Elkins Act prohibited a person or corporation from granting or receiving rebates with respect to the transportation of property in interstate commerce by common carrier. The act was not limited to conduct amounting to an omission, but included affirmative acts by "any director or officer thereof, or any receiver, trustee, lessee, agent or person acting for or employed by such corporation." Defendants were accused of paying rebates to companies shipping sugar as well as to the consignees of the sugar. The corporate defendant questioned the constitutionality of subjecting a corporation to criminal prosecution, alleging a violation of the Due Process Clause. The corporation argued that punishing a corporation would in effect be punishing innocent stockholders. Since the corporation's board of directors and stockholders could not authorize an illegal act, the corporation could not be found criminally liable. The corporation also argued that the statute deprived the corporation of the due process right to a presumption of innocence.

In affirming the applicability of the Elkins Act to a corporation, the Supreme Court authorized prosecutions against corporations for certain specific intent crimes. The Court employed a tort theory of liability and applied it in this criminal context, finding that acts of an agent, done for the benefit of the principal and within the scope of the employment, are imputed to the principal. To effectuate a public policy, the Court determined it was proper, with respect to the Elkins Act, that the corporation could be "held responsible for and charged with the knowledge and purposes of their agents, acting within the authority conferred upon them."

Although *New York Central* provides a firm basis in the law for finding a corporation guilty of an offense with an intent element, there has been significant criticism of corporate criminal liability. Critics question whether there is any deterrent effect in punishing a corporation and whether the innocent shareholders and eventual consumers will, in fact, bear the ultimate cost. Despite this criticism, it is apparent that corporate criminal liability is an accepted and growing body of law.

Legislatures do not always limit corporate criminal liability to property offenses. Crimes "against the person" have been successfully prosecuted. For example, in *Granite Construction Co. v. Superior Court of Fresno County* (Cal.App.1983), a California Appellate Court permitted a corporation to be prosecuted for manslaughter. The court chose to uphold the legislative language found in the California Penal Code, which defined "person" to include corporations. The court noted that "[i]f corporations are liable for crimes of specific intent, then they should be equally liable for crimes of negligence or recklessness."

Although corporate criminal liability has been extended to a vast array of criminal offenses, some jurisdictions have refused to extend liability to corporations for acts, like manslaughter, that are against the person. The statutory language defining the crime, as relating to human beings only, has been the determining factor for rejecting corporate criminal liability. Most courts, however, interpret the term "person" to include corporations. For example, in *State v. Richard Knutson, Inc.* (Wis.Ct.App.1995), the Wisconsin Court of Appeals found that a corporation could be prosecuted for negligent homicide by vehicle in that it was "within the class of perpetrators covered by the statute."

Corporate criminal liability has recently played a significant role in the prosecution of environmental crimes (see chap.14). Corporations can also be prosecuted for workplace deaths resulting from a willful disregard of an Occupational Health and Safety Administration (OSHA) standard. The increased penalties mandated under the federal sentencing guidelines for organizations can impact the prosecution and sentencing of corporations. (see § 24.06).

In 2003, the Department of Justice issued a policy statement on corporate prosecutions. This policy statement provides U.S. Attorneys with a list of factors to be considered in deciding whether to proceed with a criminal prosecution. For example, "pervasiveness of wrongdoing," "the corporation's past history," and "cooperation and voluntary disclosure" are some of the factors to be examined in deciding whether to prosecute a corporation. The policy statement recognizes the "unique nature of the corporate 'person'" that necessitates examination of factors beyond those used in evaluating the prosecution of individuals.

§ 2.02 Standards of Imputing Corporate Criminal Liability

The criminal liability of a corporation is predicated upon acts or omissions of its agents. Two standards have developed as to when liability should be imputed to the corporation. These can best be expressed by reference to the Model Penal Code Rule and the common law doctrine of respondeat superior.

Section 2.07 of the Model Penal Code offers a somewhat restrictive approach to corporate criminal liability. Corporate liability can only be found in one of three ways: (1) for violations (minor offenses not classified as crimes that are punishable by fine only) or offenses defined by statute outside the criminal code where the legislature has clearly imposed liability on the corporation "and the conduct is performed by an agent acting in behalf of the corporation within the scope of his office or employment;" (2) where there is an omission of a specific duty of affirmative performance imposed on corporations by law; or (3) where the offense was authorized, performed, or recklessly tolerated by the board of directors or by a high managerial agent acting in behalf of the corporation within the scope of employment.

Although this code provision restricts liability to three categories, it does not limit the criminal liability exclusively to corporations. Rather, it extends its realm to unincorporated associations. An association can be liable when there is a "specific duty of affirmative performance imposed on associations by law," or the offense is defined by statute outside the criminal code and the legislature has clearly imposed liability on the association, "and the conduct is performed by an agent of the association acting in behalf of the association within the scope of his office or employment." The exception to finding liability in this circumstance, for both the corporation and unincorporated association, is where the legislature has designated an accountable agent or has specified the circumstances of accountability. In these latter instances the legislature's designation will control.

Where the Model Penal Code restricts corporate criminal liability to three categories and provides deference only to clear legislative language for liability, it also assumes the imputation of liability to the corporation where the offense is a strict liability prohibition. Absent a clear legislative intent to reject strict liability to the corporation, offenses of this nature will be assumed to apply to corporations.

The Model Penal Code addresses individual liability for the conduct of corporate agents acting on behalf of the corporation (see § 2.05). It also provides a defense to the corporation where, absent a contrary legislative purpose, there is proof "by a preponderance of the evidence that the high managerial agent having supervisory responsibility over the subject matter of the offense employed due diligence to prevent its commission."

States that have incorporated a Model Penal Code-type provision within their statutes have experienced controversies on a variety of issues. For example, in *State v. Shepherd Construction Co.* (Ga.1981), the corporate defendant was charged with a violation of a Georgia statute that prohibited conspiracies "in restraint of free and open competition in transactions with the State." The corporation argued that the statutory provision under which they were charged only provided for imprisonment. Since a corporation was incapable of being imprisoned, the defendant argued, the legislature did not intend to include corporations.

The Georgia Supreme Court, in rejecting this argument in the *Shepherd* case, noted that the state code defined "person" to include corporations and also provided courts with the power to suspend a prison sentence and impose a fine of up to ten thousand dollars. By reading the conspiracy statute in light of existing definition sections of the state code, the court determined that it was in keeping with legislative intent to prosecute corporations for violations of this statute.

A forceful dissent in *Shepherd* by Justice Smith objected to the majority's finding of a legislative intent based upon these facts. Although supportive of corporate criminal liability, this dissent stated, "the determination that corporations are to be held accountable is for the legislature."

The Model Penal Code's application of corporate criminal liability when the offense is committed, authorized, or recklessly tolerated by "a high managerial agent acting in behalf of the corporation within the scope of his office or employment," raises questions as to (1) who is a "high managerial agent," and (2) when is that individual acting in behalf of the corporation. Although "high managerial agent" is defined in the Model Penal Code, the definition is far from being a bright line determinant. The definition provides that the agent is one "having duties of such responsibility that his conduct may fairly be assumed to represent the policy of the corporation or association."

One court refused to find a corporation liable for the acts of its managers and employees where there was no finding of complicity by the officers or directors of the corporation. In order to assess liability against the corporation, it was necessary to have evidence of criminal intent. Evidence of intent is apparent when the crime results from direct authorization of the board of directors. Where, however, the criminal act is committed by an employee and no authorization or knowledge by the corporation is presented, the criminal intent element of the statute is not met. Despite the fact that the manager handled the operations of the automobile dealership, the court found that the corporation was not subject to liability in that the president had no real knowledge and control of the day-to-day business operations. The dealership in this case was owned by a corporation that was the subsidiary of another corporation which in turn was owned by the president. *State v. Chapman Dodge Center, Inc.* (La.1983).

Another court found corporate criminal liability for conduct involving a rebate scheme in an automobile dealership where the individual directly accused of having committed the criminal acts was a salesperson and fleet manager. The Minnesota Supreme Court, finding corporate criminal liability, noted that the individual "was acting in furtherance of the corporation's business interests." The corporation, and not the individual, would be receiving the benefit of the rebate. This coupled with participation by a corporate officer and acknowledgement of the problem by the president, provided sufficient

evidence to support finding the c
criminally liable. *State v. Christy Pontiac–c*
(Minn.1984).

Federal courts apply the common law ru of
respondeat superior in assessing whether it is proper
to impute the acts of an agent to the corporation. In
contrast to the Model Penal Code, which
concentrates on whether the individual who
committed the acts is a "high managerial agent," a
court employing respondeat superior would only
examine whether the agent was acting within the
scope of his or her authority and on behalf of the
corporation. The doctrine of respondeat superior
therefore does not limit corporate criminal liability to
the upper echelon of the corporation, but rather
permits liability to be found when the criminal
actions are the result of any employee acting within
the scope of employment in behalf of the corporation.

In *Commonwealth v. Beneficial Finance Co.*
(Mass.1971), the Massachusetts Supreme Court was
presented with the question of whether the Model
Penal Code or a trial court's jury instructions
correctly reflected the law in that jurisdiction. The
corporate defendants argued that acts of a "high
managerial agent" were required for imposing
criminal liability on the corporation. In contrast, the
Commonwealth argued for the trial court's standard
that stated, "[i]t isn't the name of the office that
counts, but it's the position in which the corporation
placed that person with relation to its business, with
regard to the powers and duties and responsibilities
and authority which it gave to him which counts."
The court's instructions concentrated on whether the
"acts and the intent of the individuals were the acts

and intent of the corporation."

The Massachusetts Supreme Court adopted the trial court's view that a standard similar to the rule of respondeat superior should be employed. "The Commonwealth must prove that the individual for whose conduct it seeks to charge the corporation criminally was placed in a position by the corporation where he had enough power, duty, responsibility and authority to act for and in behalf of the corporation to handle the particular business or operation or project of the corporation in which he was engaged at the time that he committed the criminal act, with power of decision as to what he would or would not do while acting for the corporation, and that he was acting for and in behalf of the corporation in the accomplishment of that particular business or operation or project, and that he committed a criminal act while so acting." This approach to corporate criminal liability seemed more appropriate to the court in light of the evidentiary deficiencies of the Model Penal Code approach.

Use of both the Model Penal Code and respondeat superior standards raise the issue as to when an agent is acting on behalf of a corporation. According to the Fifth Circuit, corporate criminal liability requires that the conduct be for the benefit of the corporation. It does not, however, mandate that the corporation actually receive a benefit. In *Standard Oil Co. of Texas v. United States* (5th Cir.1962), the Fifth Circuit reversed convictions where the statute required the conduct to be a knowing violation. Since the individuals from whom the government was imputing knowledge to the corporation were acting to further their own criminal enterprise and not the corporations, the court found it improper to hold the corporation liable. The court stated, "[u]nder a statute requiring that there be 'a specific wrongful intent,' ... the corporation does not acquire that knowledge or possess the requisite 'state of mind essential for responsibility' through the activities of unfaithful servants whose conduct was undertaken to advance the interests of parties other than their corporate employer." Other jurisdictions have ruled in accord with this Fifth Circuit view.

The issue of when an agent is acting on behalf of a corporation is further complicated when the agent acts directly against orders given by the corporation. Courts have liberally interpreted the phrase "acting on behalf of a corporation," finding liability despite the action being contrary to a corporation's instructions. Where the offense is a regulatory nuisance offense, such as a prohibition against throwing garbage from a ship into navigable waters, the corporation can be held liable despite the fact that personnel were told not to engage in these acts. *The President Coolidge (Dollar Steamship Co. v. U.S.)* (9th Cir.1939).

In *U.S. v. Hilton Hotels Corp.* (9th Cir.1972), the Ninth Circuit concluded "that as a general rule a corporation is liable under the Sherman Act for the acts of its agents in the scope of their employment, even though contrary to general corporate policy and express instructions to the agent." The *Hilton* case involved a purchasing agent who participated in a boycott by threatening a supplier with loss of the hotel's business if the supplier refused to pay a fee to an association organized to attract conventions to the city. The agent's conduct was in direct opposition to

ourt, in
ed that
s for a
nan Act
not the
ulty the
rticular
court
uld not
of the

Where corporate criminal liability was once applicable only to strict liability offenses, as noted in the *New York Central* case, it now can apply to offenses with an intent element. As a result of this extension, the issue has arisen as to what level of culpability is required for corporate liability. Where an individual agent possesses sufficient intent, the issue becomes whether that agent's knowledge can be imputed to the corporation. As noted, the resolution of this question may depend upon whether the jurisdiction applies a respondeat superior rule or adopts a model penal code approach. More difficult is where no one corporate agent possesses the necessary intent, but rather the intent is formed as a result of collective knowledge.

In *U.S. v. Bank of New England, N.A.* (1st Cir.1987) the First Circuit examined the propriety of jury instructions that permitted the imputation of knowledge to the corporation by use of collective knowledge. The Bank of New England was convicted of thirty-one violations of the Currency Transaction

Reporting Act in failing to report transactions in excess of ten thousand dollars by a customer who used multiple checks that were each under ten thousand dollars. The customer had presented these checks to a single bank teller. One of several arguments raised on appeal contested the trial court's instructions to the jury on "willfulness," which here require knowledge of the reporting requirements.

The trial court had instructed the jury that it could "look at the bank as an institution." Its knowledge, the district court stated, "is the sum of the knowledge of all of the employees." In finding these instructions proper, the First Circuit noted that a collective knowledge instruction is appropriate when applied in the context of corporate criminal liability. The court stated, "[c]orporations compartmentalize knowledge, subdividing the elements of specific duties and operations into smaller components." One department or individual may be unaware of the operations of another unit of the corporation. The court noted that "[s]ince the Bank had the compartmentalized structure common to all large corporations, the court's collective knowledge instruction was not only proper but necessary."

§ 2.04 Dead Corporations and Noncorporate Entity Liability

Dissolved corporations can be the subject of a criminal prosecution when a state provides for the continuation of the entity after dissolution. In *Melrose Distillers, Inc. v. U.S.* (S.Ct.1959), the Supreme Court permitted a criminal action against a corporation that had dissolved. The Court predicated its decision on the fact that the applicable state statutes of Maryland and Delaware continued the corporations to make them "existing" corporations for the purposes of section eight of the Sherman Act. The Court stated, "[i]n this situation there is no more reason for allowing them to escape criminal penalties than damages in civil suits." The *Melrose* case has been used by courts to extend liability to defunct corporations when the specific statute involved contains a survival clause or permits the corporation to exist for a purpose.

Cases have also applied criminal liability to corporations despite a merger. For example, a bank was found criminally liable for failing to file currency transaction reports despite its merger with another bank. The court stated that the bank could not escape punishment by merging with another bank and assuming that bank's "corporate persona." *United States v. Alamo Bank of Texas* (5th Cir.1989).

Courts have not limited entity liability exclusively to the corporate body. In *U.S. v. A & P Trucking Co.* (S.Ct.1958), the Supreme Court reversed the dismissal of informations charging a partnership with violations of Interstate Commerce Commission regulations and the Motor Carrier Act. The Court noted that the Motor Carrier Act defined "person" to include partnerships. The Interstate Commerce Commission regulation used the term "whoever," which the Court considered defined by the "Rules of Construction" definition of "person." (1 U.S.C. § 1). The Court stated that "it certainly makes no difference whether the carrier which commits the infraction is organized as a corporation, a joint stock company, a partnership, or an individual proprietorship. The mischief is the same, and we think that Congress intended to make the consequences of infraction the same." Thus, despite language of "knowingly and willfully" in the regulations, the Court held that partnerships can be prosecuted for violations of these statutes.

§ 2.05 Overview of Personal Liability of Corporate Agents

Where corporate criminal liability evolved over time, historically corporate agents have always been held personally liable for their criminal conduct. The fact that an agent may be acting on behalf of a corporation does not release the agent from being held criminally accountable.

This principle of personal liability of a corporate agent was reinforced in the Supreme Court case of *U.S. v. Wise* (S.Ct.1962), where the government contested on direct appeal a district court's dismissal of an indictment against a corporate officer for violations of the Sherman Act. The District Court's rationale was that the Sherman Act was inapplicable to corporate officers who act in their representative capacity. In reversing this lower court decision, the Supreme Court noted that the Sherman Act's inclusion of corporations in its definition of "persons" did not serve to exclude prosecutions against individuals who have a responsible share in the criminal conduct.

The Model Penal Code (§ 2.07 (6)) imposes individual liability on the corporate agent for conduct performed on behalf of the corporation "to the same extent as if it were performed in his own name or behalf." Where there is an affirmative duty to act, the agent "having primary responsibility for the discharge of the duty is legally accountable for a reckless omission to perform the required act to the same extent as if the duty were imposed by law directly upon himself."

Where the criminal conduct is performed directly by the agent of the corporation, courts have had little difficulty in imposing liability. Even when the agent is not an officer, director, or manager, liability has been found for the criminal acts committed. Liability has been extended to agents as well as independent contractors. There have been occasional instances in which it is argued that a subordinate should not be held liable for the criminal act in that the individual was acting under the orders of a superior. In *U.S. v. Gold* (11th Cir.1984), the Eleventh Circuit found "that 'following orders' can only be a defense where a defendant has no idea that his conduct is criminal." There is, however, no consistent body of law endorsing the position taken in the *Gold* case.

When the offense involves an element of criminal intent, courts generally require that the corporate agent have personally performed, had knowledge of the acts, or have had direction or control over the conduct. For example, in *Bourgeois v. Commonwealth* (Va.1976), the Virginia Supreme Court ruled that despite the fact that the individual charged with the crime was the president of the corporation, it was necessary for the state to present evidence that this individual controlled the circumstances of the illegal acts. Absent evidence of participation in the criminal conduct or knowledge imputed from the business procedures of the corporation or the personnel, the Court found that there was no basis for imputing knowledge of wrongdoing to the president.

§ 2.06 Responsible Corporate Officer

Responsible corporate officers have been held criminally liable by a statute with a "knowing" element, despite the fact that they had no actual knowledge of the criminal conduct. *U.S. v. Johnson & Towers, Inc.* (3d Cir.1984). Willful blindness to the criminal conduct can be used to support the element of knowledge. The mere fact that one is in the position of official responsibility does not, however, constitute knowledge. *U.S. v. MacDonald & Watson Waste Oil Co.* (1st Cir.1991). However, where knowledge is an element of the offense, it often can be inferred from circumstantial evidence. This evidence may include the position and responsibilities of the corporate officer. *U.S. v. Iverson* (9th Cir. 1998).

When the offense is a strict liability offense, there is no need to concentrate on the level of knowledge held by the indicted corporate agent. The offense is imputed via the "responsible corporate officer" doctrine. This doctrine originates from the Supreme Court decision in *U.S. v. Dotterweich* (S.Ct.1943).

Dotterweich, along with the Buffalo Pharmacal Company, Inc., was charged with violating the Federal Food, Drug and Cosmetic Act. As president and general manager of the corporation, he was accused of violations involving the shipping in interstate commerce of adulterated and misbranded drugs. The drugs had been purchased from the manufacturer, repacked under the Buffalo Pharmacal Company name, and shipped in interstate commerce. Only Dotterweich was convicted after a jury trial.

Justice Frankfurter, writing for the majority, found that Dotterweich was a "person" punishable for violations of the Federal Food, Drug, and Cosmetic Act. The Court recognized the offense as a strict liability crime, thus eliminating any requirement for the government to show knowledge on the part of Dotterweich. Liability, the court found, rests upon whether the individual has a "responsible share in the furtherance of the transaction." The Court declined in this opinion to define the term "responsible share," leaving the definition to "the good sense of prosecutors, the wise guidance of trial judges, and the ultimate judgment of juries."

In a dissent written by Justice Murphy, and joined by three members of the court, it was noted that guilt was being "imputed to the respondent solely on the basis of his authority and responsibility as president and general manager of the corporation." The dissent objected to this imputation of criminality, absent clear statutory authority, and found it "inconsistent with established canons of criminal law to rest liability on an act in which the accused did not participate and of which he had no personal knowledge."

The Supreme Court elaborated on the *Dotterweich* case thirty-two years later in the case of *U.S. v. Park* (S.Ct.1975). Park, the chief executive officer of a national retail food chain, was charged with violations of the Federal Food, Drug, and Cosmetic Act. His office was located in Philadelphia, Pennsylvania while the warehouse contaminated with rodents, from which there were interstate food shipments, was located in Baltimore, Maryland. Park had been advised that steps were being taken to remedy the conditions in the warehouse. In finding defendant Park criminally liable, the Supreme Court reiterated its holding in *Dotterweich.* The Court emphasized that those who have a "responsible relationship" have a duty under the Act not only "to seek out and remedy violations" but also a duty "to implement measures that will insure that violations will not occur." A defendant is afforded the defense, and has the burden of proof if offered, of showing that he or she is " 'powerless' to prevent or correct the violation." The government is only required to show "that the defendant had, by reason of his position in the corporation, responsibility and authority either to prevent in the first instance, or promptly to correct, the violation complained of, and that he failed to do so."

The Court in *Park* examined the trial court's instructions and determined that taken as a whole they properly reflected this legal standard. The instructions did not permit a finding of guilt strictly upon Park's position in the corporation. Rather, the instructions "advised the jury that to find guilt it must find respondent 'had a responsible relation to the situation,' and 'by virtue of his position ... had ... authority and responsibility' to deal with the situation."

Three members of the Court dissenting in *Park* agreed with what it termed "the language of negligence" of the majority. The dissent, however, felt that the instructions used in the case had failed to adhere to the standard set by the Court. Whether strict liability has been abandoned for a negligence standard in applying the "responsible officer" doctrine is a subject of legal debate.

Corporate executives and employees indicted for alleged acts committed in their corporate capacity have sought reimbursement from the corporation for their attorney fees and other expenses. Likewise, if the corporate executive or employee is convicted, reimbursement has been sought for fines assessed against them. Courts have resolved issues premised upon indemnification in a variety of contexts with varying results. Executives seeking indemnification have proceeded using statutory authority, corporate policy, or an implied or express agreement between the corporation and the executive. Indemnification or payment of current expenses has been sought directly from the corporation, or alternatively pursuant to a Directors and Officers Liability Insurance Policy.

Corporate directors can be civilly obligated to institute adequate corporate compliance measures against criminal activity. *In re Caremark International Inc. Derivative Litigation* (Ct. Chancery Del. 1996). The Sarbanes Oxley Act of 2002, a legislative response to corporate improprieties, modifies the criminal law by adding new crimes, new reporting requirements, and increasing criminal penalties. (see chaps 4, 5, 6, 24). The Act is aimed at promoting "greater corporate integrity."

PART TWO

SPECIFIC OFFENSES

CHAPTER THREE

CONSPIRACY

§ 3.01 Introduction

Throughout the United States Code there are specific conspiracy statutes. Some of these statutes appear within the criminal code. [i.e., conspiracy against rights of citizens (18 U.S.C. § 241)]. Other conspiracy statutes exist outside Title 18. [i.e., conspiracy in restraint of trade (15 U.S.C. § 1); conspiracy to monopolize trade (15 U.S.C. § 2)]. In some instances conspiracy provisions are incorporated within the terms of a statute. [i.e., racketeering conspiracies (18 U.S.C. § 1962 (d)); conspiracy in bribery in sporting contests (18 U.S.C. § 224)]. The one general federal conspiracy statute, 18 U.S.C. § 371, criminalizes conspiracies to commit any offense against the United States as well as conspiracies to defraud the United States or its agencies.

Judge Learned Hand referred to conspiracy as "that darling of the modern prosecutor's nursery." *Harrison v. U.S.* (2d Cir.1925). This is especially true when placed in the context of white collar crime. Although individual acts of white collar crime are abundant, an overwhelming number of white collar criminal acts are group related. In recent years conspiracy charges have sometimes resulted in megatrials that involve many defendants and lengthy trials.

Conspiracy is an inchoate crime. One of the essential aims of conspiracy is to protect against concerted criminal activity. Conspiracy is punished as a crime to attack the special dangers resulting from group activity. ("In union there is strength").

Conspiracy charges offer prosecutors several advantages. As an inchoate crime, it provides a legal basis for stopping the effects of criminality prior to it reaching full fruition. A federal conspiracy charge under 18 U.S.C. § 371 can be filed when there is an agreement and an overt act. It is unnecessary to wait until the criminal conduct is complete to proceed with conspiracy charges.

The conspiracy offense also offers prosecutors procedural advantages. For example, a charge of conspiracy permits joinder of the co-conspirators for trial. From a practical perspective this enhances the likelihood of conviction in that the evidence to the jury will not be limited to the acts of one individual. Guilt by association can be fostered when the prosecutor presents, in the same trial, evidence of criminal conduct by those associated with the defendant.

Another procedural advantage to the prosecutor in charging conspiracy is found in the broader selection offered in choosing the forum where the case will be heard. The venue of conspiracy charges is in the location where the conspiracy was formed or where any of the overt acts took place. With several defendants and possibly several overt acts, prosecutorial discretion with respect to enhanced by charging conspiracy under section ɔ ɩ ɪ.

The conspiracy statute also can have evidentiary advantages for the prosecutor. Hearsay evidence is not permitted at trial unless it meets an exception to the hearsay rule. Federal evidence rules provide as one of the exceptions to hearsay "a statement by a co-conspirator of a party during the course and in furtherance of the conspiracy." (Federal Rules of Evidence, Rule 801(d)(2)(E)). Thus, in a conspiracy trial, statements of a co-conspirator made during the conspiracy may possibly be admitted despite the fact that the statement is hearsay. Relevant evidence also may be expanded by the presence of multiple co-conspirators and possibly several overt acts. Since many conspiracies are proved through circumstantial evidence, the increase in admissible evidence can benefit the prosecutor.

Prosecutors also have an advantage should the evidence at trial be deficient on one of several objects of a conspiracy. A general verdict on a multiple object conspiracy is proper even though the evidence on one of the objects of the conspiracy may be inadequate to support a conviction. When the inadequacy relates to inadequate evidence as opposed to being a "legal error," due process does not require setting aside the verdict. *Griffin v. U.S.* (S.Ct.1991).

The main federal conspiracy statute, 18 U.S.C. § 371, requires proof of the following elements: (1) an agreement, (2) an unlawful object, (3) knowledge and intent, and (4) an overt act. The statute provides for a penalty of up to five years imprisonment and a fine. If the unlawful object of the conspiracy is a misdemeanor then the punishment is limited to the maximum punishment provided for that misdemeanor. There is no double jeopardy violation when a defendant is prosecuted for both the substantive crime and conspiracy to commit that crime under section 371. Conspiracy to commit a crime is a separate and distinct offense from the crime itself. *U.S. v. Felix* (S.Ct.1992).

§ 3.02 Agreement

At the heart of the crime of conspiracy is the agreement. The agreement does not have to be written, oral, or explicit. It can be inferred from the "facts and circumstances of the case." *Iannelli v. U.S.* (S.Ct.1975). If the minds of the parties meet and an understanding is reached to achieve a common purpose, there is an agreement. Mere knowledge, without agreement, does not meet this element of the offense.

Incumbent to forming an agreement is, however, some knowledge. The conspirators must know of the conspiracy's purpose and must knowingly participate in it. Conspirators do not have to agree to every step of the conspiracy. An overall agreement to carry out the objectives of the conspiracy suffices.

Although it is necessary to have evidence beyond a reasonable doubt that the conspirators agreed on the "essential nature of the plan," it is not necessary to prove that all conspirators had knowledge of all the plan's details or even of the participation of all others in the conspiracy. *Blumenthal v. U.S.* (S.Ct.1947). For example, a conspiracy conviction was affirmed despite the fact that the defendant convicted of conspiracy to violate the money laundering statute (18 U.S.C. § 1956) believed the money was from narcotics trafficking and the co-conspirator believed the money came from gambling. Because the conspirators agreed on the essential scheme, to launder money, the agreement element of the conspiracy was satisfied. *U.S. v. Stavroulakis* (2d Cir.1992). The agreement must be to achieve an unlawful objective. (see § 3.04).

A defense to a conspiracy charge may be premised upon a defendant's withdrawal from the conspiracy. The defendant arguing withdrawal must prove an affirmative act of withdrawal. This can be shown through action communicated to co-conspirators that disavows or defeats the purpose of the conspiracy.

§ 3.03 Plurality

Conspiracy requires two or more parties forming the agreement. This plurality requirement does not necessitate that the government charge all members of the conspiracy. It is common to see a conspiracy case proceed against one defendant with unindicted co-conspirators mentioned in the charging document.

With plurality required, the issue arises as to whether there are in fact two or more persons to the agreement when one defendant is acquitted and another is convicted. For many years case law relative to conspiracy prohibited inconsistent verdicts. Thus, if one defendant of a two person conspiracy was acquitted, then the other defendant's conviction could not stand. Further, if all but one of the defendants of a multiple party conspiracy were acquitted, then the remaining defendant would have to be acquitted. Since the essence of a conspiracy is the agreement between two or more individuals, the elimination by acquittal of all those with whom the defendant could have conspired precluded a conspiracy conviction for the remaining defendant.

The rule prohibiting inconsistent verdicts did not apply where one defendant was tried and convicted and the other defendant was not charged with the crime. It likewise did not apply to the situation where two defendants were convicted but one was acquitted. As long as an agreement could be shown, there was no inconsistency in the verdicts. Additionally, some courts refused to extend the rule prohibiting inconsistent verdicts to situations where the defendants were tried separately. These courts only allowed for the reversal of inconsistent verdicts where the verdicts resulted from the same trial.

Many courts have now departed from the rule of prohibiting inconsistent verdicts. Reference is often made to the case of *U.S. v. Powell* (S.Ct.1984) which held that inconsistency alone is not a basis for reversing a conviction. In *Powell* the Supreme Court found it acceptable to have a defendant's conviction for the crime of using the telephone to facilitate the offense when there is an acquittal of the offense itself. (The charges were conspiracy to possess cocaine and possession of cocaine). *Powell*, however, did not directly address the issue of inconsistency in conspiracy verdicts between co-conspirators.

In *U.S. v. Bucuvalas* (1st Cir.1990) the First Circuit found that jury verdicts acquitting one alleged conspirator and convicting the sole other alleged conspirator at the same trial on the same count did not require a reversal of the appellant's conviction. The court noted that justice is met in that the appellate tribunal reviews the evidence to determine its sufficiency to support the jury's decision. In applying *Powell* to inconsistent verdicts between two alleged conspirators, the court found the "rule of consistency" no longer viable. Not all courts, however, apply *Powell* to inconsistent verdicts between alleged conspirators. Some courts see the rule of consistency between co-conspirators in a conspiracy case as an exception to *Powell*.

The requirement of plurality also raises issues of whether two parties are forming an agreement when both parties are corporations or the agreement is between a corporation and its employees. Courts have found that two corporations can form a conspiracy where the indictment involves two corporations and an individual associated with each. Plurality, likewise, exists if the conspiracy involves a corporation and one of its officers with a third party. Plurality, however, has been found not to exist when a single agent acts for both corporations. *U.S. v. Santa Rita Store Co.* (N.M.1911).

Intracorporate conspiracies have been rejected when only one human actor is involved. In *U.S. v. Stevens* (11th Cir.1990), the Eleventh Circuit reversed a conspiracy conviction where the defendant, accused of conspiring with a corporation, had been convicted of conspiracy to defraud the government pursuant to 18 U.S.C. § 371. In *Stevens* the defendant was the sole stockholder of the corporation and acted as its sole agent. The court acknowledged that outside the context of antitrust violations, corporations can be criminally liable under section 371 for conspiracies involving its officers or employees. Where, however, the conspiracy involves only one human actor, as in *Stevens*, than the crime of conspiracy is improper.

The existence of plurality also can become an issue when the offense, by its very nature, requires two individuals. For example, crimes of bribery, adultery, incest or bigamy necessitate a minimum of two individuals to achieve the substantive offense. Historically, Wharton's Rule prohibited conspiracy prosecutions "when the crime is of such a nature as to necessarily require the participation of two persons for its commission."

Wharton's Rule has been significantly limited over time. If more than the minimum number of offenders participate in the offense, the rule has been found inapplicable. Further, Wharton's Rule cannot be used if the statute only criminalizes the conduct of one of the parties to the crime. The Model Penal Code does not endorse Wharton's Rule.

The Supreme Court held in *Iannelli v. U.S.* (S.Ct.1975), that in federal court, Wharton's Rule only acts "as a judicial presumption, to be applied in the absence of legislative intent to the contrary." According to this case, Wharton's Rule requires not only that the parties to the agreement be the only parties to participate in the commission of the offense, but also that "the immediate consequences of the crime rest on the parties themselves rather than on society at large." In *Iannelli*, Wharton's Rule was held not to apply to an alleged gambling conspiracy, in that the offense, a violation of 18 U.S.C. § 1955, differed from the traditional Wharton Rule offenses. Further, the court found that the harm emanating from large gambling activities was not limited to the parties but rather sought to include the participation of additional individuals who, in the case of bettors, were not a party to the conspiracy or to the substantive offens

Plurality will not be found whe
specifically protects one party to the o
a party is legislatively protected, it is improper for
the government to charge conspiracy. Clearly victims
of a crime should not be prosecuted for conspiracy for
their unwilling participation in a crime.

Plurality is seriously jeopardized when one of the
parties to the conspiracy is a government agent.
Courts have found that there is no agreement unless
there is "at least one bona fide co-conspirator." *U.S.
v. Schmidt* (9th Cir.1991). If the only person that the
defendant conspires with is a government agent,
there is no true agreement nor a meeting of the
minds. If, however, the agreement includes a
government agent coupled with other individuals,
then a conspiracy can exist.

§ 3.04 Unlawful Object of Conspiracy

18 U.S.C. § 371 can be subdivided as follows: (1)
conspiracies to commit any **offense** against the
United States, or (2) conspiracies to **defraud** the
United States or its agencies. The offense and
defraud clauses of this statute offer alternative
methods of charging under section 371.

Under the **offense** provision, the conspiracy has as
its object the violation of other civil and criminal
statutes. For example, a conspiracy to commit mail
fraud (18 U.S.C. § 1341) and conspiracy to obstruct
justice (18 U.S.C. § 1503) would be violations of 18
U.S.C. § 371.

In contrast the **defraud** provision focuses not on
specific offense activity, but rather on conduct that

defrauds the United States. A conspiracy to defraud the United States requires a showing that the accused either cheated the government out of property or money, or interfered with or obstructed a lawful government function by "deceit, craft or trickery, or at least by means that are dishonest." *Hammerschmidt v. U.S.* (S.Ct.1924). It is not incumbent that there be an actual financial or property loss where there is an obstruction or impairment of a lawful function of a department of the government. Thus, even though the charges against the defendant did not allege that the government suffered any monetary loss, the defraud clause was applicable where a release of a cotton crop report to select market speculators obstructed or impaired the lawful delivery of the information by the government. *Haas v. Henkel* (S.Ct.1910).

The scope of the scheme to defraud in section 371 is broad in that the very language of the statute states a defrauding of the United States "in any manner or for any purpose." Courts, however, are bound to scrutinize criminal conspiracy charges carefully to make certain that its wide net does not "ensnare the innocent as well as the culpable." *Dennis v. U.S.* (S.Ct.1966). Lenity is to be used in resolving ambiguities as to the scope of the defraud clause. *Tanner v. U.S.* (S.Ct.1987).

The relationship between the offense and defraud clause of section 371 has been the subject of recent controversies. One view is that although the government can prosecute a defendant under both the offense and defraud clauses of section 371, only one conviction and one punishment is possible. *U.S. v. Bilzerian* (2d Cir.1991).

In *U.S. v. Minarik* (6th Cir.1989), however, the Sixth Circuit held that the government should be limited to the offense clause of section 371, as opposed to using the defraud clause, in those instances where Congress specifically enacted a statute that covers the wrongful conduct. The court noted that to hold otherwise would allow prosecutors to circumvent a misdemeanor penalty. By charging the offense as the felony of conspiracy to defraud the United States, the government could effectively obtain a felony punishment where the specific offense is only a misdemeanor.

More recent decisions in the Sixth Circuit limit *Minarik* to the facts presented in the case. Where the alleged conduct violates more than one specific offense, fits within the defraud clause, and the indictment provides adequate notice to the defendant of the alleged charges, the court does not require that the conspiracy be charged under the offense clause rather than the defraud clause of the conspiracy statute. *U.S. v. Kraig* (6th Cir.1996).

Even though the "object of the conspiracy" may be "impossible to achieve," as when the government intercedes and defeats the conspiracy object, a conspiracy can still exist as "conspiracy law does not contain" an "'automatic termination' rule." *U.S. v. Jimenez Recio* (S.Ct. 2003).

§ 3.05 Knowledge and Intent

Conspiracy requires both knowledge and specific intent. As previously noted, the defendant must agree to the conspiracy. This requires knowledge of the conspiracy's existence, as well as knowledge of the objective of the conspiracy. It does not, however, require knowledge by the accused of all the details of the conspiracy (see § 3.02).

In addition to knowledge, the defendant must also intend to participate in the conspiracy. The degree of mens rea required for the conspiracy is dependent upon the level of intent required for the underlying specific offense. Conspiracy to commit a specific offense only exists when there is sufficient evidence of at least the degree of criminal intent required for the substantive offense. *Ingram v. U.S.* (S.Ct.1959).

Although knowledge and intent are required, in almost all instances it is not necessary that there be knowledge of a jurisdictional element. "The concept of criminal intent does not extend so far as to require that the actor understand not only the nature of his act but also its consequence for the choice of a judicial forum." *U.S. v. Feola* (S.Ct.1975). Only in the rare circumstance where the parties need to have knowledge to establish the existence of federal jurisdiction, will it be required that there be knowledge of the federal jurisdiction for the conspiracy offense. In almost all instances, knowledge by the defendant of the existence of federal jurisdiction is not required for the substantive offense, and therefore, will not be required for a conspiracy.

§ 3.06 Overt Act

Although many state jurisdictions and some specific federal conspiracy statutes find the actus reus of a conspiracy charge to be solely the agreement, section 371 requires both an agreement and an overt act in furtherance of the agreement. The overt act does not have to be a criminal act.

Further, it does not have to be performed by the individual accused of the crime of conspiracy. As long as one member of the conspiracy committed an overt act in furtherance of the conspiracy, the element is met.

The overt act must take place during the conspiracy. For purposes of the statute of limitations for a conspiracy prosecution, the time does not commence to run until the commission of the last overt act in furtherance of the conspiracy as alleged in the charging document. It is incumbent that the government prove an overt act within the statute of limitations.

§ 3.07 Single or Multiple Conspiracies

Whether the parties are properly joined in one conspiracy and whether the acts of the parties constitute a single or multiple conspiracy, are issues raised in some conspiracy cases. The substantive, procedural, and evidentiary advantages afforded a prosecutor in charging conspiracy can be further enhanced by including in one prosecution multiple defendants and multiple acts. As a result, the government often finds itself arguing that the parties formed one general conspiracy as opposed to several smaller conspiracies, and that the acts of these parties are part of a single conspiracy as opposed to multiple conspiracies.

Although it is necessary to have one overall agreement between the parties to charge conspiracy, it is not necessary to have every participant of the conspiracy know the other individuals involved or know the specific details of every aspect of the conspiracy. When there are more than two members of a conspiracy, the question arises whether in fact all are part of the same conspiracy or perhaps some are involved in one conspiracy and others involved in a different conspiracy.

This issue arose in the case of *Kotteakos v. U.S.* (S.Ct.1946) where defendants were convicted of a conspiracy to obtain loans under the National Housing Act. One individual, Brown, conspired with many of the defendants and served as the "common and key figure in all the transactions proven." In many cases, however, the defendants did not have any relationship with each other except Brown's connection with each transaction. The Supreme Court rejected this connection as sufficient for a single conspiracy.

The *Kotteakos* court analogized these facts to the hub of a wheel with its spokes. In this case Brown served as the hub of the wheel. The spokes were the individual defendants, who in this case had no relationship to each other. Except for Brown, the individual conspirators were not interested in anything but their own loan. The conspiracies were therefore separate and disconnected with no one overriding plan. Absent a single comprehensive plan, there was no single conspiracy. Rather the defendants were involved in multiple conspiracies with Brown.

The "wheel and spoke" conspiracy has been distinguished from the "chain" conspiracy. In a "chain" conspiracy, the court looks to whether the parties serve as links in a chain. In *Blumenthal v. U.S.* (S.Ct.1947), the Supreme Court found that the parties had agreed to sell liquor at prices exceeding the ceiling set by regulations of the Office of Price

Administration.   The   Cour'
agreements were steps in t'
larger general conspiracy. By ¹.
knowledge of the plan's general scoμ.
end, the disposing of the whiskey, they
drawn together in a single conspiracy.

A single agreement with multiple criminal
objectives is one conspiracy, as opposed to several
separate conspiracies. It is improper to charge several
counts of conspiracy when only one agreement is
involved. *Braverman v. U.S.* (S.Ct.1942). This is not,
however, true when there is a single agreement to
violate different conspiracy statutes. *Albernaz v. U.S.*
(S.Ct.1981).

§ 3.08 Pinkerton Rule

In *Pinkerton v. U.S.* (S.Ct.1946), the Supreme
Court held that a conspirator can be liable for the
substantive offenses of a co-conspirator that are in
furtherance of the conspiracy. Defendant Pinkerton's
convictions for violations of the Internal Revenue
Code and conspiracy were affirmed despite the fact
that there was no evidence that he had directly
participated in or had knowledge of the substantive
offenses. The evidence showed that defendant's
brother committed these substantive offenses while
the defendant was in prison. The jury, however,
found that these substantive offenses were
committed in furtherance of the conspiracy.

Pinkerton requires that to find a conspirator liable
for the substantive offense of a co-conspirator, the
substantive offense (1) must be within the scope and
in furtherance of the conspiracy, (2) be committed by
one or more members of the conspiracy, and (3) the

ndividual accused of the substantive offense must be a member of the conspiracy at the time the specific offense was committed. It is within the province of a jury to apply this rule to the facts.

In some instances *Pinkerton* is applied when the substantive crime is a primary goal of the alleged conspiracy. *U.S. v. Alvarez* (11th Cir.1985). Other cases employ the *Pinkerton* Rule where the substantive crime "facilitates the achievement of one of the primary goals" of the conspiracy.

In *Pinkerton*, the Supreme Court noted that its holding did not encompass cases where the substantive offenses were not reasonably foreseen as a necessary or natural consequence of the unlawful agreement. Some courts have used this language to find liability where the substantive offenses were not the objective of the conspiracy, but were reasonably foreseeable by the conspirators. *U.S. v. Tilton* (5th Cir.1980). Reasonably foreseeable, but originally unintended, substantive offenses may be limited to where the conspirator "played more than a 'minor' role in the conspiracy, or had actual knowledge of at least some of the circumstances and events culminating in the reasonably foreseeable but originally unintended substantive crime." *U.S. v. Alvarez* (11th Cir.1985).

§ 3.09 Antitrust Conspiracies

Section One of the Sherman Act addresses conspiracies intended to produce an unreasonable restraint of trade or commerce. It requires plurality as well as an interstate nexus. In contrast, section two of the Sherman Act can be met absent plurality in that it prohibits "every person" from monopolizing any part of trade or commerce. Issues raised in prosecutions under section one have included whether plurality exists when there is an intra-enterprise or intra-corporate conspiracy. Alleged violators of section one have also contested the level of intent necessary for the prosecution.

Historically intra-enterprise conspiracies were subject to the Sherman Act. As early as 1947, the Supreme Court rejected arguments that a Sherman Act conspiracy could not be premised upon affiliated corporations. *U.S. v. Yellow Cab Co.* (S.Ct.1947). This position was significantly altered by the United States in 1984 when the Court issued its decision in *Copperweld Corp. v. Independence Tube Corp.* (S.Ct.1984).

In *Copperweld*, the Supreme Court held that a parent corporation and its wholly owned subsidiary were incapable of conspiring with each other for purposes of section one of the Sherman Act. Officers and employees of the same company lack the necessary plurality of actors needed for a section one conspiracy. The Court found that section one did not reach conduct that was "wholly unilateral."

The Court did not, however, resolve whether this prohibition should be extended to intra-enterprise conspiracies where the parent corporation is accused of conspiring with an affiliated corporation that it does not completely own. A Louisiana court interpreting a state antitrust statute declined to adopt the *Copperweld* position, noting that it departed from the Supreme Court's own precedent and from a prevailing decision of the Louisiana Court. *Louisiana Power and Light Co. v. United Gas Pipe Line Co.* (La.1986).

Plurality does not exist when the parties are part of the same corporation. Unlike the general conspiracy provision found in section 371, section one of the Sherman Act does not permit intra-corporate conspiracies. "A corporation cannot conspire with itself any more than a private individual can, and it is the general rule that the acts of the agent are the acts of the corporation." *Nelson Radio & Supply Co. v. Motorola, Inc.* (5th Cir.1952).

When the defendant is accused of a violation of section one of the Sherman Act, and the conduct is not per se illegal, it is necessary for the government to prove intent. In *U.S. v. United States Gypsum Co.* (S.Ct.1978), the Supreme Court held that a mens rea is the rule rather than the exception in criminal law. The trial court in *Gypsum* had erred in instructing the jury that "if the effect of the exchanges of pricing information was to raise, fix, maintain, and stabilize prices, then the parties to them are presumed, *as a matter of law*, to have intended that result." The Court found that "action undertaken with knowledge of its probable consequences and having the requisite anticompetitive effects can be a sufficient predicate for a finding of criminal liability under the antitrust laws."

If the offense is a per se violation, courts have found that there is no requirement to show that the accused intended to restrain trade. Showing that the defendant knowingly engaged in conduct that violated the law suffices. *U.S. v. Cargo Service Stations, Inc.* (5th Cir.1981). Agreements to fix prices are unlawful per se under the Sherman Act. *U.S. v. Socony–Vacuum Oil Co., Inc.* (S.Ct.1940).

CHAPTER FOUR
MAIL, WIRE AND BANK FRAUD

§ 4.01 Introduction

The mail fraud statute was one of 327 sections of the 1872 recodification of the Postal Act. Its initial emphasis was on the misuse of the postal system by way of a counterfeit scheme.

In its infancy there was a disparity of interpretation of this criminal offense with some courts reading the mail fraud statute to include any scheme that misused the postal system while others endorsed a more literal reading. Congress clarified the scope of the offense by providing in 1889 a detailed mail fraud statute that listed all imaginable counterfeit schemes that the framers of the Act could envision. Included within the array of schemes outlawed by this congressional revision were schemes dealing with "green articles," "counterfeit money fraud," and "paper goods."

Durland v. U.S. (S.Ct.1896) set the tone for future mail fraud cases by interpreting this new act broadly. Mail fraud would include "everything designed to defraud by representations as to the past or present, or suggestions and promises as to the future." *Durland's* holding was followed by a 1909 congressional revision that added to the mail fraud statute the language "or for obtaining money or property by means of false or fraudulent pretenses, representations, or promises."

53

Today, the crime of mail fraud is located in section 1341 of Title 18 of the United States Code. It requires proof of four elements: (1) a scheme devised or intending to defraud or for obtaining money or property by fraudulent means, (2) intent, (3) materiality, and (4) use or causing to use the mails (or private carrier) in furtherance of the fraudulent scheme. Unlike its predecessor, the present day offense does not require that the mails be an essential aspect of the scheme to defraud. A mailing that is "incident to an essential part of the scheme" (*Pereira v. U.S.* (S.Ct.1954)) or "a step in the plot" (*Badders v. U.S.* (S.Ct.1916)) suffices.

Due to the breadth of the statute, as well as its simplicity of proof, mail fraud is extensively used by federal prosecutors. Chief Justice Burger termed mail fraud the "stopgap" provision in his dissenting opinion in *U.S. v. Maze* (S.Ct.1974), finding that the offense served the purpose of providing criminality to new frauds until particularized legislation could be passed. In reality, however, mail fraud often serves as the charged offense despite the existence of a specific statute that criminalizes the conduct.

The felony of mail fraud carries a penalty of not more than twenty years imprisonment and a fine. Where the mail fraud affects a financial institution, the allowed penalty is increased to imprisonment of not more than thirty years and a fine of up to one million dollars.

§ 4.02 Scheme to Defraud, Intent & Materiality

The scheme to defraud element of the crime of mail fraud encompasses a myriad of frauds. The ever expanding list includes credit card fraud, divorce mill fraud, franchise fraud, insurance fraud, securities fraud, medical drug fraud and fraud premised upon political malfeasance. Rarely is conduct excluded from the bounds of this element.

The scheme to defraud element is not limited by the common law definition of fraud. Conduct characterized by the deprivation of something of value by "trick, deceit, chicane, or overreaching" are encompassed within the terms of the statute. *Hammerschmidt v. U.S.* (S.Ct.1924). Mail fraud does not, however, criminalize "all sharp conduct, manipulative acts, or unethical transactions." *U.S. v. Brown* (11th Cir. 1996).

Use of extortion does not equate with conduct included within a scheme to defraud. Thus, in *Fasulo v. U.S.* (S.Ct.1926), the Supreme Court rejected the use of mail fraud for demands of money by threat and coercion through fear and force. The Court found that a scheme premised upon threats of murder and bodily harm was not a "scheme to defraud."

Implicit within the scheme to defraud element is that the defendant have a fraudulent intent. Courts have varied on the degree of fraudulent intent necessary to support a mail fraud conviction. Some require proof of a specific intent to defraud while others have been satisfied when the defendant acts recklessly or with willful blindness. Irrespective of the standard employed, courts often allow the mens rea to be inferred from the evidence.

An intent to deceive does not, however, always coincide with an intent to defraud. For example, in *U.S. v. Regent Office Supply Co.* (2d Cir.1970), the Second Circuit rejected the use of mail fraud premised upon use of false pretenses in the preliminary stages of a sales solicitation. The defendant in *Regent* stipulated that its agents used false pretenses and representations in obtaining access to customers of stationary supplies. Argued, however, was that the price and quality of the merchandise to be sold were being honestly portrayed to the customers. The Second Circuit found that false representations which are "not directed to the quality, adequacy or price of goods to be sold, or otherwise to the nature of the bargain," do not form a scheme to defraud. Although actual defrauding is not required for conviction, the government does have to show that "some actual harm or injury was contemplated by the schemer."

In *U.S. v. D'Amato* (2d Cir.1994), the Second Circuit reversed mail fraud convictions finding insufficient evidence of intent on either a "right to control theory" or a "false pretenses theory." Rejecting the government's use of "right to control theory," the court stated that "[w]here a third party acting upon instructions from a corporate agent is charged with depriving shareholders of their right to control, the government must prove that the third party knew that the concealment would involve" "(i) information available to shareholders as provided by the state of incorporation's laws providing access to corporate books and records," "(ii) information that, if withheld or inaccurate would result in rendering information that is public materially misleading," or "(iii) information that would materially aid shareholders in enforcing management's fiduciary obligations under state law." The court also rejected a "false pretenses" theory, declining the "government's invitation to infer fraudulent intent on the part of an attorney who accepts a retainer agreement and is subsequently not called upon to perform services that the government or trier of fact deems worth the fee paid."

Materiality is an essential element of the federal mail fraud, wire fraud and bank fraud statutes. In *Neder v. U.S.* (S.Ct. 1999), the Court remanded a case to determine whether it was harmless error for the trial court to fail to instruct the jury on materiality as an element of the fraud statute. In finding materiality an element of these federal fraud statutes, the Court noted that "the common law could not have conceived of 'fraud' without proof of materiality."

§ 4.03 Intangible Rights

Schemes to defraud premised upon the deprivation of intangible rights surfaced in the 1940s and developed in the 1970s and 1980s. Public officials were charged with the crime of mail fraud for depriving the citizenry of the right to good government and honest services. During this period, mail fraud was not limited to cases where a victim suffered monetary or property loss but included breaches of an owed fiduciary duty. Routinely encompassed within the words "any scheme or artifice to defraud" were political malfeasance that deprived citizens of intangible rights. In addition to political malfeasances, the charge of mail fraud was also used in instances when an employee was alleged to have deprived an employer of honest and faithful services. *U.S. v. George* (7th Cir.1973).

McNally v. U.S. (S.Ct.1987) abruptly halted the use of an intangible rights theory. The Supreme Court reversed mail fraud convictions of three defendants who were convicted for participating in a scheme to defraud the citizens and government of Kentucky of their intangible right to have the Commonwealth's affairs conducted honestly.

Defendant Hunt, then chairperson of the state democratic party had been given de facto control over selecting the insurance agencies from which the state would purchase its policies. Hunt, together with codefendants McNally and Gray, were accused of a scheme that extracted commissions from Kentucky's worker's compensation insurance business into agencies in which the defendants had an interest.

Both the government's charge and the jury's instructions in the *McNally* case did not include language of a deprivation of the Commonwealth's money or property. The essence of the action was the fiduciary duty owed by a public official to the public and the misuse of a public office for private gain.

In reversing the convictions, Justice White stated that while the mail fraud statute protected property rights, it did not encompass the intangible right of the citizenry to good government. Absent congressional clarification, allegations of a deprivation of money or property would be required to meet the scheme to defraud element of the mail fraud statute.

Justice Stevens, joined in parts by Justice O'Connor, offered a heavily footnoted dissent in the *McNally* case. He rejected the narrow construction provided by the majority in defining the term "defraud" as contradicting the construction that the federal courts had consistently given the statute, as well as the meaning provided the term in § 371, the prohibition of conspiracies to "defraud the United

States."

In 1988, Congress accepted Justice White's invitation in the *McNally* decision for congressional clarification by enacting 18 U.S.C. § 1346. This new provision, applicable to both mail and wire fraud, defines the term "scheme or artifice to defraud" to include "a scheme or artifice to deprive another of the intangible right of honest services." Courts have been faced with challenges of vagueness of section 1346. In *U.S. v. Rybicki* (2nd Cir. 2003), an en banc Second Circuit found that the intangible right of honest service "was not unconstitutional on its face." A four person dissent stated that "the statute imposes insufficient constraint on prosecutors, give insufficient guidance to judges, and affords insufficient notice to defendants."

§ 4.04 Intangible Property

Within months of the *McNally* decision, the Supreme Court accepted and decided the case of *Carpenter v. U.S.* (S.Ct.1987). While *McNally* foreclosed the use of mail fraud premised upon intangible rights (absent the congressional redefinition in § 1346), *Carpenter* opened new doors by permitting schemes to defraud based upon intangible property.

In *Carpenter*, defendant Winans, a reporter for the Wall Street Journal, authored a highly regarded column that offered information on selected stocks and takeovers. The Wall Street Journal had an official policy and practice that before publication, the contents of the "Heard on the Street" column were the confidential information of the newspaper. Defendant Winans revealed this confidential information to co-conspirators Felis and Brant, stockbrokers, who used the advance information to buy and sell stocks based upon the probable impact of the newspaper articles on the market.

Although the contents of the newspaper articles were not altered to increase the potential profits of the conspirators, Felis and Winans were convicted for mail fraud, wire fraud and securities violations. Defendant Carpenter, a roommate of Winans, was convicted for aiding and abetting.

The Supreme Court unanimously affirmed the mail fraud and wire fraud convictions. Justice White, the author of the opinion, commenced his legal analysis of the case by reaffirming the *McNally* requirement of a deprivation of money or property for upholding mail and wire fraud convictions. He noted that although mail fraud is limited in its scope to the protection of property rights, there is no requirement that these property rights be tangible. The fiduciary obligation owed by Winans to the Wall Street Journal and the breach of that duty by exploiting the confidential business information for a personal benefit, resulted in a scheme to defraud of intangible property.

Carpenter therefore serves to reinforce *McNally's* holding requiring that a charge of mail fraud include a deprivation of "money or property" as opposed to intangible rights. It also, however, extends its reach to include both tangible and intangible property.

Normally state and municipal licenses will not constitute property. In *Cleveland v. U.S.* (S.Ct. 2000), the Supreme Court held that Louisiana's video poker licenses in the hands of the licensor were not property for purposes of the mail fraud statute.

§ 4.05 Use of the Mails in Furtherance

Besides the crime of mail fraud requiring a scheme to defraud, intent, and materiality, it is also necessary that the mails be used in furtherance of the fraudulent scheme. This second element of the offense of mail fraud requires (a) a mailing, (b) by the defendant or caused to be mailed by the defendant, (c) in furtherance of a scheme to defraud.

Historically, the use of the United States Postal System was the jurisdictional object that brought the fraudulent conduct within the bounds of a federal statute. The statute, however, was amended in 1994 to include the language "or deposits or caused to be deposited any matter or thing whatever to be sent or delivered by any private or commercial interstate carrier." Items sent using Federal Express, UPS, or similar carriers may now be subject to prosecution under the mail fraud statute.

It is unnecessary, however, for the defendant to have personally sent a letter. Use of an agent can suffice. In *Pereira v. U.S.* (S.Ct.1954), the Supreme Court set forth the test to decide whether the defendant had caused the mails to be used. The Court held that "[w]here one does an act with knowledge that the use of the mails will follow in the ordinary course of business, or where such use can reasonably be foreseen, even though not actually intended, then he 'causes' the mails to be used."

In addition to a mailing by the defendant, or caused to be mailed by the defendant, it is also necessary that there be a nexus between the scheme to defraud and the mailing. This is reflected in the requirement that the mailing be "in furtherance" of the scheme to defraud. This latter subpart has been the subject of several controversies presented to courts.

§ 4.06 Limitations to "In Furtherance"

Historically, cases reflected four legal limitations to a mailing being in furtherance of a scheme to defraud. Mailings which conflicted with the scheme, were an imperative command of duty imposed by the state, occurred prior to commencement of the scheme, or occurred after fruition of the scheme, were found not to be in furtherance of the scheme to defraud.

In *U.S. v. Maze* (S.Ct.1974), the defendant's conviction for mail fraud was reversed in that the mailings were "not sufficiently closely related to the respondent's scheme to bring his conduct within the statute." The defendant was alleged to have stolen his roommate's credit card and used the card for the purchase of food and lodging in his travels to various states. The four counts of mail fraud were based upon the merchant's mailing of the sales slips of purchase to the bank issuing the credit card.

In *Maze*, the Supreme Court rejected the use of mail fraud, finding that the mailing of the credit card slips conflicted with the defendant's purpose and that the mailing occurred after fruition of the scheme to defraud. As a result of *Maze*, mailings that aid in the detection of the fraud or are counterproductive to the scheme to defraud are considered as not within the legal limits of being "in furtherance" of the scheme to defraud.

In *Parr v. U.S.* (S.Ct.1960), the Supreme Court rejected the use of mail fraud as not being in furtherance of the scheme to defraud because the mailings were an imperative duty to the state. Also alleged was that the mailings in *Parr* were after the scheme to defraud had reached fruition. The twenty count indictment for mail fraud and conspiracy to commit mail fraud in *Parr* was based upon defendant's alleged scheme to defraud a school district of money through misappropriation and embezzlement. The mailings included letters for the assessment and collection of school taxes. The Court rejected the use of mail fraud stating that mailings "under the imperative command of duty imposed by state law" are not criminal for the purposes of mail fraud "even though some of those who are so required to do the mailing for the District plan to steal."

It is rare that courts have supported the legal duty limitation to the "in furtherance" aspect of mail fraud, as enunciated in *Parr*, when there has been no showing of the mailing being dispatched after completion of the scheme to defraud. Thus, charges of mail fraud for the mailing of fraudulent tax returns are for the most part not barred by the "legal duty" limitation.

Mailings prior to commencement of the scheme or after fruition of the scheme, were recognized by courts as not in furtherance of the scheme to defraud. In *U.S. v. Beall* (N.D.Cal.1954), the Northern District of California Court found mailings of a fund raising campaign for the Infantile Paralysis Foundation to be a part of a lawful fund raising effort. A later misappropriation of the money was therefore embezzlement and not mail fraud. In that the mailing was prior to any fraud, it was not in furtherance of the scheme to defraud.

Kann v. U.S. (S.Ct.1944) showed the Supreme Court's initial adoption of an after-the-fact mailing not being in furtherance of the scheme to defraud. Defendant Kann, president of a corporation that manufactured munitions, was indicted with fellow workers for allegedly divesting company funds on government contracts for their personal benefit. The mailings that formed the basis of the charges were checks cashed by defendants that were presented to the drawee banks for purposes of collection. The nexus between the mailing and the scheme to defraud was lacking in that the scheme was completed at the time of the mailing.

Like *Kann*, the mailings in *Parr* and *Maze* were also mailings to collect on funds. In all these cases, the scheme had reached fruition and thus the mailings were immaterial to defendants' continuation of the scheme to defraud. *Kann, Parr,* and *Maze* contained forceful dissents by justices of the Supreme Court.

A recognized exception to after the fact mailings being considered "in furtherance" of the scheme is where the mailings serve to "lull" the victims into the defendant's scheme. *U.S. v. Sampson* (S.Ct.1962). In *U.S. v. Lane* (S.Ct.1986), the Supreme Court rejected respondent's claim that there was insufficient evidence to support mail fraud convictions based upon insurance claims mailed after fruition of the scheme to defraud. In referring to *Sampson*, the *Lane* Court concluded that the after-the-scheme mailings met the "in furtherance"

element in that they "were designed to l[
victims into a false sense of security."

§ 4.07 The "In Furtherance" Test

In 1989 the Supreme Court in *Schmuck v. U.S.*
(S.Ct.1989) enunciated a new test for determining
whether a mailing was in furtherance of a scheme to
defraud. The Court stated that a mailing is in
furtherance if it "is part of the execution of the
scheme as conceived by the perpetrator at the time."

In *Schmuck*, the defendant was convicted of twelve
counts of mail fraud in a scheme of selling
automobile dealers vehicles with rolled back
odometers at prices artificially inflated as a result of
the altered low-mileage. The mailings were twelve
title applications submitted by the automobile dealers
on behalf of their customers to the Wisconsin
Department of Transportation.

The Supreme Court, in addition to rejecting
defendant's argument that he was entitled to have
the jury instructed on the lesser charge of odometer
tampering, also rejected defendant's claim that the
mailings were not in furtherance of the scheme to
defraud.

Justice Blackmun, writing the opinion for the
majority noted that the use of the mails need not be
an essential element of the scheme. It is, likewise,
irrelevant if it is later shown that the mailings were
counterproductive to the scheme. Unlike *Kann, Parr,*
and *Maze*, the mailings did not resemble post-fraud
accounting. The Court found that the evidence in the
Schmuck case supported a rational finding that the
mailing was part of the execution as conceived by the

defendant at the time. The title application was essential to the successful passage of title to the customers and thus to the continuity of the scheme. A failure in the passage of title would have jeopardized the defendant's "trust and goodwill with the retail dealers upon whose unwitting cooperation" the scheme depended.

A four person dissent criticized the majority in *Schmuck* for discarding precedent and for making mail fraud into a crime of "mail" and "fraud" as opposed to mailings that are in furtherance of the fraud. Whether the decision will create "problems for tomorrow," as predicted by the dissenters, remains to be seen. Likewise uncertain, is the viability of the four limitations to in furtherance previously recognized by courts.

§ 4.08 Wire Fraud

The wire fraud statute, 18 U.S.C. § 1343, was passed in 1952 and operates parallel to mail fraud. Like mail fraud, the emphasis of the crime is on the scheme to defraud as opposed to the means used in effectuating the deception. Wire fraud does, however, require a transmittal in interstate or foreign commerce by means of wire, radio, or television communication of writings, signs, signals, pictures or sounds.

Although there is a requirement of an interstate transmission, there is no requirement that the defendant know or foresee of the transmission going interstate. In *U.S. v. Bryant* (8th Cir.1985), defendants sent two telegrams from Kansas City, Missouri to Bridgetown, Missouri. The telegrams, however, were routed through Middletown, Virginia.

The Eighth Circuit affirmed the defendants' convictions for wire fraud finding that the defendant need not know or foresee that the communication would be interstate. The necessity for an interstate transmittal is merely a jurisdictional requirement to satisfy the constitutional limitation on congressional acts over intrastate activities pursuant to the Commerce Clause of the United States Constitution.

§ 4.09 Bank Fraud

In response to the increase in financial frauds, Congress in 1984 passed the bank fraud statute (18 U.S.C. § 1344). This statute criminalizes the conduct of one who "knowingly executes, or attempts to execute, a scheme or artifice to defraud a financial institution, or to obtain ... property owned by, or under the custody or control of, a financial institution, by means of false or fraudulent pretenses, representations, or promises." Like mail fraud's provision relative to financial institutions, bank fraud today carries a penalty of up to thirty years imprisonment and a maximum fine of one million dollars.

The term "scheme to defraud" mirrors the term as seen in the mail and wire fraud statutes. In interpreting this element in the context of bank fraud, a court remarked that a scheme to defraud is incapable of precise definition. It requires case by case analysis to determine whether the scheme demonstrates a "departure from fundamental honesty, moral uprightness, or fair play and candid dealings in the general life of the community." *U.S. v. Goldblatt* (3d Cir.1987). In some cases, check kiting has been found to be a scheme to defraud that can be prosecuted as bank fraud. Courts have not, however, ruled consistently on whether the term "execute" should be interpreted to refer to the entire series of acts or whether multiple counts for each act can be charged.

Where money is legally withdrawn from a bank by victims of a confidence scheme, the bank fraud statute was held to be inapplicable. Despite the existence of a scheme to defraud, the Second Circuit found no violation of section 1344. "Where the victim is not a bank and the fraud does not threaten the financial integrity of a federally controlled or insured bank, there seems no basis in the legislative history for finding coverage under section 1344(a)(2)." *U.S. v. Blackmon* (2d Cir.1988). It is not, however, necessary that the financial institution actually suffer a loss.

§ 4.10 Mail Fraud and Other Crimes

Mail fraud is often used in place of or in conjunction with a statute that is specifically tailored to meet the prohibited conduct. It is rare that courts find it inappropriate to use mail fraud in these scenarios.

For example, in *U.S. v. Computer Sciences Corp.* (4th Cir.1982), the Fourth Circuit concluded that the district court had erred in dismissing mail and wire fraud charges being prosecuted in conjunction with a charge pursuant to the false claims statute (18 U.S.C. § 287). The court found no language in the statutes that revealed "mutual exclusivity insofar as the prosecution is concerned."

Mail fraud is used in cases where the crimes could be prosecuted under the Bankruptcy Act, Landum–Griffin Act, Jenkins Act, National Stolen Property Act, Truth in Lending Act and the Federal Trade Commission Act. Mail fraud is often an alternative to a securities violation. In *Edwards v. U.S.* (S.Ct.1941) the Supreme Court rejected the argument that securities laws preempt the use of the mail fraud statute. The Court noted that "[t]he two can exist and be useful, side by side."

A rare instance of finding the use of mail fraud as overcharging by a prosecutor is seen in the case of *U.S. v. Henderson* (S.D.N.Y.1974). This 1974 decision of the United States District Court of the Southern District of New York involved charges of attempted evasion of taxes and mail fraud for the mailing of the tax returns. The court rejected the joint charges as a "pyramiding of sentences" that was "utterly unrealistic." Use of mail fraud to reach the same conduct prohibited by the Internal Revenue Code was found to be "beyond the intent of Congress."

The *Henderson* court view has been rejected by the majority of courts deciding issues of a similar nature. The Department of Justice did, however, recently add a guideline requiring department approval prior to bringing a mail fraud prosecution that is premised upon mailed tax returns. This guideline provides that authorization for this type of prosecution will only be granted in exceptional circumstances.

Mail fraud has historically been one of several statutes used to prosecute health care fraud. Recently, Congress enacted 18 U.S.C. § 1347, a statute which specifically targets health care fraud.

The statute includes the same "scheme or artifice" language found in mail, wire, and bank fraud. It provides for imprisonment of up to ten years, imprisonment of up to twenty years if the violation results in serious bodily injury, and a term of years or life if the violation results in death.

Congress also, as part of the Sarbanes Oxley Act, added a new securities fraud crime to the criminal fraud statutes (18 U.S.C. § 1348). The Sarbanes Oxley Act is allows for the prosecution of attempts and conspiracies under these fraud statutes (18 U.S.C. § 1349).

CHAPTER FIVE

SECURITIES FRAUD

§ 5.01 Introduction

An overlap between civil and criminal law is apparent in examining cases involving securities fraud. An individual violating securities statutes can be subject to civil and administrative proceedings, criminal prosecution, or dual civil and criminal actions (see chap. 18). The Supreme Court, however, held in *Central Bank of Denver v. First Interstate Bank of Denver* (S.Ct.1994), that a private plaintiff could not use 18 U.S.C. § 2, the aiding and abetting statute, as the basis of their suit under § 10(b) of the Securities Exchange Act. To sustain a criminal prosecution it is necessary that the accused acted willfully.

Securities violations are typically investigated by the Securities and Exchange Commission (SEC). Most often criminal prosecutions arise when the SEC refers the matter to the Department of Justice for criminal prosecution. (15 U.S.C. § 78 u(d)). Selective enforcement of violations occurs both in the referring of matters to the Department of Justice and in their decision of whether to prosecute.

Although securities violations may arise under an array of federal acts, most often prosecutions under securities law emanate from the Securities Act of 1933 and the Securities Exchange Act of 1934. These acts are found in Title 15 of the United States Code.

Section 24 of the Securities Act of 1933 (15 U.S.C. § 77x) provides criminality to willful violations of provisions under the Act or rules and regulations of the Commission. It also prohibits, in a registration statement filed under the Act, the making of any untrue statement of material fact or omitting to state any material fact required to be stated or necessary so as to keep a statement from being misleading. This felony offense authorizes a fine and imprisonment up to five years.

The Securities Exchange Act of 1934, likewise, provides criminality to willful violations of the civil provisions of the Act. A willful violation of a provision of this Act, or rule or regulation thereunder, can result in criminal penalties. Additionally, false or misleading statements of material facts made willfully and knowing in "any application, report, or document required to be filed" by the Act are subject to criminal prosecution with individuals eligible to receive fines up to five million dollars and imprisonment up to twenty years. In the case of persons other than natural persons, the fine may be increased to twenty-five million dollars. The authorized term of imprisonment cannot be imposed if the defendants prove that they had no knowledge of the rule or regulation violated. The penalty provision also differs for a violation of 15 U.S.C. § 78dd–1, the statute pertaining to the prohibited foreign trade practices by issuers.

Prosecutions of securities fraud have concentrated on violations of section 17(a) of the Securities Act of 1933 and section 10(b) of the Securities Exchange Act of 1934 and its accompanying Rule 10b–5. In recent years, prosecutions under these provisions have been the subject of significant publicity with increased government investigations into insider trading. Legislative response to insider trading is seen in the passage of two congressional acts. The Insider Trading Sanctions Act (ITSA) and the Insider Trading and Securities Fraud Enforcement Act (ITSFEA) include provisions that increase the penalties to individuals engaged in improper insider trading.

Other securities sections have also served as the basis of a criminal prosecution. For example, prosecutions have been brought under section 5 of the Securities Act of 1933 for failure to register the sale of securities. Failure to file reports or the filing of false reports are among the prosecutions brought under the Securities Exchange Act of 1934.

As part of the Sarbanes Oxley Act of 2002, a new securities fraud statute exists. This statute is located in the criminal fraud statutes and carries a penalty of up to twenty-five years. (18 U.S.C. § 1348) The Sarbanes Oxley Act also added a new statute for failure of corporate officers to certify financial reports (18 U.S.C. § 1350) and a statute that allows prosecutions of attempts and conspiracies under the fraud statutes in title 18. (18 U.S.C. § 1349).

Prior to the passage of the Sarbanes Oxley Act, securities fraud was not prosecuted exclusively under specific securities statutes. The government would sometimes use general criminal provisions such as mail fraud. Other general criminal statutes that have been employed include wire fraud, false statements, perjury, obstruction of justice, interstate transportation of stolen property, and conspiracy to commit an offense against the United States or to defraud the United States. The extent that prosecutions will use the securities fraud statute found in 18 U.S.C. § 1348 as the exclusive basis for a criminal securities fraud prosecution remains to be seen.

§ 5.02 Mens Rea

Willfulness is necessary for a criminal prosecution under the Securities Act and Securities Exchange Act. This mens rea precludes prosecutions when the accused acted through mistake, excusable neglect, or inadvertence. Acts that are deliberate and intentional have been found sufficient to meet the willfulness requirement. Although willfulness does not necessitate that the defendant be aware of the applicable statute or rule, some circuits require that the prosecutor establish "a realization on the defendant's part that he was doing a wrongful act." *U.S. v. Peltz* (2d Cir.1970).

Although most courts find mere negligent conduct insufficient, reckless indifference has been found to be an intentional misrepresentation. Courts have found it proper to charge a jury "that the specific intent to deceive may be found from a material misrepresentation of fact made with reckless disregard of the facts." *U.S. v. Boyer* (3d Cir.1982).

One who acts with willful blindness can also be found culpable. When a person standing in a position of authority takes a "hands off" position, it has been found proper for the court to give a "conscious avoidance" instruction. *U.S. v. Langford* (11th Cir.1991).

Usually willfulness is proven through circumstantial evidence. A jury may infer this intent from the evidence presented. The experience and intellect of the accused, as well as the cumulative effect of all the evidence presented, have been factors used in supporting a jury determination of willfulness. *U.S. v. White* (2d Cir.1941).

In *U.S. v. Weiner* (9th Cir.1978), the Ninth Circuit upheld securities convictions entered against auditors of Equity Funding Corporation of America. Defendants argued that they were victims of the fraud perpetrated by Equity Funding officers. In finding sufficient evidence to support these convictions, the court noted the lack of backup documentation to support entries. The court found that either the auditors failed to follow accepted auditing standards or that they cooperated with Equity Funding officials. The amount of fraud involved and the lengthy time period over which it extended could lead to the conclusion that the defendants "were totally inept or, more likely, were at least partly aware of the false inflation of Equity Funding's accounts." The instruction given in *Weiner* advised the jury that good faith constituted a complete defense.

A defendant who asserts a defense premised upon good faith opens themselves to cross-examination as to the basis for their understanding that their actions were legal. In *U.S. v. Bilzerian* (2d Cir.1991), the defendant made a motion in limine requesting that he be permitted to testify at trial as to his good faith belief in the lawfulness of his conduct, without being subjected to cross-examination on communications with his attorney. The Second Circuit upheld the trial court's declining to rule on the motion in limine in the abstract, finding that the judge's ruling did not preclude the defendant from denying criminal intent and from arguing a good faith defense in opening and closing statements and through the examination of witnesses. The appellate court in *Bilzerian* noted that it lacked a specific factual basis to determine prejudice to the defendant in that he chose not to testify and thus, no privileged communications were admitted into evidence.

A person can be found culpable for willfully violating a statute, rule, or regulation of the Securities Act of 1933 and Securities Exchange Act of 1934 absent knowledge of the existence of the applicable statute, rule, or regulation. Knowledge, however, is required under the Securities Exchange Act of 1934 when the criminal charge is premised upon a false or misleading statement of any material fact in any application, report, or document required to be filed under the Act. *U.S. v. Dixon* (2d Cir.1976). Thus, the government must prove that the accused acted both willfully and knowingly when proceeding under the second clause of section 32(a) of the Securities Exchange Act of 1934.

When a defendant, convicted under the Securities Exchange Act of 1934, has no knowledge of the violated rule or regulation, the court is precluded by statute from entering a sentence of imprisonment. The defendant, however, has the burden to demonstrate a lack of knowledge. Since the no knowledge proviso is directed toward sentencing, it has been found not to place an unconstitutional burden on the defendant to disprove an element of the offense. *U.S. v. Mandel* (S.D.N.Y.1969).

A defendant, who plead guilty to a violation of Rule 10b–5, was precluded from obtaining the benefits of the no knowledge proviso in *U.S. v. Lilley* (S.D.Tex.1968). The court found that the "no knowledge" clause meant that the accused had no knowledge that their conduct was contrary to law. The court stated that it does not mean that the defendant did not know "the precise number or common name of the rule, the book and page where it was to be found, or the date upon which it was promulgated. It does not even mean proof of a lack of knowledge that their conduct was proscribed by rule rather than by statute." The court found that by pleading guilty to securities fraud, the "defendants admitted that they knew securities fraud was prohibited, which is the substance of Rule 10b–5. No more knowledge is required."

§ 5.03 Insider Trading

There is an "expectation of the securities marketplace that all investors trading on impersonal exchanges have relatively equal access to material information." *Securities and Exchange Commission v. Texas Gulf Sulphur Co.* (2d Cir.1968). Insider trading, although not specifically defined by any statute, arises when an insider, with material nonpublic information, trades in securities without first disclosing the material inside information to the public. Issues arise as who is an insider and when it is necessary to disclose nonpublic information. Issues can also arise as to whether the information is material.

Insider trading prosecutions have been at the forefront of white collar crime cases. Investment bankers, lawyers, arbitragers, and financial executives have been among the many that have been indicted and convicted for violations of securities laws. In many instances the individuals reached plea agreements that required government cooperation in further investigations. Significant publicity has surrounded many of the insider trading cases.

Insider trading cases are usually prosecuted under section 10(b) of the Securities Exchange Act of 1934 and its accompanying Rule 10b–5. The government has the burden of proving that the accused willfully employed a scheme to defraud, or misrepresented or failed to disclose a material fact, or engaged in a course of business which operated as a fraud, in connection with the purchase or sale of any security. *U.S. v. Koenig* (S.D.N.Y.1974). Federal jurisdiction is attained by showing that the accused used a means or instrumentality of interstate commerce, the mails, or any facility of any national securities exchange.

In *Chiarella v. U.S.* (S.Ct.1980), the Supreme Court reversed a criminal conviction that was predicated on a violation of Rule 10b–5. Petitioner Chiarella worked as a "markup man" for a financial printer engaged in the printing of announcements of corporate takeover bids. Although the documents delivered to the printer did not initially disclose the names of the target companies, petitioner deduced this information and purchased stock in the target companies prior to this information being disclosed to the public. Chiarella's profits from the purchase and sale of these stocks exceeded thirty thousand dollars.

Justice Powell, writing the opinion for the majority, examined the effect of silence on the part of a person holding nonpublic market information. The Court reaffirmed the position taken in the Securities and Exchange Commission case of *Cady, Roberts & Co.* (1961), which held that a corporate insider must abstain from trading in the shares of the corporation unless the corporate insider has first disclosed all known material inside information. The obligation to disclose, however, rested upon one having the affirmative "duty to disclose arising from a relationship of trust and confidence between parties to a transaction."

Distinguishing petitioner's conduct from this precedent, the Court noted that Chiarella was not a corporate insider and that he had not received confidential information from the target company. The Court found error that the trial court "[i]n effect ... instructed the jury that petitioner owed a duty to everyone; to all sellers, indeed, to the market as a whole." Not being an agent, fiduciary, or person in whom the sellers had placed their trust and confidence petitioner did not have a duty to disclose. To hold otherwise, the Court believed would create a "general duty between all participants in market transactions to forego actions based on material, nonpublic information."

The Court in *Chiarella* refused to speculate on what duty may be owed to anyone other than the seller, in that the issue had not been submitted to the jury. The dissenting opinions, however, addressed this second question finding that the jury instructions properly charged a violation of Section 10(b) and Rule 10b–5. Chief Justice Burger, in his dissenting opinion, expressed the view that Chiarella had "misappropriated—stole to put it bluntly—valuable nonpublic information entrusted to him in the utmost confidence."

The Court expounded upon the ramifications of the disclosure of information in the case of *Dirks v. Securities and Exchange Commission* (S.Ct.1983). Dirks, a securities analyst, received inside information from a former officer of Equity Funding of America. This information, of alleged overstatement of assets by the company as a result of fraudulent corporate practices, was given to Dirks for the purpose of verification and disclosure to the public. Dirks received a censure from the SEC for disclosure of this inside information to clients and investors. The SEC took the position that a tippee "inherits" the duty to disclose the information or abstain whenever the tippee receives the information from an insider. By passing the information to traders the SEC found that Dirks had breached this fiduciary duty.

In reversing the SEC position, that had been upheld by the lower courts, the Supreme Court in a 6–3 decision found that Dirks had no duty to abstain from using this information. Justice Powell, writing the majority opinion, found that "[t]he tippers received no monetary or personal benefit for revealing Equity Funding's secrets, nor was their purpose to make a gift of valuable information to Dirks." Since the motivation was the exposure of the fraud, the Court found no breach of duty to shareholders by the insider. Absent a breach of duty by the insider, there was no derivative breach by Dirks.

§ 5.04 Development of the Misappropriation Theory

In both *Chiarella* and *Dirks* the Court concentrated on the duty owed to shareholders by an insider and by individuals receiving information from the insider. Absent a duty owed, the Court was not willing to extend insider trading liability. Some appellate courts, however, permitted the bounds of insider trading to be extended through the use of a misappropriation theory.

The doctrine of misappropriation arose in Chief Justice Burger's dissenting opinion in the *Chiarella* case. He expressed the view "that a person who has misappropriated nonpublic information has an absolute duty to disclose that information or to refrain from trading." In *U.S. v. Newman* (2d Cir.1981), the Second Circuit accepted and applied this misappropriation theory. Newman was accused of participating in a scheme to misappropriate confidential information regarding upcoming tender offers. He, along with two co-conspirators, employees of two investment banking firms, were alleged to have gathered and traded on nonpublic information.

The prosecution's indictment in the *Newman* case focused on the issue unresolved in *Chiarella*, that being, duties owed to persons other than the sellers. The government's case specifically rested upon a duty allegedly owing to the defendant's employers and their employers' clients. The court in *Newman* reversed the district court's dismissal of the indictment, finding that Rule 10b–5 contained "no specific requirement that fraud be perpetrated upon the seller or buyer of securities." The court noted that in other areas of the law, deceitful

misappropriation of confidential information by a
fiduciary, was considered a crime. The court found
that this same standard should be applied to conduct
under the Securities Acts.

The tenuous status of the misappropriation theory
was highlighted by the fact that the *Newman* case
was not a unanimous decision. A concurring and
dissenting opinion, written by Senior District Judge
Dumbauld, noted that "[t]he culprits in the case at
bar (as in *Chiarella*) owed no duty to the sellers of
the target company securities which they purchased."
Despite the deceptive and improper violation of a
fiduciary duty to employers and customers of the
employers, Judge Dumbauld stated that these parties
had not at the time actually purchased or sold any
target securities.

Later decisions in the second circuit, however,
affirmed the use of the misappropriation theory in
the context of an employee misappropriating
confidential information. In *Securities and Exchange
Commission v. Materia* (2d Cir.1984), the Second
Circuit affirmed an injunction and disgorgement of
unlawfully obtained profits where an employee of a
printing company misappropriated confidential
information concerning tender offers and
subsequently traded on the information. The court
found that the misappropriation of material
nonpublic information by an employee, perpetrated
a fraud upon the employer that was prohibited by the
antifraud provisions of the Securities Exchange Act
of 1934.

In *U.S. v. Carpenter* (2d Cir.1986), the Second
Circuit revisited the misappropriation theory in the
context of convictions of a newspaper reporter,

former newspaper clerk, and stockbroker for violations of section 10(b) of the Securities Exchange Act of 1934 and Rule 10b–5. The Supreme Court accepted certiorari on this case but affirmed the securities violations by an equally divided court. Defendants' convictions for mail and wire fraud were unanimously affirmed in a landmark Supreme Court case that held that the "money or property" clause of the mail fraud statute included both tangible and intangible property (see chap. 4).

In affirming the district court's judgment of conviction on the securities fraud counts, the Second Circuit in *Carpenter* examined the misappropriation theory as applied to an insider trading scheme that misappropriated information from the Wall Street Journal prior to its publication. Although *Newman* and *Materia* involved corporate clients of the employer, the court found that the misappropriation theory "broadly proscribes the conversion by 'insiders' or *others* of material non-public information in connection with the purchase or sale of securities."

The Supreme Court directly addressed and endorsed the misappropriation theory in its decision in *U.S. v. O'Hagan* (S.Ct. 1997). Justice Ginsberg's majority opinion initially distinguishes the "classical theory" from the "misappropriation theory." "The classical theory targets a corporate insider's breach of duty to shareholders with whom the insider transacts; the misappropriation theory outlaws trading on the basis of nonpublic information by a corporate 'outsider' in breach of a duty owed not to a trading party, but to the source of the information." "In lieu of premising liability on a fiduciary relationship between company insider and purchaser or seller of the company's stock, the misappropriation theory premises liability on a fiduciary turned trader's deception of those who entrusted him with access to confidential information."

Finding "deception" through nondisclosure "central" to a misappropriation theory, the Court noted "if the fiduciary discloses to the source that he plans to trade on the nonpublic information, there is no 'deceptive device' and thus no § 10(b) violation—although the fiduciary turned trader may remain liable under state law for breach of a duty of loyalty." The Court also noted that the element "in connection with the purchase or sale of [a] security" is met "because the fiduciary's fraud is consummated, not when the fiduciary gains the confidential information, but when, without disclosure to his principal, he uses the information to purchase or sell securities." *U.S. v. O'Hagan* (S.Ct. 1997).

CHAPTER SIX

OBSTRUCTION OF JUSTICE

§ 6.01 Introduction

Most of the obstruction of justice offenses are found in chapter 73 of Title 18. Here one finds a conglomerate of specific statutes that protect proceedings in the three branches of government in addition to the individuals connected with these proceedings. There has been a growth and restructuring of these offenses in recent years to increase the protection afforded witnesses, victims, and informants as well as provide smoother federal audits and examinations of financial institutions.

The breadth of protection provided by the obstruction of justice statutes in chapter 73 is seen by examining these specific offenses. Criminalized by specific statutes are obstructive conduct involving an assault on a process server (§ 1501), resistance to an extradition agent (§ 1502), influencing a juror through a writing (§ 1504), theft or alteration of a record or process (§ 1506), picketing, parading, using sound equipment, or demonstrating in or near a courthouse or "a building or residence occupied or used by such judge, juror, witness, or court officer" (§ 1507), "[r]ecording, listening to, or observing proceedings of grand or petit juries while [they are] deliberating or voting" (§ 1508), obstruction relating to court orders (§ 1509), and obstruction pertaining to state and local law enforcement (§ 1511).

Section 1503 has historically served as the focal point of the obstruction charges. Although its original protection was for officers, jurors, and witnesses, the passage of the Victim and Witness Protection Act in 1982 transferred the specific reference to witnesses in section 1503 into new provisions of this chapter. Despite the elimination in section 1503's language of obstruction against witnesses, the section remains a noteworthy provision in that it contains an omnibus clause that prohibits obstruction of the "due administration of justice."

The Victim and Witness Protection Act also modified section 1505. This section pertains to obstruction under the Antitrust Civil Process Act and proceedings before departments, agencies, and committees of the government. This section plays a crucial role in the prosecution of obstructions related to proceedings before Congress and federal agencies. In *U.S. v. Poindexter* (D.C.Cir.1991), the District of Columbia held the term "corruptly," as used in section 1505, to be "too vague to provide constitutionally adequate notice that it prohibits lying to the Congress." The court stated that, "neither the legislative history nor the prior judicial interpretation of § 1505 supplies the constitutionally required notice that the statute on its face lacks." In 1996 Congress modified this section by including in § 1515, the definitions section of the obstruction statutes, that the term "corruptly" as used in § 1505 "means acting with an improper purpose, personally or by influencing another, including making a false or misleading statement, or withholding, concealing, altering, or destroying a document or other information." (18 U.S.C. § 1515(b)).

Originally, section 1505 criminalized obstructive conduct directed against both witnesses and parties. As a result of the Victim and Witness Protection Act, witnesses and parties are now incorporated into the new obstruction statutes. Untouched by the 1982 amendment, however, is the omnibus clause of section 1505 that protects "the due and proper administration of the law under which any pending proceeding is being had before any department or agency of the United States."

Two of the provisions created by the Victim and Witness Protection Act, sections 1512 and 1513, heighten the scrutiny provided to obstruction involving witnesses, victims, and informants. Section 1512 criminalizes conduct that uses intimidation, physical force, or threats, or conduct that involves corruptly persuading another person to withhold testimony, destroy objects of an official proceeding, evade legal process, or be absent from an official proceeding. This section includes conduct involving attempts to kill and actual killing of a person to prevent that individual from testifying, producing evidence, or communicating information about the commission of a crime or a violation of probation, parole, or release. As part of the Sarbanes Oxley Act, section 1512 was amended to include document destruction by the accused.

Section 1512 is applicable to incidents within the United States, as well as providing extraterritorial federal jurisdiction. Additionally, the government is given discretion to bring an action for violation of this section in either the district of the official proceeding, or alternatively, the location where the alleged offense occurred.

Where section 1512 concentrates on obstruction prior to a proceeding, section 1513 focuses on retaliation against witnesses, victims, and informants. Section 1513 prohibits conduct that causes or threatens to cause "bodily injury to another person" as retaliation for being a witness, providing evidence in an official proceeding, or giving information relating to an offense to a law enforcement officer. Section 1513 also applies to acts both inside and outside the United States. The Sarbanes Oxley Act of 2002 amended this section to include retaliation against whistleblowers who provide information to law enforcement.

Also added to the obstruction offenses by the Victim and Witness Protection Act of 1982 is a provision that permits a government attorney to bring a civil action to restrain harassment of a victim or witness. (§ 1514). This section provides for a temporary restraining order and issuance of protective order where "there are reasonable grounds to believe that harassment of an identified victim or witness in a Federal criminal case exists or that such an order is necessary to prevent and restrain an offense under section 1512 of this title, other than an offense consisting of misleading conduct, or under section 1513 of this title."

Another key provision for the government's prosecution of obstructive conduct is found in section 1510 of title 18. This section prohibits obstruction of criminal investigations by means of bribery. It criminalizes obstruction of criminal investigations by officers of financial institutions and obstruction by those involved in the business of insु

This recent focus on financial crim्.
reflected not only in section 1510, but also by sु
other additions to the obstruction statutes. These are
section 1516, a provision criminalizing obstruction of
a federal audit and section 1517, making it a criminal
offense to obstruct the examination of a financial
institution. The focus on health care fraud is
reflected in the addition of section 1518, a section
relating to obstruction of criminal investigations of
health care offenses.

The Sarbanes Oxley Act added section 1519 and
1520 to the obstruction statutes. Section 1519, which
carries a penalty of up to twenty years imprisonment
pertains to the "destruction alteration, or
falsification of records in Federal investigations and
bankruptcy."   Section 1520, a statute with a
maximum penalty of ten years, relates to
"destruction of corporate audit records."

Penalties for obstruction of justice vary dependent
upon the specific statutory offense employed.   For
example, the basic sentence for a violation of § 1503,
is up to ten years imprisonment, but can be increased
with imprisonment of up to twenty years in the case
of an attempted killing or where the offense is
against a petit jury and a class A or B felony has been
charged. An actual killing can result in a sentence of
death. Where the offense "occurs in connection with
a trial of a criminal case, and the act in violation of
this section involves the threat of physical force or
physical force, the maximum term of imprisonment
which may be imposed for the offense shall be the
higher of that otherwise provided by law or the
maximum term that could have been imposed for any

offense charged in such case."

§ 6.02 Overview of Section 1503

Section 1503 of Title 18 is a contempt statute emanating from the Act of March 2, 1831. Section one of the Act of 1831 pertained to contemptuous conduct occurring in the presence of the court. Section two of this act focused on conduct away from the court. This predecessor statute was eventually split into two distinct offenses with 18 U.S.C. § 401 being obstruction in the court's presence and 18 U.S.C. § 1503 being obstruction away from the court. *U.S. v. Essex* (1969).

Section 1503 originally served as the focus of obstruction offenses for obstructive acts against witnesses, parties, jurors, or court officers. The Victim and Witness Protection Act removed witnesses and parties from the language of section 1503 making the specific emphasis of the statute on acts occurring against grand and petit jurors and judicial officers. The Victim and Witness Protection Act did not, however, modify the catch-all clause of section 1503 that prohibits obstruction of the "due administration of justice." Thus, today, section 1503 can be divided into two categories; (a) acts of obstruction to jurors or court officers, and (b) obstruction of the "due administration of justice."

Acts of obstruction against jurors or court officers includes threats or force that endeavor to "influence, intimidate, or impede any grand or petit juror" or court officer in the discharge of their duties or alternatively, acts of obstruction that injure jurors or court officers. "Jurors" has been interpreted to include prospective jurors, and federal district court judges have been found to be included within the category of "officer[s] in or of any court."

The most noteworthy aspect of section 1503 still remains the omnibus clause that covers conduct impeding the "due administration of justice." In order to sustain a conviction under the omnibus clause of section 1503 the government must show that the accused (1) "corruptly or by threats or force," (2) endeavored, (3) "to influence, obstruct, or impede, the due administration of justice." These elements are not always distinct entities, but are often intertwined, with the same evidence being sufficient to meet several aspects of the offense.

§ 6.03 Corruptly or by Threats or Force—Section 1503

Section 1503 requires that the defendant engage in conduct "corruptly, or by threats or force, or by any threatening letter or communication." Courts have generally interpreted these provisions in the alternative finding it only necessary for the government to have evidence of either the accused acting "corruptly" or using some type of "threats or force."

Controversy has existed as to the level of proof required to meet the statutory requisite of "corruptly." Some courts find the term "corruptly" not to be an element of the offense that necessitates specific proof. It can be met by a showing of any attempt to influence a juror or court officer. For example in *U.S. v. Ogle* (10th Cir.1979) the Tenth Circuit agreed with the trial judge's position that "an endeavor to influence a juror in the performance of his or her duty or to influence, obstruct or impede the due administration of justice is per se unlawful and is tantamount to doing the act corruptly." The court in *Ogle* noted "that the term 'corruptly' does not superimpose a special and additional element on the offense such as a desire to undermine the moral character of a juror." Some courts admit that the term "corruptly" is capable of "different meanings in different connections," but then conclude that as used in section 1503 it includes "any endeavor to influence a witness or to impede and obstruct justice." *U.S. v. Cohen* (D.Conn.1962).

In contrast, other courts have made "corruptly" a separate element that the government must specifically prove. "The offending conduct must be prompted, at least in part, by a 'corrupt motive'.... and if there is a fair doubt as to whether the defendants' conduct is embraced within the prohibition, the policy of lenity requires that the doubt be resolved in favor of the accused." *U.S. v. Brand* (11th Cir.1985). In this context, "corruptly" can require a showing that the accused acted "for an evil or wicked purpose." *U.S. v. Ryan* (9th Cir.1971). In some instances the "evil or wicked purpose" is met by a showing that the accused acted intentionally or willfully.

In *U.S. v. Thomas* (11th Cir.1990), the Eleventh Circuit combined some of the varying approaches used in defining the element of "corruptly." The court found "corruptly" to be "the specific intent of the crime," but noted that its meaning can vary with the prosecution. The court stated that, "[g]enerally, the government must show that the defendant knowingly and intentionally undertook an action from which an obstruction of justice was a reasonably

foreseeable result.... Although the gover,
required to prove that the defendant had
purpose of obstructing justice ... it mus
that the conduct was prompted, at least in   , ~y a
'corrupt motive.' "

A wide assortment of activities have been found to
meet the definition of "corruptly." For example "the
destruction or concealment of documents can fall
within the prohibition of the statute." *U.S. v.
Rasheed* (9th Cir.1981). Although acts of bribery are
not required to meet this element of the offense,
when there is evidence of bribery, courts have found
that there is per se evidence of acting "corruptly."
Fraudulent conduct by the accused also can form the
basis of this element. As stated in *U.S. v. Polakoff* (2d
Cir.1941), "[i]t is as 'corrupt' to persuade a public
officer by lies as by bribes."

In *Cole v. U.S.* (9th Cir.1964), the Ninth Circuit
discussed the relationship between advising someone
to claim the constitutional privilege against
self-incrimination and violating section 1503.
Although exercising this constitutional right is
lawful, where one "bribes, coerces, forces or
threatens a witness to claim it, or advises with
corrupt motive the witness to take it," it can be
found to be an obstruction of justice. In affirming the
defendant's conviction in *Cole*, the court noted that
the jury had been instructed "that only *corrupt*
methods were prohibited; that *corrupt* influence was
the only influence proscribed;—that only any act
committed *corruptly* was to be considered."

The question of whether a defendant endeavored to
influence a witness "corruptly" has been held by one
court to be a "mixed question of law and fact, if not

one of fact alone." *U.S. v. Fayer* (2d Cir.1975). Another view is that whether the endeavor was "corrupt" is a question for the jury to determine. *U.S. v. Fasolino* (2d Cir.1978).

§ 6.04 Endeavors—Section 1503

For the crime of obstruction of justice, an actual obstruction is not required. It is only necessary that the accused "endeavored" to obstruct justice. "[A]n endeavor within the statute ... is very similar to a criminal solicitation statute ... and does not require proof that would support a charge of attempt." *U.S. v. Fasolino* (2d Cir.1978).

In *U.S. v. Silverman* (11th Cir.1984), the Eleventh Circuit stated that "'[e]ndeavor' ... describes any effort or assay to accomplish the evil purpose the statute was enacted to prevent.... The government is not required to prove, however, that the defendant harbored the specific purpose of obstructing the due administration of justice; all the government has to establish is that the defendant should have reasonably foreseen that the natural and probable consequence of the success of his scheme would achieve precisely that result." Thus, one does not have to succeed in the endeavor for there to be a successful prosecution for obstruction of justice.

Discussion of whether the defendant endeavored to obstruct justice has occasionally come into play when there is an issue related to the obtaining or giving of a false statement to a court officer. Reversed by the Eleventh Circuit was a conviction where the false statement was not submitted to the prosecutor and it was shown that the false statement never in fact existed. *U.S. v. Brand* (11th Cir.1985). Where, however, the false statement actually existed, the government relied upon its existence, and there was evidence that it was likely that the statement would be produced in court and justice would be obstructed, it has been found sufficient to satisfy the "endeavor" element. The fact that the false statement was never actually used in court does not bring the conduct outside the purview of the statute. *U.S. v. Fields* (11th Cir.1988).

§ 6.05 To Influence, Obstruct or Impede the Due Administration of Justice—Section 1503

To meet the element of influencing, obstructing, or impeding the due administration of justice, there must be (1) a pending proceeding, (2) that the accused knew or had notice of, and (3) that the accused intended to influence, obstruct, or impede its administration. Here again, an actual obstruction, although helpful, is not required. The "conduct must be such, however, that its natural and probable effect would be the interference with the due administration of justice." *U.S. v. Thomas* (11th Cir.1990).

Although a "pending proceeding" is required for application of the omnibus clause of section 1503, courts have liberally construed the term. The term "proceeding" is not limited to an actual court trial. Rather, conduct relating to grand jury proceedings and conduct occurring while a matter is proceeding on appeal have been found sufficient to support an obstruction of justice charge.

Some courts have interpreted "pending proceeding" to include acts occurring after at least a complaint has been filed with the magistrate or a grand jury impaneled. Thus, obstruction of FBI, IRS, or other government agency investigations would not by itself be sufficient to meet the "judicial proceeding" requirement.

Even though a grand jury has been impaneled, however, does not mean that the "pending proceeding" element has always been satisfied. Courts vary on the level of activity required by the grand jury to meet this element. Where an impaneled grand jury has issued no subpoenas, has not been apprised of the alleged criminal conduct, and there has been no showing that the defendant has knowledge of the federal grand jury proceeding, it has been found there was insufficient activity to meet the pending judicial proceeding element. In contrast, where subpoenas have been issued by the Assistant United States Attorney, even though the grand jury has no knowledge of the subpoena or criminal conduct, there was activity sufficient to form the basis of an obstruction charge. *U.S. v. Simmons* (3d Cir.1979). If the subpoena, however, is merely to furnish documents for an agency investigation, as opposed to an actual grand jury investigation, it has been found insufficient to meet the requirement of a proceeding for purposes of section 1503.

Most courts find that perjury and false statements alone do not constitute an obstruction of justice. *U.S. v. Essex* (6th Cir.1969). "To show an obstruction of justice based on false testimony, the government must establish a nexus between the false statements and the obstruction of the administration of justice." *U.S. v. Thomas* (11th Cir.1990).

Recently, in *U.S. v. Aguilar* (S.Ct.1995), the Supreme Court reexamined the "nexis" required between the act and the judicial proceeding, finding that the "act must have a relationship in time, causation, or logic with the judicial proceedings." The Court rejected use of § 1503 where the evidence was limited to "uttering false statements to an investigating agent ... who might or might not testify before a grand jury." The Court stated that, "what use will be made of false testimony given to an investigating agent who has not been subpoenaed or otherwise directed to appear before the grand jury is far more speculative." The Court in *Aguilar* found this could not "be said to have the 'natural and probable effect' of interfering with the due administration of justice."

Besides there being a pending judicial proceeding, it is incumbent that the accused have knowledge or notice of that fact. In *Pettibone v. U.S.* (S.Ct.1893), a case involving a conspiracy to obstruct the due administration of justice, the Court stated that " ... a person is not sufficiently charged with obstruction or impeding the due administration of justice in a court unless it appears that he knew or had notice that justice was being administered in such court."

Cases after *Pettibone* have held that there is no requirement that there be direct evidence of knowledge. Information or a reasonably founded belief can be sufficient. Further, knowledge can be inferred from the evidence. Although knowledge is required, the government does not have to prove that the defendant knew that it was a federal proceeding.

Knowledge or notice of the pending proceeding must be accompanied by an intent to impede its administration. *U.S. v. Guzzino* (7th Cir.1987). Although a specific intent to impede the administration of justice is an essential element of the offense, direct evidence of this intent is not required. A jury may use circumstantial evidence and may infer the intent from the evidence provided. The level of intent necessary may depend upon what definition a court gives to the term "corruptly."

§ 6.06 Section 1503 as it Relates to Other Obstruction Statutes

Along with the passage of the Victim and Witness Protection Act also came a restructuring of some of the obstruction offenses found in chapter 73. Removed from section 1503 was specific language relating to witnesses and parties. This excluded language formed the basis for the new offenses found in sections 1512 and 1513. As a result of this reorganization, courts have found it necessary to resolve controversies pertaining to the use of the omnibus clause of section 1503 when the new statutes might more specifically criminalize the conduct. In examining the existing cases that have resolved this issue, it is evident that there is a jurisdictional dichotomy. Some courts take the position that section 1503 can be charged alternatively or in conjunction with section 1512 when the conduct involves obstruction against a witness. Others take the position that the general obstruction charge of section 1503 is overridden by the specific victim and witness protection provided in section 1512. There is an added complexity to this issue as a result of an additional modification made to the statute in 1988 by Congress that added the word "corruptly" to section 1512(b).

In *U.S. v. Lester* (9th Cir.1984), the Ninth Circuit examined the propriety of the government charging a violation of both section 1503 and 1512. The defendant questioned the use of section 1503 for witness tampering in light of the enactment of the Victim and Witness Protection Act. The government contended that despite the passage of a new statute, section 1503's omnibus clause remained intact for conduct that "endeavors to influence, obstruct, or impede, the due administration of justice."

In accepting the government's position, the *Lester* court dissected section 1503 into two parts; the part originally established to protect witnesses and the latter portion used to prevent a miscarriage of justice by corrupt methods. Reading the omnibus clause as a separate aspect to this statute, the court determined "that Congress enacted section 1512 to prohibit specific conduct comprising various forms of coercion of witnesses, leaving the omnibus provision of section 1503 to handle more imaginative forms of criminal behavior, including forms of witness tampering, that defy enumeration."

The *Lester* court mentioned in the decision that it believed this position was in harmony with the view expounded by the Second Circuit in *U.S. v. Hernandez* (2d Cir.1984). The *Hernandez* case, however, had held that it was improper to use section 1503 with section 1512 conduct in that "congress affirmatively intended to remove witnesses entirely from the scope of section 1503." The *Hernandez* decision also stated that "by enacting [the Act] in 1982, Congress intended that *intimidation and harassment* of witnesses should thenceforth be prosecuted under § 1512 and no longer under §

1503." Using this latter sentence from *Hernandez*, the *Lester* court reconciled its position by finding that section 1503 was still operative with respect to witnesses when the conduct was outside the realm of "intimidation and harassment of witness." Since *Lester* involved conduct that was not on its face an intimidation or harassment of witnesses, but was directed toward the administration of justice, it was proper to use the omnibus clause of section 1503.

Initially the weight of authority appeared to express the view taken by *Lester*, allowing prosecutions under section 1503 when the conduct involved witness tampering. Left for the minority was the more restrictive approach expressed by the Second Circuit in *Hernandez*. In 1985 the Supreme Court denied certiorari in a case that could have resolved this jurisdictional dichotomy. Three justices dissenting on the denial of the petition for writ of certiorari remarked how two large circuits, the fifth and second, had "contrary interpretations" of this statute. *Cooper v. U.S.* (S.Ct.1985).

This issue takes on a new dimension with the passage of a 1988 amendment to section 1512(b) adding the word "corruptly." This permits a section 1512(b) prosecution when the conduct is noncoercive witness tampering. The Second Circuit in *U.S. v. Masterpol* (2d Cir.1991) found this statutory addition further support for the *Hernandez* view that Congress, in adding section 1512, "affirmatively intended to remove witnesses entirely from the scope of § 1503." Most circuits, however, reject the position taken by the Second Circuit finding that "[t]he fact that § 1512 more specifically addresses improper conduct involving a witness does not preclude application of § 1503." *U.S. v. Kenny* (4th Cir.1992).

CHAPTER SEVEN
BRIBERY AND EXTORTION

§ 7.01 Introduction

Official corruption is often prosecuted by charges premised upon the statutory offenses of Bribery of Public Officials and Witnesses (18 U.S.C. § 201), the Hobbs Act (18 U.S.C. § 1951) or the Travel Act (18 U.S.C. § 1952). Although federal offenses, these three statutes are often used in corruption cases involving state and local officials. As one might suspect, this use has raised arguments of the implications on federalism.

The line between each of these three offenses is not always discernible and often a prosecutor has a choice in deciding what statute to use in prosecuting specific conduct. In the United States Supreme Court decision of *Evans v. U.S.* (S.Ct.1992), Justice Thomas, joined by Chief Justice Rehnquist and Justice Scalia, cautioned in their dissent that "[b]y stretching the bounds of extortion to make it encompass bribery, the Court today blurs the traditional distinction between the crimes." Permitting Hobbs Act charges when the conduct is in essence bribery serves to provide federal jurisdiction for what otherwise might be a state crime. Courts have found that bribery and extortion are not mutually exclusive.

The Foreign Corrupt Practices Act (FCPA) serves to combat bribery of foreign officials. The Act, originally passed in 1977, is incorporated into provisions of the Securities Exchange Act of 1934. Under the FCPA, certain corporations are subject to accounting requirements that include the keeping of records "in reasonable detail [to] accurately and fairly reflect the transactions and disposition of the assets of the issuer." (15 U.S.C. § 78 m(b)(2)(A)). The crux of the FCPA provides for the prosecution of those who bribe foreign officials. (15 U.S.C. § 78 dd–1 et. seq.) (see § 1.04). Other countries have joined in the fight against international bribery in passing the Convention on Combating Bribery of Foreign Public Officials in International Business Transactions. The United States in keeping with this international convention passed the International Anti-Bribery and Fair Competition Act of 1998.

§ 7.02 Overview of Bribery

The first federal bribery statute of general application was passed in 1853 and titled "An Act to Prevent Frauds Upon the Treasury of the United States." Although today there are many federal bribery offenses in the federal criminal law, the most prominent is section 201 of Title 18. This statute pertains to bribery (§ 201 (b)) and gratuities (§ 201 (c)).

Congress enacted section 201 in 1962 "as part of an effort to reformulate and rationalize all federal criminal statutes dealing with the integrity of government." *Dixson v. U.S.* (S.Ct.1984). The statute focuses on criminalizing conduct of those who improperly seek preferential treatment from government officials and also those who improperly use their public office for their personal gain. The statute also covers bribes and gratuities given to witnesses for influencing their testimony or absenting themselves from a proceeding. Section 201 criminalizes the conduct of the person giving the bribe as well as the person who receives it.

Bribery (§ 201 (b)(1)) requires the government to show that (1) something of value was given, offered, or promised (2) to a federal public official (3) corruptly to influence an official act. Subsection two of this provision concerns those instances when the offender committing the bribery is the public official. The remaining two subsections of part (b) criminalize conduct of bribing a witness in a federal proceeding or seeking or accepting a bribe as such a witness.

Subsection (c) of section 201 pertains to gratuities. When one is the public official charged with demanding or accepting a gratuity, it is incumbent for there to be a showing that the public official personally sought or accepted something of value. A distinguishing factor separating bribery from gratuities is the level of intent. The gratuity statute does not require proof of a quid pro quo. Unlike bribery, it "may constitute merely a reward for some future act that the public official will take (and may have already determined to take) , or for a past act that he has already taken." *U.S. v. Sun-Diamond Growers of California* (S.Ct. 1999).

The gratuities section does not apply to government offers of leniency in exchange for testimony from witnesses and co-defendants. In *U.S. v. Singleton*, (10th Cir. 1999), an en banc Tenth Circuit stated that "18 U.S.C. § 201(c)(2) does not apply to the United States or an Assistant United States Attorney functioning within the official scope of the office." The court did note that this does not "permit[ ] an agent of the government to step beyond the limits of his or her office to make an offer to a witness other than one traditionally exercised by the sovereign."

Bribery carries a maximum penalty of fifteen years imprisonment and a fine. Additionally it permits disqualification from public office. In contrast, the gratuities provision of this statute provides for a maximum imprisonment of two years.

§ 7.03 Bribery—Things of Value

A liberal construction has been given to the requirement of the bribery payment being "anything of value." Actual commercial value is not necessary. It is the "value which the defendant subjectively attaches to the items received," which controls. Thus, loans and a promise of future employment to an official in financial straits can be value for purposes of the statute. *U.S. v. Gorman* (6th Cir.1986).

In *U.S. v. Williams* (2d Cir.1983), Senator Harrison Williams was convicted of charges, including bribery, as a part of Operation Abscam. The Second Circuit found that defendant's acceptance of stock in corporations that he believed had value, was sufficient to support the "anything of value" element and the jury instruction, despite defendant's argument of the stock having no commercial value.

§ 7.04 Bribery—Public Official

The public official element of the bribery statute includes both federal public officials and "persons who have been selected to be public officials." These terms are descriptively defined by the statute.

Further, courts have expansively interpreted these definitions.

In *Dixson v. U.S.* (S.Ct.1984), petitioners were charged with bribery for their acceptance of kickbacks from contractors seeking work on a project arising as part of an urban renewal program. The City of Peoria, the recipient of two federal block grants from the Department of Housing and Urban Development, designated a social service organization as subgrantee in charge of administering the funds. Petitioners served in a supervisory capacity with this agency with certain fiscal and contracting authority. The issue before the Supreme Court was "whether officers of a private, nonprofit corporation administering and expending federal community development block grants are 'public officials' for purposes of the federal bribery statute."

The Supreme Court affirmed the convictions of the petitioners finding them to be "public officials." The Court was clear, however, to state that the "mere presence of some federal assistance" or being an employee of a local organization responsible for administering a federal grant does not make one a "public official." The Court found that to be a "public official," one "must possess some degree of official responsibility for carrying out a federal program or policy."

Those individuals who may not meet the "public official" element of this statute are not necessarily immune from federal prosecution. In 1984 Congress passed 18 U.S.C. § 666, an act that now extends federal criminality to agents of state and local organizations that receive ten thousand dollars or more in federal funds. Congress stated that the purpose of the act was "to augment the ability of the United States to vindicate significant acts of theft, fraud and bribery involving Federal monies which are disbursed to private organizations or State and local governments pursuant to a Federal program." Under section 666 it is not necessary for the government "to prove the bribe in question had any particular influence on federal funds." *Salinas v. U.S.* (S.Ct. 1997).

When the prosecution of the public official entails a member of the federal Congress, an issue that may arise is the effect of the Constitution's Speech and Debate Clause. Established to protect the independence of the legislature, this constitutional provision provides that "for any Speech or Debate in either House, they [Senators and Representatives] shall not be questioned in any other place."

In *U.S. v. Brewster* (S.Ct.1972), the Supreme Court rejected the use of the Speech and Debate Clause in a case charging Senator Brewster with bribery under section 201. The Court stated that "a Member of Congress may be prosecuted under a criminal statute provided that the Government's case does not rely on legislative acts or the motivation for legislative acts." The taking of a bribe, the Court stated is not a legislative act and is not "part of or even incidental to the role of a legislator."

§ 7.05 Bribery—Corruptly to Influence Official Acts

When the charge pertains to bribery of a public official, it is incumbent that the government prove that the defendant acted corruptly to influence an official act. The statute defines "official act" as "any decision or action on any question, matter, cause, suit, proceeding or controversy, which may at any time be pending, or which may by law be brought before any public official, in such official's official capacity, or in such official's place of trust or profit." Despite the extensiveness of this definition, courts have not always found a defendant's conduct sufficient to meet this element.

In *U.S. v. Muntain* (D.C.Cir.1979), the charges against the defendant included illegal gratuities pursuant to section 201. Muntain, employed as the Assistant to the Secretary for Labor Relations at the United States Department of Housing and Urban Development, was convicted after a jury trial based upon evidence of "his involvement in a private scheme to sell group insurance to labor unions as a negotiated benefit in union contracts." Defendant argued on appeal that his actions were not "official acts" in that they did not involve matters that would be brought before him in his official capacity. The District of Columbia Circuit Court of Appeals accepted this argument, finding that the promotion of group automobile insurance was not a matter that would be brought before Muntain in his capacity as the Secretary of Labor Relations at HUD. Thus, although the court found the conduct reprehensible, it did not find it sufficient to meet the element of influencing an official act.

The "official act" language is not limited to future acts. Rather, the legislature's use of the words "at any time" precludes a defendant from escaping "liability for bribe-solicitation by proving that he had successfully hidden the truth of past performance from the bribe-payer." Bribery does not require that the public official actually have the power to perform the act for which the money was received. The crux of the offense is that money is solicited or received on the representation that it is for the purpose of influencing an official act. *U.S. v. Arroyo* (7th Cir.1978).

Although the bribe must be offered with a corrupt intent to influence any official act, the public official does not need to be aware of the bribe. *U.S. v. Traitz* (3d Cir.1989). It is, likewise, immaterial to some courts whether the act could or would ever be performed. Thus, a defense of "playacting" would not negate the charge. A public official who gives false promises of assistance to individuals offering money, cannot avoid section 201's criminality claiming that the official's subjective intent was not corrupt. *U.S. v. Myers* (2d Cir.1982).

Bribery does, however, require proof of an actual or intended quid pro quo. Arguments claiming insufficiency of the quid pro quo mandate are common to cases where the defendant believes that the charge of gratuity, as opposed to bribery, more aptly describes the conduct. Considering the difference in sentencing options for these two offenses, (bribery–15 years, gratuities–2 years) the issue is significant. In distinguishing the bribery offense from the gratuity offense, the Fourth Circuit in *U.S. v. Muldoon* (4th Cir.1991), stated that "[b]ribery requires proof that the payor acted corruptly with the intent of influencing any official act, influencing a public official to defraud the government, or to do or omit an act in violation of his official duties." In contrast, the court found that proof of a gratuity "need not show that the payor intended to exact action by the recipient, although it must show that the payor gave the gratuity because of the act."

§ 7.06 Overview of Hobbs Act

The Anti–Racketeering Act of 1934 was the predecessor extortion statute of the Hobbs Act. Congress modified this initial act in 1946 in reaction to a United States Supreme Court decision that restrictively applied the 1934 Act to exclude the payment of wages by a bona fide employer to a bona fide employee. *U.S. v. Local 807* (S.Ct.1942). Although the predecessor statute criminalized extortion activity, the Supreme Court's ruling in *Local 807* permitted labor unions using coercive extortion to escape liability under the statute if the conduct involved wages paid to a bona fide employee. To correct this deficiency, Congress enacted the Hobbs Act, a new statute that specifically contained a "definition of the term 'extortion' and for the first time proscribed 'extortion' in specific language." *U.S. v. Mazzei* (3d Cir.1975).

The elements of the present day offense are (1) interference with commerce and (2) robbery or extortion. Extortion is defined within the statute as "the obtaining of property from another, with his consent, induced by wrongful use of actual or threatened force, violence, or fear, or under color of official right." Despite the predecessor statute's emphasis on racketeering activities, 18 U.S.C. § 1951 has no requirement that the government prove racketeering as an element of the offense. *U.S. v. Culbert* (S.Ct.1978). The statute permits prosecutions for actual acts of robbery or extortion as well as attempts and conspiracies to rob or extort.

Section 1951 carries a maximum term of imprisonment of not more than twenty years and a fine. The significant prison term afforded by this statute makes its use highly desirable to the government.

§ 7.07 Hobbs Act—Interstate Commerce

It is rare that a court rejects a section 1951 prosecution as not meeting the jurisdictional requirement of interstate commerce. The statute merely requires a showing that one "in any way obstructs, delays, or affects commerce or the movement of any article or commodity in commerce." Interstate commerce has been found where there is criminal activity "affecting commerce" even when the effect is "de minimus." In *U.S. v. Rabbitt* (8th Cir.1978), the Eighth Circuit stated that, "[i]f the resources of a business which affects interstate commerce are depleted and diminished as a result of extortion, then interstate commerce is affected." An actual or prospective depletion of assets has been found sufficient.

In *U.S. v. Pascucci* (9th Cir.1991), Defendant Pascucci was convicted after a jury trial of two offenses, one of which was the Hobbs Act. In support of the charge of attempted extortion, the government presented evidence at trial that included the defendant's threat to deliver an audio tape of the victim's marital infidelity to the victim's employer.

The majority opinion, by the Ninth Circuit, in *Pascucci,* noted the necessity of having a threat transmitted in interstate commerce in order to have a Hobbs Act violation. The court found that "[b]y showing that the defendant made a credible threat to deliver embarrassing materials *directly* to the victim's employer, who was then engaged in interstate commerce, the Government demonstrated that [defendant] introduced a potential impact on interstate commerce." The fact that the defendant's scheme was unsuccessful because he was caught did not dissolve the criminal liability. In addition to the fact that Pascucci was charged with the crime of attempted extortion, it is sufficient if "the scheme, if successful, would have affected commerce."

Circuit Judge Ferguson, dissenting in *Pascucci*, found the nexus with interstate commerce insufficient in this case. The dissent rejected the argument that because the defendant's "victim was employed by a firm engaged in interstate commerce, the jurisdictional nexus is established." Judge Ferguson stated that the "[i]nterstate commerce must be affected by extortion, not by a result of extortion."

U.S. v. Elders (7th Cir.1978) is an example of the rare instance when the interstate commerce element was not met by the government. The case involved alleged kickbacks to a local public official for contracts on tree removal work. Following a jury conviction, the defendant argued on appeal that his tree removal company (IST) was not involved in interstate commerce. The government, arguing a de minimus effect on commerce, claimed "(1) that the use of equipment purchased or manufactured out-of-state was sufficient to establish jurisdiction; (2) that IST engaged in out-of-state work during the period in question; and (3) that either the extortionate payments depleted the assets of IST and/or the inflated prices paid by Maywood depleted its treasury, thereby impairing the ability of either or both to do business interstate."

Despite the *Elders* court's recognition that the nexus with interstate commerce may be de minimus, the court did require that it exist and that "the connection with/or effect on interstate commerce must have been at least a 'realistic probability' at the time of the extortionate act." In *Elders*, the Seventh Circuit rejected all of the governments' arguments noting first that the out-of-state purchases of equipment were well in advance of the alleged extortions and there was no showing by the government of a "realistic probability" of additional equipment being purchased. The court also rejected the government's claim of IST doing out of state work as a basis for interstate commerce in that the few out of state jobs presented as evidence by the government had no connection with the alleged extortions. Finally, the court rejected the depletion of assets argument noting that not only was this issue not presented at trial but "the affect still must be more than a speculative attenuated 'one step removed' kind of effect."

Some courts require that if the government is proceeding on a depletion of assets theory premised upon the victim's purchase of interstate goods, it is necessary for the purchasing to be continuing in nature. "Where the victim of an extortion scheme *customarily* obtains supplies through interstate commerce, the diminution of the victim's resources impairs his purchasing power and may therefore be found to affect interstate commerce for the purpose of the Hobbs Act." *U.S. v. Merolla* (2d Cir.1975).

A depletion of assets premised merely upon the receipt of government (FBI) funds as an extortion payment does not establish an actual effect on interstate commerce. This, however, does not mean that the government would be precluded from proceeding on a charge of attempt under the Hobbs Act. *U.S. v. DiCarlantonio* (6th Cir.1989).

Although a jury decides if the facts presented by the government occurred, the trial judge can determine if the conduct affected commerce. In *U.S. v. Kuta* (7th Cir.1975), the Seventh Circuit rejected the argument that an instruction given in a trial that charged the defendant with a violation of the Hobbs Act was erroneous because it did not include a definition of commerce. The court stated that "a definition was not necessary, ... because what constitutes interstate commerce and whether it was affected were matters of law that the trial court resolved."

Challenges premised on insufficient evidence of "interstate commerce" were asserted by defendants after the Supreme Court decisions in *U.S. v. Lopez* (see § 1.02) and *U.S. v. Morrison* (S.Ct. 2000), cases that enforce a requirement of a substantial effect on interstate commerce.   The lower courts have distinguished the statutes from these two Supreme Court cases when applied to an alleged Hobbs Act violation, finding that a de minimis nexus on interstate commerce is sufficient for maintaining a Hobbs Act prosecution. *U.S. v. Clausen* (3rd Cir. 2003).

§ 7.08 Hobbs Act—Robbery or Extortion

Section 1951 requires a showing of either robbery or extortion. Robbery is defined by the statute as "the unlawful taking or obtaining of personal property from the person or in the presence of another, against his will, by means of actual or threatened force, or violence, or fear of injury, immediate or future, to his person or property, or property in his custody or possession, or the person or property of a relative or member of his family or of anyone in his company at the time of the taking or obtaining." Despite the specificity of this statute, in the case of *U.S. v. Nedley* (3d Cir.1958), the Third Circuit applied the common law definition of the term "robbery." Where a defendant argued on appeal that the common law definition of robbery should have been given as a jury instruction, the appellate court found that use of "the Hobbs Act definition of robbery was not plain error." *U.S. v. Thomas* (11th Cir.1993).

More commonly, the statute is used with acts of extortion. Prior to the 1970s, Hobbs Act extortion prosecutions were premised upon conduct by force, violence, or fear. In recent years there has been a growth and acceptance of prosecutions where the extortion is "under color of official right."

Property extorted from another by "wrongful use of actual or threatened force, violence or fear" is the first of two clauses that a prosecutor can use in alleging extortion. In making a determination as to whether fear exists, one looks at whether "fear was created in the victim's mind, if such fear was a reasonable one, and if the defendants by making use of that fear extorted money or property." *Callanan v.*

U.S. (8th Cir.1955). "Fear" can be met by a showing of the victim being placed in fear of economic loss.

In *U.S. v. Capo* (2d Cir.1987) the government charged the defendant under the Hobbs Act for conduct involving payments made to the defendant as part of a job selling scheme. The victims were alleged to have paid defendants sums of money for contacting the personnel officer at Eastman Kodak Company for favorable treatment on their job applications. On appeal of the Hobbs Act convictions, the government contended that the charge was premised upon fear of economic loss.

In rejecting the economic fear argument as presented by the government, the Second Circuit in *Capo* stated that "[t]he absence or presence of fear of economic loss must be considered from the perspective of the victim, not the extortionist; the proof need establish that the victim reasonably believed: first, that the defendant had the power to harm the victim, and second, that the defendant would exploit that power to the victim's detriment." Since the evidence in the *Capo* case failed to show any negative influencing on jobs on the part of defendants and failed to show that any victims feared a detriment to them by defendants actions, the requirement of "preclusion or diminished opportunity" had not been satisfied.

The court in *Capo* stressed the necessity of keeping state offenses away from federal prosecutors. The court stated that "[b]ecause these 'victims' faced no increased risk if they did not pay, but rather, stood only to improve their lots by paying defendants, this case is a classic example of bribery."

§ 7.09 Hobbs Act—"Under Color of Official Right"

Extortion "under color of official right" is an alternative basis upon which a prosecutor can claim extortion. It "includes the misuse of one's office to induce payments not due the person or his office. The official need not control the function in question if the extorted party possesses a reasonable belief in the official's powers." *U.S. v. Rabbitt* (8th Cir.1978). As noted in *Evans v. U.S.* (S.Ct.1992), there is no need for an affirmative act of inducement. Merely accepting a bribe to misuse one's office is sufficient. The element "under color of official right" has been the subject of two recent Supreme Court cases that involved extortion as related to public officials' campaign contributions.

In *McCormick v. U.S.* (S.Ct.1991), petitioner McCormick was a member of the West Virginia House of Delegates who sponsored and spoke on behalf of legislation that would exempt foreign medical school graduates with significant work experience from having to take the state licensing examination. McCormick allegedly received cash payments from the doctors both before and after the passage of this legislation. Evidence presented at trial was that he failed to list the funds received as campaign contributions and likewise failed to report it on his income tax return.

Petitioner McCormick was charged with five counts of violating the Hobbs Act and one count of filing a false income tax return. The Supreme Court reversed petitioner's conviction, finding that a quid pro quo is necessary for a conviction that is predicated upon receiving a campaign contribution. The Court stated that "to hold that legislators commit the federal crime of extortion when they act for the benefit of constituents or support legislation furthering the interests of some of their constituents, shortly before or after campaign contributions are solicited and received from those beneficiaries, is an unrealistic assessment of what Congress could have meant by making it a crime to obtain property from another, with his consent, 'under color of official right.' "

The Supreme Court in *McCormick* was clear to note that not all campaign contributions would be outside the scope of the Hobbs Act. "Political contributions are of course vulnerable if induced by the use of force, violence, or fear. The receipt of such contributions is also vulnerable under the Act as having been taken under color of official right, but only if the payments are made in return for an explicit promise or undertaking by the official to perform or not to perform an official act."

This latter form of extortion was the conduct displayed in the case of *Evans v. U.S.* (S.Ct.1992). Petitioner Evans was a member of the Board of Commissioners of DeKalb County, Georgia. Petitioner was approached by an undercover FBI agent who sought petitioner's assistance on a rezoning. The agent paid petitioner eight thousand dollars, of which petitioner reported a one thousand dollar check as a campaign contribution but failed to include the cash payment in the sum of seven thousand dollars on his state campaign financing disclosure form or his federal income tax return. Evans was charged with a Hobbs Act violation and a tax violation of failure to report income.

The Supreme Court in *Evans* accepted the majority view as expressed by eight circuits that an "affirmative act of inducement by a public official, such as a demand," is not required for extortion "under color of official right." The Court stated, "[w]e hold today that the Government need only show that a public official has obtained a payment to which he was not entitled, knowing that the payment was made in return for official acts." Thus passive acceptance of a benefit by a public official can meet the extortion element of the Hobbs Act when "the official knows that he is being offered the payment in exchange for a specific requested exercise of his official power."

The Supreme Court in this six to three decision also reaffirmed its prior ruling in *McCormick*, finding the instruction given in the *Evans* case sufficient to meet the quid pro quo requirement. The Court stated that "because the offense is completed at the time when the public official receives a payment in return for his agreement to perform specific official acts; fulfillment of the *quid pro quo* is not an element of the offense."

In *U.S. v. Blandford* (6th Cir.1994), the Sixth Circuit examined the effect of the *Evans* case on *McCormick* in the context of a Hobbs Act charge against the Speaker of Kentucky's House of Representatives. The court in *Blandford* concluded that "[p]ut simply, *Evans* instructed that by 'explicit' *McCormick* did not mean 'express.' "

Courts have also considered the applicability of *McCormick*'s requirement for a *quid pro quo* outside the context of campaign contributions. Some courts have found that a *quid pro quo* was not required or that a "relaxed *quid pro quo* standard" should be used with non-campaign contribution cases. In *Blandford* the court noted that "a strong argument could be advanced for treating campaign contribution cases and non-campaign contribution cases disparately." In the context of the gratuities statute, the Supreme Court held that "in order to establish a violation of 18 U.S.C. § 201(c)(1)(A), the Government must prove a link between a thing of value conferred upon a public official and a specific 'official act' for or because of which it was given." *U.S. v. Sun-Diamond Growers of California* (S.Ct. 1999).

§ 7.10 Travel Act

The Travel Act, passed in 1961, was aimed at "organized crime." Then Attorney General Robert Kennedy stated that federal legislation "was needed to aid state and local governments which were no longer able to cope with the increasingly complex and interstate nature of large-scale, multiparty crime." *Perrin v. U.S.* (S.Ct.1979). The statute used the Commerce Clause of the United States Constitution to reach state and local criminality that had an interstate nexus.

The Travel Act can be seen as a precursor to crimes such as the Racketeer Influenced and Corrupt Organization Act in its use of the commerce power to criminalize what are essentially state offenses. Initially the statute concentrated on unlawful activity in the form of business activities involving gambling, liquor, narcotics, and extortion and bribery that violated state law. The statute was later expanded to include conduct related to controlled substances and arson that violated state law. In 1986 the scope of this offense was again enlarged to encompass the Bank Secrecy Act and the money laundering offenses of sections 1956 and 1957.

18 U.S.C. § 1952, the Travel Act, requires proof of three elements: (1) interstate or foreign travel, or using the mail or any facility in interstate or foreign commerce, (2) intent to promote, direct, or manage illegal business, and (3) an overt act in furtherance of the unlawful activity.

Interstate travel, the jurisdictional element of this offense, mandates that the activity involve at least two states. A state is defined to include "a State of the United States, the District of Columbia, and any commonwealth, territory, or possession of the United States." The required nexus between interstate activity and the criminality is less clear.

In *Rewis v. U.S.* (S.Ct.1971) the Supreme Court reversed a section 1952 conviction involving a gambling operation that was frequented by out-of-state bettors. The Court, in examining the legislative history of the statute, found that it strongly suggested "that Congress did not intend that the Travel Act should apply to criminal activity solely because that activity is at times patronized by persons from another State."

Eight years later the Supreme Court chose to take a less restrictive approach to the Travel Act when deciding the case of *Perrin v. U.S.* (S.Ct.1979). Petitioner and co-defendants were charged with a violation of section 1952 for their involvement in a scheme to exploit geological data stolen from a company. The unlawful activity alleged in the indictment was the use of interstate commerce for the purpose of promoting a commercial bribery scheme in violation of state law.

The Supreme Court in *Perrin* rejected petitioner's argument that bribery should be limited to bribery of a public official. The statute, the Court held, would include "bribery of individuals acting in a private capacity." The Court distinguished *Perrin* from *Rewis* finding the interstate nexus that was lacking in *Rewis* sufficient in this case. The Court stated, " ... so long as the requisite interstate nexus is present, the statute reflects a clear and deliberate intent on the part of Congress to alter the federal-state balance in order to reinforce state law enforcement."

Cases have held that requisite to meeting the "business enterprise" element of this offense is a showing of continuity of the activity. Thus, a single action involving the transportation of drugs would not sustain a conviction. *U.S. v. Bates* (11th Cir.1988). Where there was a showing of three drug deliveries and a drug distribution enterprise, the Fifth Circuit found sufficient continuity to meet the "business enterprise" element. *U.S. v. Carrion* (5th Cir.1987).

The Travel Act requires that the accused "thereafter performs or attempts to perform" an act as specified in the statute. Although an overt act is required by the statute, the Second Circuit stated in *U.S. v. Jenkins* (2d Cir.1991) that the government does not have to show that the accused took a substantial step in furtherance of the intended unlawful activity. "Rather, ... to establish a Travel Act violation the government must prove that the defendant used a facility of interstate or foreign commerce to 'make easier or facilitate' the intended unlawful activity, and thereafter did one additional act in furtherance of the unlawful activity."

CHAPTER EIGHT

RACKETEER INFLUENCED AND CORRUPT ORGANIZATIONS (RICO)

§ 8.01 Introduction

The Racketeer Influenced and Corrupt Organizations Act (RICO) is Title IX of the Organized Crime Control Act of 1970. It was enacted by Congress as a tool to combat organized crime. In the initial years after passage, RICO was seldom used by prosecutors. Today, however, it is common for federal prosecutors to bring RICO charges. The addition of RICO as a criminal charge provides the government with federal criminal enforcement in areas that were previously within the state police powers. Its penalty and forfeiture provisions offer the government a strong incentive for using this statute (see § 8.07).

Although some believe that Congress intended RICO to serve as a weapon against organized crime, courts have not required proof to support a RICO charge, of the defendant being a member of organized crime. RICO is "dependent upon behavior and not status." *U.S. v. Mandel* (D.Md.1976).

The RICO statutes are found in 18 U.S.C. § 1961 through § 1968. Section 1961 of Title 18 serves as a definitions statute for the terms used in the remaining RICO statutes. In defining these terms, it lists nine state and over thirty federal offenses that can serve as predicate acts for a RICO charge. Although it offers basic definitions for most of the elements of the offense, court interpretations have provided language to further assist in this regard.

Section 1962, subsections (a), (b), (c), and (d), provides four separate and distinct types of prohibited conduct. These are: (a) using income from a pattern of racketeering activity to acquire an interest in an enterprise engaged in, or the activities of which affect interstate or foreign commerce; (b) acquiring or maintaining through a pattern of racketeering activity an interest in an enterprise engaged in, or the activities of which affect interstate or foreign commerce; (c) conducting or participating in the conduct, through a pattern of racketeering activity, of such affairs of an enterprise affect interstate or foreign commerce; and (d) conspiring to further any of the activities listed in (a), (b), or (c). Although it is only necessary for there to be one of these four prohibited activities for a RICO offense, some prosecutions use more then one type of prohibited activity in the charging document.

Although most RICO prosecutions involve racketeering activity, this statute can also be used by the government when the criminal activity involves the collection of an unlawful debt. Section 1961 defines the term "unlawful debt" to mean debts relating to either gambling or usurious loans that are incurred in connection with an illegal gambling business or in connection with a business of lending money where the usurious rate is at least twice the enforceable rate.

The essence of a RICO charge is in proving that the defendant, (1) invested the proceeds of a pattern of racketeering in, or acquired or maintained an interest in through a pattern of racketeering, or participated in through a pattern of racketeering, (2) an enterprise, (3) engaged in, or the activities of which affect, commerce. The intricacies of this statute appear, when each of these elements are dissected relative to the four different types of prohibited conduct. One finds that not only do jurisdictions approach these elements differently, but that courts will vary within the same jurisdiction dependent upon the prohibited conduct that has been charged.

Section 1963 provides the penalties available in a RICO prosecution. A maximum term of imprisonment of up to twenty years is provided for by this statute. This term may be increased to life where the violation is based upon racketeering activity that has a maximum penalty of life imprisonment. In addition to imprisonment and fines, RICO also provides for asset forfeiture. RICO not only serves as a criminal statute, but also provides private parties and the government with a civil cause of action. (18 U.S.C. § 1964).

§ 8.02 Enterprise

RICO requires that the defendant have invested in, maintained an interest in, or participated in the affairs of an enterprise. The term "enterprise" is defined in section 1961(4) as including "any individual, partnership, corporation, association, or other legal entity, and any union or group of individuals associated in fact although not a legal entity." The expansiveness of this definition is seen upon examining cases.

In *U.S. v. Turkette* (S.Ct.1981), the accused successfully argued in the appellate court that RICO was solely intended to protect legitimate businesses and thus criminal participation in an association that performed only illegal acts, and had not infiltrated or attempted to infiltrate a legitimate enterprise, could not form the basis for a RICO charge. The Supreme Court, in reversing the appellate court, conceded that the congressional purpose of RICO was to combat organized crime that infiltrated legitimate businesses. The Court noted, however, that this did not preclude RICO charges where the enterprise was illegal. Since neither the language of the statute nor the structure of RICO limited its application to legitimate enterprises the Court found it proper to follow Congress' intent for RICO to have a broad reading. To hold otherwise, the Court noted, would omit whole areas of organized criminal activity from the reach of the statute. RICO does not, however, require that the enterprise or predicate acts have an economic motive. *National Organization For Women, Inc. v. Scheidler* (S.Ct.1994).

In addition to allowing both legitimate and illegitimate enterprises, courts have permitted the enterprise to be a governmental body. For example, in *U.S. v. Thompson* (6th Cir.1982), defendants entered conditional guilty pleas arguing that it was improper to use the "The Office of Governor" of the State of Tennessee as the enterprise for RICO. The Sixth Circuit in an en banc ruling found that the language and plain meaning of the statute did not exclude governmental offices as RICO enterprises.

Although the court in *Thompson* permitted the use of governmental bodies as RICO enterprises, it noted in dicta its dislike of this practice. The court reflected upon the disruption of comity in federal-state relations and the needless unfair reflection on innocent individuals. The court offered as a better course that prosecutors treat the group of defendants as a group of individuals associated in fact although not a legal entity. Despite this advice, prosecutors have continued to charge RICO with a government entity as the enterprise, and courts have continued to uphold the use of governmental bodies as RICO enterprises.

Courts have disagreed over the necessary structure of an enterprise consisting of a "group of individuals associated in fact although not a legal entity." (§ 1961(4)). They generally agree that attributes of this entity include a common purpose and functioning as a continuing unit. Some courts will even go so far as to require that there be an ascertainable structure. This latter position was taken in *U.S. v. Bledsoe* (8th Cir.1982).

In *Bledsoe* the Eighth Circuit rejected a position taken by some courts that any confederation of two or more persons, no matter how loose or temporary it may be, can be an association of individuals and thus, an enterprise. The court held that the term "enterprise" is meant to signify an association different from the acts that form the pattern of racketeering activity. In addition to commonality of purpose, an enterprise must "function as a continuing unit," and have an "ascertainable structure." Finding only a loose association without structure, the court in *Bledsoe* reversed the conviction.

The approach taken in *Bledsoe* is rejected by other circuits. Reference is often made to *Turkette's* holding that the enterprise be separate from the pattern of racketeering. Proof of the enterprise, however, may "coalesce" with the proof of the pattern. *U.S. v. Perholtz* (D.C.Cir.1988).

Actions brought pursuant to 1962(c) require that the enterprise must be separate and distinct from the person-defendant. RICO separateness can be shown when the defendant is a president and sole shareholder of a closely held corporation. In *Cedric Kushner Promotions, LTD v. King,* (S.Ct. 2001), the Court, in a civil RICO case, found that "separateness" is met for purposes of RICO when there is an individual and a corporation, even if the corporation has only one shareholder and is a closely held corporation as the "corporate owner/employee, a natural person, is distinct from the corporation itself, a legally different entity with differing rights and responsibilities due to its different legal status."

§ 8.03 Interstate Commerce

The jurisdiction for the RICO statute is found in its requirement of interstate commerce. In *U.S. v. Robertson* (S.Ct.1995), the Supreme Court held that the enterprise's activities could either be "engaged in" or "substantially affect" interstate commerce. The Court found that Robertson had purchased supplies and equipment from out of state, had workers brought in from out of state, and took some of the gold mine's output out of state. The Court found that the activities of the enterprise were engaged in interstate or foreign commerce.

§ 8.04 Pattern of Racketeering Activity

The definitions section of RICO defines a "pattern of racketeering activity" as requiring "at least two acts of racketeering activity, one of which occurred after the effective date of this chapter and the last of which occurred within ten years (excluding any period of imprisonment) after the commission of a prior act of racketeering activity." Courts and the legislature have provided guidance as to what constitutes a pattern and what acts are permissible as racketeering activity.

There are nine state and over thirty federal offenses specifically listed in section 1961 as racketeering activity. The nine state offenses are murder, kidnapping, gambling, arson, robbery, bribery, extortion, dealing in obscene matter, or dealing in narcotics or other dangerous drugs. The statute requires that the state offense be chargeable under state law and punishable by imprisonment for more than one year.

Although it is necessary that the state offense be chargeable under state law, it is unimportant what label is placed on the state statute. In defining the nine state offenses, the legislature intended that a generic definition be used. Thus, violations of the Illinois official misconduct statute can fit a general definition of bribery, and thus form a RICO predicate. *U.S. v. Garner* (7th Cir.1987).

It is not necessary that the accused actually be charged with the state offense. Further, procedural problems that might preclude the filing of a state charge do not serve as an impediment to the filing of a RICO charge. Courts have held that it is only necessary to show that the offense can be chargeable under state law.

Where the defendant has been charged with the state predicate in state court, the federal courts have still permitted RICO charges to be brought in federal court using the same state act as a RICO predicate offense. This has been allowed even in some instances where the state trial resulted in an acquittal of the state offense. The dual sovereignty rule provides concurrent jurisdiction to both the state and federal governments so collateral estoppel does not apply. The double jeopardy clause also has not barred a subsequent RICO prosecution based upon a federal predicate offense previously used to prosecute the defendant. Since RICO requires proof of a pattern of racketeering, courts have found that it is not the same offense as the predicate act. *U.S. v. Pungitore* (3d Cir.1990).

Over thirty federal offenses are listed as possible predicate acts for a RICO charge. These offenses are listed in the definitions provision of RICO (18 U.S.C. § 1961), using both the statutory numbers of the offense and descriptions of the conduct. For example, section 201 contains the parenthetical "relating to bribery." Courts have interpreted this language to be merely a description of the statute and not to serve as a limit to the actual statutory provision. Thus, section 201's bribery and gratuities offenses are both included as possible predicate acts.

The expansiveness of RICO is demonstrated by noting the federal offenses included as possible predicate acts. For example, mail fraud, wire fraud, and obstruction of justice are among the list of offenses. Certain drug offenses and currency reporting crimes can also serve as predicate acts of a RICO charge. Federal RICO predicates have been added since the passage of the initial legislation. For example, in the "Uniting and Strengthening America by Providing Appropriate Tools Required to Intercept and Obstruct Terrorism Act of 2001" (Patriot Act) Congress included acts of terrorism as a RICO predicate.

Although RICO requires at least two predicate acts within the applicable time period, having merely two acts does not make RICO automatically available. Further, the existence of numerous predicate acts does not conclusively imply satisfaction of the pattern of racketeering element of RICO. The statute requires both the requisite number of acts and a pattern. Courts have provided guidance in defining the term "pattern."

The Supreme Court in the case of *H.J. Inc. v. Northwestern Bell Telephone Co.* (S.Ct.1989), defined "pattern of racketeering" as requiring "continuity plus relationship." The Court stated that " 'continuity' is both a closed-and open-ended concept." Continuity is achieved by proving related acts extending over a substantial period of time or by acts that demonstrate a threat of continued racketeering activity. Predicate acts over a few weeks or months that do not entail a threat of future criminal conduct do not meet the continuity requirement. Where the acts are over a short period of time, but demonstrate a "specific threat of repetition extending indefinitely into the future" or are part of an "ongoing entity's regular way of doing business," they can satisfy continuity.

The Court in *H.J. Inc.* defined the "relationship" requirement by referring to another provision of the Organized Crime Control Act of 1970. (18 U.S.C. § 3575 (e)). "[C]riminal conduct forms a pattern if it embraces criminal acts that have the same or similar purposes, results, participants, victims, or methods of commission, or otherwise are interrelated by distinguishing characteristics and are not isolated events."

Although the Court in *H.J. Inc.* provided a standard for reviewing cases to determine the existence of a pattern of racketeering, it admitted that a precise method of determination could not be fixed in advance. The development of cases applying specific facts to the "continuity plus relationship" test is needed to see the full effect of this definition. Four justices concurring in this opinion, criticized the "continuity plus relationship" test finding it as helpful to the conduct of affairs as saying "life is a fountain." Although these justices invite a future challenge based upon statutory vagueness, certiorari has been denied when the issue has been brought to the Supreme Court.

§ 8.05 Nexus Between Pattern of Racketeering and Enterprise

In the case of 1962(a) and 1962(b) there is no need to reflect upon the nexus requirement in that the statute specifically incorporates the nexus between the racketeering and the enterprise. In 1962(a) a person is using income from a pattern of racketeering activity to acquire an interest in an enterprise and in 1962(b) the accused is acquiring or maintaining through a pattern of racketeering an interest in an enterprise. Thus, in these two provisions the relationship between the racketeering and enterprise is apparent.

Although prosecutions under section 1962(c) also require a nexus between the enterprise and the racketeering activity, the basis of that nexus is less obvious. Section 1962(c) prohibits conducting or participating in conducting, through a pattern of racketeering activity, the affairs of an enterprise affecting interstate commerce. Prior to 1993, a jurisdictional dichotomy existed as to what relationship was required between the enterprise and the racketeering activity or person engaged in the racketeering activity.

In 1993, in the case of *Reves v. Ernst & Young* (S.Ct.1993), the Supreme Court resolved the jurisdictional dichotomy. The Court held that 1962(c) required that one participate in the operation or management of the enterprise. The Court noted, however, that the "operation or management" test would not be limited to upper management. "An enterprise is 'operated' not just by upper management but also by lower-rung participants in the enterprise who are under the direction of upper management. An enterprise also might be 'operated' or 'managed' by others 'associated with' the enterprise who exert control over it as, for example, by bribery." The Court did not resolve "how far § 1962(c) extends down the ladder of operation."

§ 8.06 RICO Conspiracy

Section 1962(d) prohibits a conspiracy to commit the conduct stated in sections (a), (b), or (c). Unlike the general conspiracy statute (18 U.S.C. § 371), a

RICO conspiracy is not focused upon the agreement to commit a specific offense or defraud the government. Rather, the object of a RICO conspiracy is on the conspiracy to violate a substantive RICO provision. For example, a conspiracy to violate section 1962(c) would have as the object of the offense an agreement to conduct or participate in the affairs of an enterprise through a pattern of racketeering. It would not have as the object of the offense, an agreement to commit the individual predicate acts required for a pattern of racketeering. *U.S. v. Elliott* (5th Cir.1978). In *Salinas v. U.S.* (S.Ct.1997) the Supreme Court held that a RICO "conspiracy may exist even if a conspirator does not agree to commit or facilitate each and every part of the substantive offense." An overt act is not necessary for a RICO conspiracy.

§ 8.07 Forfeiture

In addition to fines and imprisonment, the RICO statute provides for forfeiture of property. Section 1963(a)(1) provides for forfeiture of "any interest the person has acquired or maintained in violation of section 1962." Additionally, any interest in an enterprise in which the person participated in, that violated section 1962, is subject to forfeiture under § 1963(a)(2). Finally, property from the proceeds of racketeering activity or the unlawful collection of a debt in violation of 1962, is subject to forfeiture under § 1963(a)(3). Property forfeitable under RICO relates back to property owned at the time of the commission of the section 1962 violations. (18 U.S.C. § 1963(c)).

Both tangible and intangible property can be forfeited. Real property, as well as things affixed to it, are subject to forfeiture under § 1963(a)(1). In *Russello v. U.S.* (S.Ct.1983) the Supreme Court held that profits and income were an "interest" and therefore subject to forfeiture. The Court noted that although the statute did not specifically define the term "interest," the ordinary meaning of the word encompassed profits or proceeds. The *Russello* Court found that Congress, wanted "to remove the profit from organized crime by separating the racketeer from.... dishonest gains." Thus, reading the statute as applying only to interests in an enterprise, would limit its effectiveness and place whole areas of organized criminal activity beyond the reach of the statute. Section 1963(a)(3) codified *Russello* in providing for the forfeiture of the "proceeds" of racketeering activity.

Contract rights are also subject to forfeiture. An example of the forfeiture of a contract right is seen when the court orders an individual to forfeit a union position. The court may not, however, extend this forfeiture to precluding the person from seeking to reattain their office. *U.S. v. Rubin* (5th Cir.1977).

In *U.S. v. Caporale* (11th Cir.1986), the Eleventh Circuit found it permissible under the forfeiture provisions of the statute to impose joint and several liability. The government, the court noted, is not required to trace racketeering proceeds to specific assets. All that is necessary is for the government to show the "amount of the proceeds and identify a finite group of people receiving the proceeds."

In personam forfeitures are, however, subject to Eighth Amendment challenges under the Excessive

Fines Clause. In *Alexander v. U.S.* (S.Ct.1993), the Supreme Court remanded a forfeiture order for the lower court to consider whether the penalty was excessive.

§ 8.08 Civil RICO

In addition to criminal RICO actions, the RICO Act provides a statutory basis for both the government and civil litigants proceeding with a civil cause of action. (18 U.S.C. § 1964). Unlike criminal RICO actions that provide penalties including imprisonment, those premised upon section 1964, the civil RICO statute, have remedies of damages. The government, in pursuing civil RICO actions, can also request equitable relief. The applicability of injunctive relief to private plaintiffs remains an unresolved issue. The statute does provide that "[a]ny person injured in his business or property by reason of a violation of section 1962 ... may sue ... and shall recover threefold the damages he sustains and the cost of the suit, including a reasonable attorney's fee."

Most civil RICO actions do not require that the defendants be convicted of the predicate acts used to form the basis of the pattern of racketeering. *Sedima, S.P.R.L. v. Imrex Co., Inc.* (S.Ct.1985). The right to sue for treble damages under RICO, however, does require a showing of injury to the plaintiff, and that the defendant's actions in violation of the statute were the proximate cause of that injury. Therefore, the plaintiff must show a direct relationship between the conduct alleged and the injury asserted in the complaint. *Holmes v. Securities Investor Protection Corp.* (S.Ct.1992). Congress amended § 1964(c) so that a civil RICO action could not be premised upon "conduct that would have been actionable as fraud in the purchase or sale of securities" unless the individual was criminally convicted in connection with the fraud.

CHAPTER NINE

FALSE STATEMENTS

§ 9.01 Introduction

A myriad of statutes exist today that prohibit the making of false statements. Most of these offenses are specifically tailored to meet explicit prohibited conduct. For example, false statement offenses exist with regard to making false statements under the Federal Trade Commission Act (15 U.S.C. § 50), presenting a false deed, power of attorney or other contract writing that defrauds the United States (18 U.S.C. § 495), presenting a false invoice with the intent to smuggle (18 U.S.C. § 545), making a false statement to obtain a federally backed loan (18 U.S.C. § 1014) and making a false statement with respect to work performed on a highway project (18 U.S.C. § 1020).

Despite the volume of tailored legislation, the most pervasively used provision is the generic false statement statute located in section 1001 of Title 18. Section 1001 has been effectively employed to combat public corruption. The simplicity of proof necessary to obtain a conviction, as well as the substantial penalty provided, has made it a beneficial charge for the government's use.

18 U.S.C. § 1001 emanates from an 1863 Act that made it a criminal offense for a person in the United States armed forces to make a fraudulent claim

against the government. In subsequent years the statute was expanded to encompass "every person" and not just those in the military. A 1934 revision modified the language to include fraudulent claims "in any matter within the jurisdiction of any department or agency of the United States." In 1948 the legislature divided the statute designating 18 U.S.C. § 287 as the false claims statute and 18 U.S.C. § 1001 as the prohibition against the making of false statements. As part of the False Statements Accountability Act of 1996, the statute was amended to include "any matter within the jurisdiction of the executive, legislative, or judicial branch" of the United States government.

Section 1001 is divisible into three types of conduct. It can apply to one who "[1] falsifies, conceals or covers up by any trick, scheme or device a material fact, [2] makes any materially false, fictitious, or fraudulent statement or representation, or [3] makes or uses any false writing or document knowing the same to contain any materially false, fictitious, or fraudulent statement or entry."

False statements require proof of the following elements: (1) a statement, (2) falsity, (3) materiality, (4) made knowingly and willfully, (5) within the executive, legislative, or judicial branch of the United States government. Commission of an act prohibited by section 1001 carries a penalty of not more than five years imprisonment and a fine.

§ 9.02 Statements

Section 1001 statements can take a variety of forms. They can be written or oral, sworn or unsworn. False statements that relate to past, present or future activity are covered by the statute. The statement also may be either voluntary or made pursuant to a requirement of law.

If proceeding under the first type of conduct described in the false statement statute ("falsifies, conceals or covers up by trick, scheme or device a material fact"), then an actual statement is not necessary. In this instance it is sufficient to show an affirmative act in which the defendant has used a trick, scheme or device that conceals, covers up or results in a failure to disclose. Thus, a failure to provide information on a government form where there is a duty to disclose the information can serve as the basis for a charge under section 1001. It is "incumbent on the Government to prove that the defendant had the duty to disclose the material facts at the time [the defendant] was alleged to have concealed them." *U.S. v. Irwin* (10th Cir.1981).

In *Brogan v. U.S.* (S.Ct.1997) the Supreme Court held that the "the plain language of § 1001 admits of no exception for an 'exculpatory no.'" Prior to this decision, lower courts had accepted in varying degrees an exception to the false statement element of the statute, when the accused replied with a "mere negative response[ ] to questions propounded to him by an investigating agent during a question and answer conference," that was not initiated by the accused. In *Brogan* the Court rejected the self-incrimination claim finding that there is no Fifth Amendment "privilege to lie."

§ 9.03 Falsity

Falsity can be achieved through either the making of a false statement or by the concealment of a material fact. Where the alleged conduct is premised upon the making of a false statement, it is incumbent upon the government to prove actual falsity. *U.S. v. Hixon* (6th Cir. 1993). Literally true statements, as well as statements that are merely misleading, have been found insufficient. Although the issue of falsity is a question of fact for a jury to decide, a statement that is subject to more than one interpretation places a burden on the government to refute the meaning attributed by the defendant.

Concealment of a material fact also can provide a basis for the crime of false statements. When proceeding under the concealment aspect of the statute, the government must prove that the defendant's affirmative act in failing to disclose a material fact was by means of trick, scheme or device.

§ 9.04 Knowledge and Intent

Section 1001 requires that the government prove the defendant's knowledge of the falsity of the statement, or that the defendant's action was taken for the purpose of concealing or covering up a material fact. Additionally, proof of willfulness is required.

The level of knowledge required of the defendant can be met by evidence of a reckless disregard of the truth or by a conscious avoidance in learning the truth. Actual knowledge of the statement's falsity is not required. In meeting the knowledge requirement, the government may employ circumstantial evidence.

Willfulness does not mandate proof of an intent to defraud. The false statement statute contains language in the disjunctive: "false, fictitious **or** fraudulent." Thus, willfulness is met with proof that a defendant intended to deceive. Where the government's indictment specifically characterizes the defendant's conduct as fraudulent, as opposed to being false or fictitious, then courts have required that the government prove the allegation.

When proceeding under the concealment provision of the false statement statute, it is also necessary for the government to present sufficient proof of intent to deceive. Additionally, when the indictment is premised upon concealment, it is necessary for the government to substantiate that the defendant knew of the duty to disclose and intentionally failed to comply with that duty.

Although a knowledge and willfulness are required for a violation of section 1001, there is no necessity to show that the defendant had actual knowledge of federal agency jurisdiction. In *U.S. v. Yermian* (S.Ct.1984), the Supreme Court resolved a then existing jurisdictional dichotomy on whether it was necessary for the government to prove that the defendant actually knew that the matter was before a government agency.

Defendant Yermian was convicted of three counts of making false statements based upon false information supplied to his employer in connection with a Department of Defense security questionnaire. Defendant failed to disclose his mail fraud conviction on the submitted form and additionally listed employment with two companies that had never employed him. The defendant "signed a certification stating that his answers were 'true, complete and correct to the best of [his] knowledge' and that he understood' that any misrepresentation or false statement ... may subject [him] to prosecution under section 1001 of the United States Criminal Code.' "At trial, defendant admitted to the falsity of the statements, but contended that he did not have actual knowledge that the statements would be given to a federal agency.

The Supreme Court, in a 5–4 decision, found no basis for requiring proof of actual knowledge of federal agency jurisdiction. The Court held that the term "knowingly" following the phrase "in any matter within the jurisdiction of any department or agency of the United States," is merely a jurisdictional requirement. The Court found that "[a]ny natural reading of § 1001, therefore, establishes that the terms 'knowingly and willfully' modify only the making of false, 'fictitious or fraudulent statements,' and not the predicate circumstance that the statements be made in a matter within the jurisdiction of a federal agency."

Unresolved by *Yermian* was whether a lesser degree of mens rea would be required with respect to the element of federal agency jurisdiction. In a footnote in the *Yermian* decision, the Supreme Court remarked that the jury had been instructed, without objection from the government, that proof was required that defendant "knew or should have known" that statements were made within the jurisdiction of a federal agency. In this footnote, the Court specifically remarked on the narrowness of the issue being decided. Since the only question before the Court in *Yermian* was whether proof of *actual* knowledge of federal agency jurisdiction was mandated, resolution of the level, if any, of culpable mental state of federal agency jurisdiction remains for future determination. Also left for future interpretation is whether specific inclusion of "executive, legislative, or judicial branch" in the statute alters the required level of knowledge.

In *U.S. v. Green* (9th Cir.1984), the Ninth Circuit found no abuse of discretion in a trial court's failure to give an instruction on jurisdictional knowledge. The appellate court held that "[n]o culpable mental state must be proved with respect to federal agency jurisdiction in order to establish a violation of section 1001." Other jurisdictions have ruled in accord with this Ninth Circuit decision.

§ 9.05 Materiality

Originally materiality was only listed in the concealment clause of section 1001. ("Falsifies, conceals or covers up by a trick, scheme or device a *material* fact"). The remaining two misrepresentation clauses of the statute omitted the term. ("[2] makes any false, fictitious or fraudulent statements or representations, or [3] makes or uses any false writing or document knowing the same to contain any false, fictitious or fraudulent statement or entry.") Despite the failure to explicitly require materiality in the second and third clauses of the statute, most courts required proof of materiality to sustain a false statement conviction. Materiality was added to sections 2 and 3 of the statute as part of the False Statements Accountability Act of 1996.

In determining whether a false statement or concealment is material, courts examine whether the statement has "a natural tendency to influence, or [be] capable of influencing, the decision of the decisionmaking body to which it is addressed."

Kungys v. U.S. (S.Ct.1988). It is not necessary to prove that the government agency was actually influenced or that the statement was relied upon by the government. There is also no requirement that the statement be made directly to a federal official.

In *U.S. v. Gaudin* (S.Ct.1995), the Supreme Court found that the issue of materiality is a mixed question of law and fact that should properly be submitted to the jury. The defendant in *Gaudin* was accused of making false statements on federal loan documents. The district court ruled as a matter of law that the statements were material. The Ninth Circuit, en banc, reversed finding that the issue of materiality should have been submitted to the jury. In affirming the Ninth Circuit, Justice Scalia wrote that "[t]he Constitution gives a criminal defendant the right to have a jury determine, beyond a reasonable doubt, his guilt or every element of the crime with which he is charged."

In *Gaudin*, the parties had "agreed that materiality was an element of 18 U.S.C. § 1001, but disputed whether materiality was a question for the judge or jury." In *U.S. v. Wells* (S.Ct.1997), the Supreme Court found that 18 U.S.C. § 1014, a statute pertaining to false statements to a federally insured financial institution, did not require the government to prove materiality.

§ 9.06 Matters Within the Jurisdiction of the Executive, Legislative, or Judicial Branch

It is first necessary to consider the scope of the term "jurisdiction." In *U.S. v. Rodgers* (S.Ct.1984), the United States Supreme Court held that "jurisdiction," although undefined in the statute, does not suggest support for a narrow construction. Section 1001 "expressly embraces false statements made 'in *any* matter within the jurisdiction of *any* department or agency of the United States.' "Thus, a man who lied to the F.B.I. by telling them his wife had been kidnapped and lied to the Secret Service in telling them his wife was involved in a plot to kill the President, was not entitled to a dismissal of a false statement charge as not within the bounds of the term, "jurisdiction," as used in section 1001. Since the F.B.I. is authorized to investigate crimes, including kidnapping, and the Secret Service is charged with protecting the President, statements to these agencies were within their statutory bases. The Court noted that reading section 1001 broadly furthered the "valid legislative interest in protecting the integrity of [such] official inquiries."

For many years courts struggled with the limits of the term "department or agency." In *U.S. v. Bramblett* (S.Ct.1955), the Supreme Court found that the Disbursement Office of the House of Representatives was, in fact, a "department or agency of the United States." Defendant Bramblett, a former member of Congress, was charged with falsely representing to the Disbursement Office that an individual was entitled to compensation for being his official clerk. The Court, providing guidance on how to interpret the term "department," stated that "as used in this context, [it] was meant to describe the executive, legislative and judicial branches of the government." *Bramblett* permitted the term "department" to include numerous government agencies, sub-agencies, and boards. In *Hubbard v. U.S.* (S.Ct.1995), however, the Supreme Court overruled *Bramblett* finding that a court was not an agency or department for purposes of § 1001.

The False Statements Accountability Act of 1996 modifies the statute to explicitly provide "the jurisdiction of the executive, legislative, or judicial branch" of the United States government. The section, however, specifically excludes "statements, representations, writings or documents submitted by" a party or counsel in a judicial proceeding. The new provision also limits the scope of matters of the legislative branch by stating that it applies only to administrative matters or certain Congressional investigations or reviews.

§ 9.07 Other Crimes

In examining the surge of cases relating to government procurement fraud, it is evident that a myriad of criminal statutes may be used in prosecuting the criminal conduct. False statements pursuant to section 1001 has traditionally been a major offense used in procurement fraud cases. In 1988 Congress passed the Major Fraud Act (18 U.S.C. § 1031) that created the specific offense of procurement fraud for government contract fraud involving one million dollars or more.

Also used when proceeding against procurement fraud is the false claims statute located in 18 U.S.C. § 287. This offense, originally combined with the false statements statute, was separated by Congress in 1948. The false claims statute is more restrictive in its application than section 1001 in that it applies only to false claims to the government. False claims actions can be presented by private individuals acting on behalf of the United States. Section 3730 of Title 31 permits qui tam plaintiffs the right to bring civil actions on behalf of themselves and the government for violations of the False Claims Act.

When false statements under section 1001 are charged in conjunction with another criminal offense, courts are left to decide the propriety of the prosecutor's selection of multiple charges. In *U.S. v. Woodward* (S.Ct.1985), the Supreme Court considered the acceptability of indictments under 18 U.S.C. § 1001 and 31 U.S.C. § 1058, 1011 for willfully failing to report the carrying of cash in excess of five thousand dollars. The charges arose from the defendant's response of "no" on a customs form followed by a search and finding of monies in excess of five thousand dollars on the defendant and his wife. The Supreme Court found substantiation of Congress' intent to punish under both 18 U.S.C. § 1001 and 31 U.S.C. §§ 1058, 1101 "by the fact that the statute's 'are directed to separate evils.' "

A court has, however, refused to permit a conviction and sentence to stand when the same conduct was being punished under two different false statement statutes. In *U.S. v. Avelino* (2d Cir.1992), the Second Circuit held that it was a violation of the double jeopardy clause to convict and sentence a defendant for both false statements pursuant to section 1001 and making false statements to Customs officials pursuant to 18 U.S.C. § 542. The court noted that "every element needed to prove a crime under Section 1001 is an element of a Section 542 offense and that there is no clear indication of a congressional intent to provide for cumulative punishments for Sections 1001 and 542."

CHAPTER TEN

PERJURY AND FALSE DECLARATIONS

§ 10.01 Introduction

Perjury statutes exist throughout the United States Code. They are evident in Title 18, as well as in sections of the Code that are not focused predominantly upon crimes. For example, in Title 26 one observes a tax offense that is predicated upon the filing of a perjurious tax return (26 U.S.C. § 7206). In some instances the statute will authorize an individual to give an oath and refer violations of the oath to the perjury provisions found in Title 18. For example, Title 8 contains a statute pertaining to false evidence or swearing before the Immigration and Naturalization Service (8 U.S.C. § 1357) and authorizes prosecution pursuant to the criminal perjury statute. (18 U.S.C. § 1621).

Key statutes related to false and perjurious testimony are located at 18 U.S.C. § 1621 (perjury) and 18 U.S.C. § 1623 (false declarations). Today's perjury statute (§ 1621) dates back to statutes enacted by Congress for the purpose of criminalizing all false swearing. *U.S. v. Smull* (S.Ct.1915). The false declarations statute (§ 1623) was added by Congress in 1970 as part of the Organized Crime Control Act of 1970 to "facilitate perjury prosecutions and thereby enhance reliability of testimony before federal courts and grand juries." *Dunn v. U.S.* (S.Ct.1979). Although this new statute eased the evidentiary requirements in prosecuting perjury, it's scope was limited to proceedings before or ancillary to federal courts or grand juries.

Perjury (18 U.S.C. § 1621) requires the government prove that the defendant: (1) under oath, by one authorized to administer the oath; (2) before a competent tribunal, officer, or person; (3) made a false; (4) material statement; (5) willfully and with knowledge of its falsity. Perjury carries a penalty of not more than five years imprisonment and a fine.

False declarations (18 U.S.C. § 1623) requires the government prove that the defendant: (1) under oath; (2) before or ancillary to any court or grand jury of the United States; (3) made a false; (4) material statement; (5) with knowledge of its falsity. False declarations carries a penalty of not more than five years imprisonment and a fine.

Perjury and false declarations permit prosecutions of statements that are made both inside or outside the United States. Further, these statutes incorporate 28 U.S.C. § 1746, thereby permitting certain unsworn statements to be subject to prosecution.

The key distinctions between these two offenses are noted in examining the scope, defenses, and evidentiary rules surrounding the two statutes. Most notable is the fact that perjury includes a broader range of proceedings than false declarations. Where perjury applies to false statements before any "competent tribunal, officer, or person," false declarations is limited to statements "before or ancillary to any court or grand jury of the United States."

An additional distinction between these two statutes is noted in the fact that unlike the perjury statute, the false declarations statute does not require two witnesses. Also, the false declarations statute permits the use of inconsistent statements to prove falsity, without specification as to which statement is false. Finally, the false declarations statute provides for a recantation defense in certain circumstances.

When sections 1621 and 1623 both apply to the applicable criminal conduct, prosecutors have discretion to choose under which offense to proceed. Defense attorneys have unsuccessfully contested the use of the perjury statute when the statement was before a court or grand jury, and therefore subject to a false declarations charge. Arguments that the government has deprived the defendant of the recantation defense, by proceeding with a perjury charge, have failed to merit reversals. In one case, however, the Ninth Circuit treated a charge pursuant to section 1621 as if it had been filed under section 1623. *U.S. v. Clizer* (9th Cir.1972).

Immunization of a witness does not preclude a perjury or false declarations charge against that witness. The federal immunity statute, 18 U.S.C. § 6002, specifically excepts "a prosecution for perjury, giving a false statement, or otherwise failing to comply with the order." Both the truthful and untruthful immunized testimony may be used in a subsequent false swearing prosecution for making false statements in the immunized testimony. *U.S. v. Apfelbaum* (S.Ct.1980) (see § 19.12).

§ 10.02 Oath

Both perjury (18 U.S.C. § 1621) and false declarations (18 U.S.C. § 1623) require proof that the defendant's statement was under oath. In most circumstances this oath will be a sworn declaration. It is possible, however, to prosecute for perjury or false declarations, absent an oath, when the criteria encompassed in 28 U.S.C. § 1746 have been met.

Congress passed section 1746 of Title 28 in 1976. That same year the legislature amended sections 1621 and 1623 to incorporate this alternative to the sworn oath requirements of the perjury and false declarations statute. Section 1746 provides that where a law, "rule, regulation, order, or requirement made pursuant to law" permits or requires an oath, then an unsworn declaration can suffice. The unsworn declaration must, however, be in substantially the same form as specifically set forth in the text of section 1746. The form provided includes a declaration, under penalties of perjury, that the statement is true and correct. The statute offers alternative forms for the unsworn declaration dependent on whether it is executed inside or outside the United States.

Although sections 1621 and 1623 of Title 18 require an oath, there is no necessity that the indictment allege the name of the person administering the oath. In *U.S. v. Debrow* (S.Ct.1953), the Supreme Court reversed a district court's dismissal of a perjury indictment that failed to state the name and authority of the individual administering the oath. The Court found that the oath requirement could be met by the indictment's allegations "that the defendant had 'duly taken an oath.' "The term "duly taken" was interpreted by the Court to mean "an oath taken according to a law which authorizes such oath."

Although the indictment does not have to name the person who administered the oath, a court has required that it be proven in a section 1621 prosecution. In *Smith v. U.S.* (5th Cir.1966), the Fifth Circuit found insufficient evidence of the oath requirement where the government's case consisted of a court clerk identifying a certified copy of the transcript containing the alleged perjury. The clerk in *Smith* failed to state that he was present at the hearing or that he observed the administration of an oath to the defendant. The court found that "the bare statement in the transcript, unsupported by testimony, that the defendant had been duly sworn was insufficient evidence to support a conviction of perjury."

In contrast, one court held that the false declarations statute (18 U.S.C. § 1623) does not make the identity of the one who administered the oath an essential element of the offense. In *U.S. v. Molinares* (11th Cir.1983), the Eleventh Circuit discussed the distinction in proof required for 1621 and 1623. The court found that section 1621 required greater proof of the oath in that the statute used the language "taken an oath before a competent tribunal, officer, or person ...". In contrast, section 1623, the false declarations statute, merely required "the government prove that the maker of a knowingly false declaration before a court be under oath at the time of the statement." The court in *Molinares* found direct evidence by two witnesses of the administration of the oath, coupled with a transcript of the proceedings indicating the defendant being duly sworn prior to testifying, sufficient evidence for sustaining a prosecution pursuant to section 1623.

Although courts require that the oath be taken before an individual authorized to administer the oath, the person may be a de facto officer. A prosecution involving a violation of 18 U.S.C. § 1623 was predicated upon false testimony given under an oath administered by an "assistant" deputy foreperson of a grand jury. The court had designated an assistant deputy foreperson due to the absence of the foreperson. In response to the defendant's challenge of this oath, the Eastern District of Virginia found the use of the word "assistant" to be mere surplusage. The court stated that "generally it is considered immaterial whether the person administering the oath is an officer de jure or de facto, if his act takes place in the presence of the Court or one authorized to administer the oath, and with its apparent sanction." *U.S. v. Allen* (E.D.Va.1975).

§ 10.03 Within Tribunals and Proceedings

Section 1621 requires that the statement be made before "a competent tribunal, officer, or person, in any case in which a law of the United States authorizes an oath to be administered." In contrast, section 1623 is more limited in that the statement has to be "in any proceeding before or ancillary to any court or grand jury of the United States."

The competency of the person administering the oath has been challenged in several section 1621 cases. Courts have found district court judges, deputy clerks, Senate subcommittees, an internal revenue agent, and public notaries as competent tribunals, officers, or persons authorized to administer an oath.

Even a court proceeding that is later found to be premised upon a defective indictment can serve as a competent tribunal for purposes of section 1621. All that is required is court power to proceed to a determination on the merits. Thus, a later showing of a statute being unconstitutional or a holding of insufficient evidence to prove the crime will not bar a prosecution of false testimony presented at the trial. *U.S. v. Williams* (S.Ct.1951). A false declaration indictment, however, was found to be improper when based upon a declaration made two days after the grand jury term had expired. *U.S. v. Fein* (2d Cir.1974).

The scope of proceedings is more restrictive in section 1623 than in section 1621. In *Dunn v. U.S.* (S.Ct.1979), the Supreme Court found that a sworn statement taken at an interview in a private attorney's office did not constitute a proceeding ancillary to a court or grand jury. The Court in *Dunn* examined the legislative history surrounding section 1623 and also noted a comment of the Department of Justice on the proposed legislation "that the scope of the inconsistent declarations provision was 'not as inclusive' as the perjury statute." Despite this comment, the government argued that since pre-trial depositions were covered in a letter sent by Senator McClellan to the Assistant Attorney General, it could also be interpreted that affidavits and certificates were meant to be included. The Court in *Dunn* agreed with the Court of Appeal's conclusion that the interview in this case "lacked the degree of formality required by § 1623." Implied throughout this decision, however, is that depositions, taken pursuant to Rule 15 of the Federal Rules of Criminal Procedure and 18 U.S.C. § 3503 can be ancillary proceedings for the purposes of a section 1623 prosecution.

§ 10.04 Falsity

Prosecutions of both perjury and false declarations require a false statement. Actual falsity has been demanded by the courts. Thus, literally true but misleading statements will not constitute falsity. Likewise, ambiguous questions that call for varying interpretations cannot be used as the basis for obtaining a perjury or false declarations conviction.

Bronston v. U.S. (S.Ct.1973), is the Supreme Court's seminal decision holding that literally true statements cannot be the basis of a perjury conviction. In *Bronston*, the defendant was being questioned in a bankruptcy hearing by a lawyer representing a creditor. The questions sought to elicit whether the defendant, sole owner of Bronston Productions, had any Swiss bank accounts. The attorney first asked defendant if he had any Swiss bank accounts. To this question the defendant answered "no." The attorney for the creditor then asked defendant Bronston, "[h]ave you ever?" The defendant responded that "[t]he company had an account there for about six months, in Zurich." The defendant failed, however, to mention that although he presently had no bank accounts in Switzerland, he had held such an account for the past five years. Thus, although defendant's answers were literally true, in that he did not presently have an account and the company did at one point have one, he had failed to respond specifically to whether he had a Swiss bank account in the past.

In rejecting the government's use of this second question as the basis for a perjury conviction, the Court stated that it is the responsibility of the "questioner to pin the witness down to the specific object of the questioner's inquiry." Even though the witness may be deliberately avoiding the question, "it is the lawyer's responsibility to recognize the evasion and to bring the witness back to the mark, to flush out the whole truth with the tools of adversary examination." Literally true, but unresponsive answers should not be the subject of a federal perjury prosecution.

Falsity is a question to be determined by the jury. In making this determination, the jury should examine the answer to the question objectively. "The jury should determine whether the question—as the declarant must have understood it, giving it a reasonable reading—was falsely answered." *U.S. v. Lighte* (2d Cir.1986).

In *U.S. v. Shotts* (11th Cir. 1998) the Eleventh Circuit stated that "[a] perjury conviction must rest on the utterance by the accused of a false statement; it may not stand on a particular interpretation that the questioner places upon the answer." In *U.S. v. DeZarn* (6th Cir. 1998), however, the Sixth Circuit held that a perjury inquiry can examine the contextual setting of the statement. The court stated, "[a] perjury inquiry which focuses only upon the precision of the question and ignores what the Defendant knew about the subject matter of the question at the time it was asked, misses the very point of perjury: that is, the Defendant's intent to testify falsely and, thereby, mislead his interrogators."

Falsity cannot exist when the question itself is "fundamentally ambiguous." A test for determining if a question is "fundamentally ambiguous" is set forth in the case of *U.S. v. Lattimore* (D.D.C.1955), where the District Court for the District of Columbia found vagueness in a phrase that "is not a phrase with a meaning about which ordinary men of ordinary intelligence could agree, nor one which could be used with mutual understanding by a questioner and answerer unless it were defined at the time it were sought and offered as testimony."

To determine if a statement is "fundamentally ambiguous" it is necessary to examine the statement in its context. The asking of some ambiguous questions does not preclude a perjury conviction. *U.S. v. Lighte* (2d Cir.1986). Further, a question in not "fundamentally ambiguous" just because some of the words used in the question may have different meanings.

The false declarations statute (18 U.S.C. § 1623) specifically provides that in certain circumstances a defendant who knowingly makes "two or more declarations, which are inconsistent to the degree that one of them is necessarily false, [the indictment] need not specify which declaration is false ..." The statute specifies that each declaration must be material to the point in question, and the declarations must be made within the applicable statute of limitations for the offense being charged. It is a defense if the accused believed the declaration to be true at the time it was made.

§ 10.05 Materiality

Materiality is an element of both perjury and false declarations. Although required, the element is met with minimal evidence. "The test of materiality is whether the false testimony was capable of influencing the tribunal on the issue, or whether the false testimony would have the natural effect or tendency to influence, impede, or dissuade the Grand Jury from pursuing its investigation." *U.S. v. Gremillion* (5th Cir.1972). The statement does not have to actually influence the tribunal or impede the investigation. It suffices when it is capable of this result.

The government bears the burden of proving materiality. *U.S. v. Bednar* (8th Cir.1984). It need only be proven as of the time the statements were given. Materiality does not require that the statement relate to a main issue in the case. Statements relating to subsidiary matters have been found to be material.

§ 10.06 Knowledge and Willfulness

It is incumbent in a perjury or false declarations prosecution that the defendant have acted with knowledge of the statement's falsity. Although the statutes differ in this mens rea terminology, (perjury uses "not believe to be true," false declarations uses "knowingly"), courts have been consistent in finding that both provisions require that the defendant must have believed when delivering the testimony that it was untrue. *U.S. v. Reveron Martinez* (1st Cir.1988).

Whether the accused acted with knowledge of the statement's falsity is a question for the jury to resolve. Oftentimes circumstantial evidence is presented to satisfy the knowledge requirement. "The trier of fact may infer this element of knowledge from the surrounding circumstances." *U.S. v. Larranaga* (10th Cir.1986).

Willfulness is an element of a section 1621 offense. It is not, however, used in the statutory language found in section 1623. Refusal of a defendant's willfulness instruction in a section 1623 prosecution has been upheld by an appellate court, since willfulness is not an element of a section 1623 offense. *U.S. v. Fornaro* (2d Cir.1990).

§ 10.07 Two Witness Rule

Perjury prosecutions are subject to a two-witness rule. *Hammer v. U.S.* (S.Ct.1926). This evidentiary rule bars a conviction for perjury that is based solely upon one witness. *Weiler v. U.S.* (S.Ct.1945). The rule requires "that the falsity of the defendant's statements must be proved by the testimony of two witnesses or the testimony of one witness, plus corroborating evidence." *U.S. v. Davis* (9th Cir.1977).

The two-witness rule is not applicable to charges brought pursuant to section 1623, the false declarations statute. Congress specifically stated in the false declarations statute that although proof beyond a reasonable doubt would be sufficient for a conviction, it would not be necessary that such proof include a particular number of witnesses or evidence.

The policy rationale offered for adoption of a two-witness rule in perjury prosecutions is that it prevents a perjury conviction resting solely on one person's oath against another. Further, the rule encourages witnesses to come forward in that it prevents witnesses from being harassed or subjecting themselves to a possible false perjury prosecution.

Although called the two-witness rule, in actuality it does not require two separate witnesses. The rule can be satisfied either with two witnesses, or alternatively, one witness and sufficient corroborative evidence. Jurisdictions have differed over the precise level of sufficiency required for corroboration.

Generally, the corroborating evidence does not have to be sufficient for a conviction. It cannot, however, consist of merely peripheral testimony not tending to show the falsity of the accused's statements while under oath. *U.S. v. Diggs* (7th Cir.1977). Most courts require that the corroborative evidence "be inconsistent with the innocence of the accused and must tend to show the perjury independently of the testimony which it is intended to corroborate." *U.S. v. Forrest* (5th Cir.1981). Independent evidence has been defined as "evidence coming from a source other than that of the direct testimony." *U.S. v. Diggs* (7th Cir.1977).

Some jurisdictions, however, have not mandated that the corroborative evidence, taken by itself, be inconsistent with the innocence of the accused. These courts find it sufficient if the corroborative evidence, taken in conjunction with the direct testimony, is inconsistent with the innocence of the accused.

Courts have accepted circumstantial evidence as corroboration. The evidence must, however, be trustworthy. Some jurisdictions have permitted the defendant's own statements and conduct to serve as the corroboration. The jury decides the weight to be accorded to the corroborative evidence.

§ 10.08 Recantation

The false declarations statute, section 1623, permits a limited defense of recantation. The statute provides one with the opportunity to admit false testimony and avoid a false declarations prosecution. The statute requires that the admission be made in the same continuous court or grand jury proceeding of the original declaration. The statute, however, is only applicable in certain circumstances.

Congress offered this recantation defense in an effort to "encourage truthful testimony by witnesses appearing before courts and grand juries." *U.S. v. Moore* (D.C.Cir.1979). The House Committee on the Judiciary reported that recantation "serves as an inducement to the witness to give truthful testimony by permitting him voluntarily to correct a false statement without incurring the risk [of] prosecution by doing so."

Recantation does not apply to perjury prosecutions under section 1621. Defendants have unsuccessfully raised the issue that the government has deprived them of their right of recantation by charging perjury when the conduct could have been charged pursuant to the false declarations statute. In *U.S. v. Kahn* (2d Cir.1973), the Second Circuit expressed concern with the prospect of prosecutors using section 1621 when a recantation existed and section 1623 when it did not. In *Kahn* the court found it unnecessary to reach the merits of this argument in that even if the defendant had been charged pursuant to the false declarations statute, he would not have been entitled to a recantation defense.

Eligibility for a recantation defense is statutorily limited in that "at the time the admission is made, the declaration has not substantially affected the proceeding, or it has not become manifest that such falsity has been or will be exposed." Despite the disjunctive wording of this provision, most courts hold that "and" should be substituted for the "or" in section 1623(d). Thus, a defendant desiring a recantation defense must avail themselves of the opportunity before it substantially affects the proceeding and prior to it being exposed. The Eighth Circuit, however, found that "or" should be given "its ordinary meaning, reading the statute as setting forth two alternative conditions, satisfaction of either of which will allow a declarant to employ the recantation defense to bar prosecution for perjury." *U.S. v. Smith* (8th Cir.1994).

The rationale as to why most courts require both conditions for a recantation defense is seen in examining the statute's aim of truthtelling in judicial proceedings. To permit a defendant the right to recant upon realization of a possible prosecution, would encourage a witness to initially lie. Only when threatened with exposure or prosecution would the witness come forward to recant. *U.S. v. Fornaro* (2d Cir.1990).

In *U.S. v. Moore* (D.C.Cir.1979), the defendant initially testified before a grand jury investigating police corruption. Learning of a tape recording that contradicted his testimony, he attempted to recant his prior grand jury statements. The government, however, stopped a rehearsal of this recantation claiming his new version to be lacking credibility. The district court dismissed defendant's indictment when the government refused to permit defendant Moore the opportunity to reappear before the grand jury to recant his prior statements.

On appeal, the District of Columbia Circuit Court reversed and remanded, finding that the defendant was not entitled to a recantation defense when the government was already aware that Moore had lied to the grand jury. The court recognized that the recantation defense was premised upon a New York statute that used a conjunctive interpretation. It permitted a recantation defense only when the falsity had not substantially affected the proceeding and when it had not become manifest that such falsity had been or would be exposed.

In addition to these two conditions, courts have precluded a recantation defense when a defendant is using this avenue to attempt to explain prior inconsistent testimony. Outright retraction and repudiation of the prior statement has been required. *U.S. v. Tobias* (9th Cir.1988). Implicit recantation, such as claiming memory loss, has been held not to suffice.

A recantation defense must be raised by the defendant prior to trial. Courts differ, however, on which party bears the burden of proving recantation. Some find that once the defendant raises the issue, then the prosecution has the burden of proving the inapplicability of the recantation defense beyond a reasonable doubt. Other courts place the burden on the defendant to prove proper recantation pursuant to section 1623(d). It is, however, clear that recantation is a question of law for the court.

CHAPTER ELEVEN

TAX CRIMES

§ 11.01 Introduction

White collar crime prosecutions commonly include tax charges. Title 26 of the United States Code provides an array of available offenses. Additionally, tax offenses can sometimes be prosecuted through general criminal statutes found in Title 18.

Charges are often premised on attempts to evade or defeat tax. (26 U.S.C. § 7201). Also noteworthy to criminal tax prosecutions are charges of failure to file a return or pay a tax (26 U.S.C. § 7203), and the filing or aiding and assisting in the filing of a false tax return. (26 U.S.C. § 7206). On occasion the prosecution also will include a charge of delivering a fraudulent return. (26 U.S.C. § 7207).

Fewer prosecutions have been premised on other tax offenses, such as a willful failure to collect or truthfully account for and pay over any tax (26 U.S.C. § 7202), a willful furnishing of a fraudulent statement or failing to furnish a statement to employees as required by section 6051 of the Internal Revenue Code (26 U.S.C. § 7204), and a willful failure to supply withholding information or the supplying of false withholding information to an employer (26 U.S.C. § 7205).

166

Section 7212 criminalizes two types of behavior. Under section 7212(a) one who corruptly or by force or threats of force endeavors to interfere with the administration of the internal revenue laws is subject to prosecution. Section 7212(b) criminalizes forcible rescue of property seized under the Internal Revenue Code. A tax offense also exists specifically to combat offenses such as extortion and obstruction by officers and employees "of the United States acting in connection with any revenue law of the United States." (26 U.S.C. § 7214).

There are also statutes for specific criminal conduct that arises in the context of tax issues. For example, false statements to purchasers or lessees relating to tax (26 U.S.C. § 7211), failure to obey a summons pursuant to certain sections of the Internal Revenue Code (26 U.S.C. § 7210), and disclosure or use of information by preparers of returns can in certain circumstances result in misdemeanor penalties (26 U.S.C. § 7216).

Criminal statutes located in the crimes section of the United States Code also provide a basis for the prosecution of tax charges. For example, a conspiracy (18 U.S.C. § 371) charge can be used where the accused conspires with another to commit an offense defined in other federal statutes or conspires to defraud the United States. *U.S. v. Helmsley* (2d Cir.1991). As previously noted, conspiracy under this general conspiracy statute requires an overt act in furtherance of the conspiracy. (see chap. 3).

False statements (18 U.S.C. § 1001), false claims (18 U.S.C. § 287), perjury (18 U.S.C. § 1621), and mail fraud (18 U.S.C. § 1341) have also been used when the conduct involves tax violations. The

Department of Justice, however, restrains prosecutorial discretion by internally limiting the application of mail fraud charges to tax offenses. Authorization is required to prosecute tax violations as mail fraud. Further, the Department of Justice Guideline states that this authorization will only be given in "exceptional circumstance[s]." This restriction not only serves to limit the prosecution of tax violations through mail fraud charges, but also limits tax violations that might be prosecuted under the Racketeer Influenced and Corrupt Organization Act (RICO). Because mail fraud serves as one of the possible predicate acts for a RICO offense, but tax violations do not, the restriction has the effect of precluding most tax violations from being used in RICO prosecutions. This guideline, however, is not enforceable as a matter of law in that it is merely an internal guideline of the Department of Justice.

§ 11.02 Willfulness

An element common to the tax fraud offenses (§§ 7201–7207) is the mens rea element of willfulness. Although willfulness is not defined in these sections, the Supreme Court has ruled that it has the same meaning in each section. Thus, irrespective of whether the offense is a misdemeanor or a felony, the level of willfulness required remains the same. *U.S. v. Bishop* (S.Ct.1973). Although the willfulness element remains consistent in all tax fraud prosecutions, it "is a word of many meanings, its construction often being influenced by its context." *Spies v. U.S.* (S.Ct.1943).

Historically courts interpreted willfulness to mean acts done with "bad purpose or evil intent," *U.S. v.*

Murdock (S.Ct.1933), "evil motive and want of justification in view of all the financial circumstances of the taxpayer," *Spies v. U.S.* (S.Ct.1943), or "willful in the sense that he knew that he should have reported more income than he did." *Sansone v. U.S.* (S.Ct.1965). This historical view is outlined in the Supreme Court's decision in *U.S. v. Bishop* (S.Ct.1973).

Bishop, a lawyer convicted of three counts of the felony of filing a false return (26 U.S.C. § 7206(1)), contested the failure of the trial court to give his requested instruction on the misdemeanor offense of delivering a fraudulent return (26 U.S.C. § 7207). He argued that section 7207 was a lesser included offense of the felony and that "willfully" as found in the misdemeanor statute should be construed to require less scienter than the term would require in the felony offense.

In rejecting defendant's argument, the Supreme Court in *Bishop* stated that " 'willfully' has the same meaning in § 7207 that it has in § 7206(1)." While adhering to the historical standard of willfulness, the Supreme Court in *Bishop* also stated that willfully "connotes a voluntary, intentional violation of a known legal duty."

In *U.S. v. Pomponio* (S.Ct.1976), the Supreme Court elucidated upon its holding in *Bishop*. Petitioners in *Pomponio* were convicted of willfully filing false income tax returns (26 U.S.C. § 7206(1)). The Supreme Court reversed the appellate court's ruling that the jury had been improperly instructed concerning willfulness. The instruction given by the trial court had not required a finding of bad purpose or evil motive. The Court in *Pomponio* stated that

Bishop did not require "proof of any motive other than an intentional violation of a known legal duty." Thus, the trial court did not err in failing to instruct the jury on bad purpose or evil motive.

Although courts continue to refer to bad purpose and evil motive, it is clear that the government is not required to present such proof in establishing the element of willfulness. It is, however, incumbent upon the government to prove beyond a reasonable doubt that the accused intentionally and voluntarily violated a known legal duty.

Whether the accused acted with the requisite intent is a question of fact subject to jury determination. Often the prosecution offers circumstantial evidence as proof of this mens rea. A jury may infer willfulness from the facts presented. In practice, juries are often provided with evidence of the accused engaging in fraudulent type conduct ("badges of fraud").

Negating the element of willfulness can be a crucial aspect of the defense. In the landmark case of *Cheek v. U.S.* (S.Ct.1991), the Supreme Court resolved the standard to be used by a jury in deciding whether a defendant had a good faith misunderstanding of the law that negated willfulness.

Petitioner Cheek, a commercial airline pilot, was convicted by a jury of six charges of failing to file federal income tax returns (26 U.S.C. § 7203) and for alleged tax evasions (26 U.S.C. § 7201). Petitioner, acting pro se at trial, argued that he acted without willfulness in that he believed his actions were lawful and further that he believed that the tax laws were being unconstitutionally enforced.

The district court instructed the jury on three occasions regarding aspects of willfulness. The latter two occasions were as a result of questions submitted to the court by the jury. On appeal Cheek argued that the trial court erred in instructing the jury "that only an objectively reasonable misunderstanding of the law negates the statutory willfulness requirement." The Seventh Circuit rejected Cheek's argument and affirmed his convictions.

The Supreme Court granted certiorari and thereafter vacated the judgment of the Court of Appeals and remanded the case for further proceedings consistent with its opinion. Justice White, writing the majority opinion, commenced by noting that the term "willfully" as used in federal criminal tax offenses served to "carv[e] out an exception to the traditional rule" that ignorance of the law or mistake of law is no defense to criminal prosecution. The Court further reaffirmed that the standard for willfulness is the "voluntary, intentional violation of a known legal duty."

In resolving the issues presented in this case, the Court concentrated on the "knowledge" requirement of willfulness. The government must prove that the defendant is "aware of the duty at issue, which cannot be true if the jury credits a good-faith misunderstanding and belief submission, whether or not the claimed belief or misunderstanding is objectively reasonable." To characterize a belief as not objectively reasonable transforms the question to a legal issue and precludes the jury from properly resolving this factual question. It was, therefore, improper for the trial court to instruct the jury in such a way that they were precluded from considering petitioner's asserted beliefs that wages were not income and that he was not a taxpayer within the meaning of the Internal Revenue Code. The Court determined that these are rightfully issues to be decided by a jury in considering whether Cheek had acted willfully.

The Court in *Cheek*, however, rejected the defendant's claim that he had a good-faith belief that the income tax laws were unconstitutional as applied to him. Claims of unconstitutionality reveal that the accused's conduct is not arising from innocent mistakes. Rather, it provides a showing of full knowledge of the law. A defendant's view of the law is irrelevant to the issue of willfulness. It was, therefore, not error in this case for the trial court to instruct the jury to disregard defendant's claims that the tax laws were unconstitutional.

In his concurring opinion, Justice Scalia voiced his dissatisfaction with the Court's test for willfulness. He argued that willfulness should not be interpreted so "that belief in the nonexistence of a textual prohibition excuses liability, but belief in the invalidity (*i.e.*, the legal nonexistence) of a textual prohibition does not."

A dissent authored by Justice Blackmun, and joined by Justice Marshall, criticized the Court for exceeding the limits of common sense. The dissent expressed the view that a person of defendant's intelligence should not be permitted to assert, as a defense to willfulness, that the wages he receives for labor is not income.

On retrial, defendant Cheek argued a good faith belief premised upon his reliance on the advice of counsel. The trial court, however, refused defendant's request for an instruction on advice of counsel. The Seventh Circuit affirmed, finding insufficient evidence to warrant the giving of the instruction. *U.S. v. Cheek* (7th Cir.1993).

Willfulness also can be negated when there is uncertainty in the tax law. *James v. U.S.* (S.Ct.1961). In *U.S. v. Garber* (5th Cir.1979), the Fifth Circuit in an en banc rehearing examined the defendant's conviction for tax fraud that stemmed from her alleged failure to report income from the sale of her blood. The court reversed and remanded this section 7201 conviction finding that the district court had acted improperly in failing to permit experts from testifying on the question of whether the income was taxable. The court also found it improper for the trial court to have refused to instruct the jury that a reasonable misconception of tax law would negate defendant's intent. Because of the novel and unsettled nature of the law, the defendant should have been afforded the opportunity to present this position.

Some jurisdictions adhere to the position taken in *Garber*, finding uncertainty in the law as a proper defense to a tax charge. Subsequent Fifth Circuit cases, however, have limited *Garber* to the facts of that case. *U.S. v. Burton* (5th Cir.1984). Additionally, not all jurisdictions accept the position expressed in *Garber*. For example, in *U.S. v. Curtis* (6th Cir.1986), the Sixth Circuit rejected this view in part because it placed in the hands of the jury a legal question that should be resolved by the court. In *Curtis* the court expressed the view that a jury should not be asked "to read and interpret statutes to determine whether or not the governing law is uncertain or debatable."

§ 11.03 Tax Evasion

Tax evasion is considered the "capstone" of the tax offenses. Its purpose is to "induce prompt and forthright fulfillment of every duty under the income tax law and to provide a penalty suitable to every degree of delinquency." *Spies v. U.S.* (S.Ct.1943). The elements of a charge pursuant to 26 U.S.C. § 7201 are: (1) the existence of a tax deficiency, (2) an affirmative act of evasion or attempted evasion of tax, and (3) willfulness. The felony of tax evasion carries a penalty of not more than five years imprisonment and a fine, although pending legislation seeks to increase the sentence for this offense. When the evasion is by a corporation, the fine can be higher than that for an individual.

The government is required to prove beyond a reasonable doubt the existence of a tax deficiency. Courts often require that the deficiency be "substantial." In *U.S. v. Marashi* (9th Cir.1990), however, the Ninth Circuit rejected defendant's *de minimis* argument. The court stated that "[t]he language of section 7201 does not contain a substantiality requirement. It simply states that willful attempts to evade 'any tax' under the Tax Code is a felony." In reality, the Justice Department seldom prosecutes a tax evasion case absent a showing of a sufficient level of tax due and owing.

A mere tax deficiency, however, will not suffice to sustain an evasion conviction. It is also essential that the government show an affirmative act of evasion and willfulness. The evidence supporting these latter two elements often coalesces.

In *Spies v. U.S.* (S.Ct.1943), the Supreme Court examined the predecessor evasion statute as it relates to the misdemeanor of willful failure to pay a tax. According to the Court, the factor that distinguishes these two offenses is the "affirmative action implied from the term 'attempt,' as used in the felony subsection." While the misdemeanor can be a willful omission, the felony of evasion requires a positive attempt to evade tax.

The willful attempt to defeat or evade tax can be accomplished "in any manner." In *Spies* the Court offered illustrations of conduct (so-called "badges of fraud") from which a willful attempt could be inferred. The examples provided were "keeping a double set of books, making false entries or alterations, or false invoices or documents, destruction of books or records, concealment of assets or covering up sources of income, handling of one's affairs to avoid making the records usual in transactions of the kind, and any conduct, the likely effect of which would be to mislead or conceal." The filing of a false tax return has been found to be a sufficient affirmative commission to satisfy this element. *Sansone v. U.S.* (S.Ct.1965).

§ 11.04 Methods of Proof

It is necessary for the government to prove a tax deficiency for a prosecution under section 7201. One way this can be accomplished is through the direct or specific item method. Alternatively, the government can use indirect methods of proof. The indirect methods include the net worth method, the expenditures method, and bank deposit method.

The direct or specific item method is considered the simplest method of proving a tax deficiency. It employs specific items to prove the underpayment.

For example, a defendant's records could be used to prove that a specific deduction listed on the return was improper.

Indirect methods of proving a tax deficiency use circumstantial evidence to establish this element. One such method is the net worth method that examines the defendant's net worth at the beginning of a year in contrast to the net worth at the end of the year.

In *Holland v. U.S.* (S.Ct.1954), the Supreme Court examined the use of the net worth method. The Court noted the flaws inherent in this method, but upheld its legality cautioning that it be subject to the "exercise of great care and restraint." It is essential that the government establish the net worth at the beginning of the year with "reasonable certainty." Because the net worth method rests solely on circumstantial evidence, courts require the government to investigate all reasonable explanations offered by the defendant that are inconsistent with guilt.

Using the cash expenditures method, a variant of the net worth method, the government shows that the defendant's expenditures exceeded the reported income. Presumably the source of funds for these expenditures must be taxable income.

Finally, the government can use the bank deposit method for proving the tax deficiency. The government examines the bank deposits of the defendant, excluding deposits that are not taxable income. These deposits are then compared to the reported income of the accused. The excess in the amount deposited over the reported income represents the unreported income.

The government also may use a combination of methods. In *U.S. v. Scott* (7th Cir.1981), the defendant William J. Scott, former Attorney General for the State of Illinois, was convicted of one count of violating section 7206(1). The government used the net worth, cash expenditures, and specific items methods to prove that Scott had falsely reported his adjusted gross income for 1972.

§ 11.05 Failure to File a Return or Pay a Tax

Section 7203 criminalizes the willful failure to pay any tax, make any return, keep any records, or supply any information as required by law or regulations. The government must prove beyond a reasonable doubt that the accused, (1) willfully, (2) failed to make a return, to pay a tax, to keep records or supply information, (3) having a legal duty to do so, (4) at the time required by law. This misdemeanor offense carries a penalty of up to one year imprisonment and a fine, although this may be changed by pending legislation. In the case of a corporation, this fine can be higher. If, however, the failure to pay involves an estimated tax, the section is inapplicable if there is no addition to tax under section 6654 or 6655. The statute becomes a felony offense where the willful violation involves section 6050I of the Code. (see § 12.06). In this circumstance the offense carries a penalty of up to five years imprisonment.

This section is commonly employed to prosecute tax protesters who fail to file a return or who file incomplete returns. It is rare that the government proceeds with a section 7203 case absent a certain threshold of unpaid tax. Failure to file can be proven by testimony of an individual from the Internal Revenue Service stating that a search was made of the government's records and no return was found. As with other tax offenses, the government is required to prove that the accused acted willfully.

§ 11.06 False Returns

Section 7206 is divided into two separate offenses. Subsection one is a perjury tax offense in that it prohibits one from willfully making and subscribing a return, statement, or other document under penalties of perjury which the person did not believe to be true and correct as to every material matter. Subsection two criminalizes the conduct of one who aids or assists in the preparation of a false return.

In order to sustain a conviction under section 7206(1), the government must prove that the accused: (1) willfully, (2) signed a return, statement, or other document, (3) under penalties of perjury, (4) that the return, statement, or document was materially false, and (5) that the accused did not believe it to be true and correct. Section 7206(2) requires the government to prove that the accused: (1) willfully, (2) aided or assisted in, or procured, counseled or advised the preparation or presentation of any document in connection with any matter arising under the internal revenue laws, (3) which document is materially false.

Both subsections to this statute are felony offenses. They carry penalties of up to three years imprisonment and a fine, although this may be increased if pending legislation passes. In the case of a corporation, the fine can be higher.

Unlike the tax evasion statute, there is no requirement for the government to prove a tax deficiency. It is only necessary to show that the return is materially false.

In *U.S. v. DiVarco* (7th Cir.1973), defendants' convictions included violations of section 7206(1). Defendants argued on appeal that the government's failure to show that they understated their income precluded the use of this statutory provision. The Seventh Circuit noted that although most cases involving misstatement of source of income also involve an understatement of taxable income, "the purpose behind the statute is to prosecute those who intentionally falsify their tax returns regardless of the precise ultimate effect that falsification may have." In *DiVarco*, the court found that misstatement of the source of one's income could be a material matter.

In *U.S. v. Greenberg* (2d Cir.1984), the Second Circuit rejected defendant's argument that the misstatements were not material in that "they resulted in, at most, minimal underpayments of taxes." The court found that materiality referred to the impact the statement may have on the ability of the agency to perform its assigned functions. "The question is not what effect the statement actually had, ... rather whether the statement had the potential for an obstructive or inhibitive effect." The court in *Greenberg* found the false statements of income material, even though they resulted in the minimal underpayment of taxes.

Courts have not ruled consistently on whether materiality under § 7206 is a question of law to be decided by the court, or a question of fact to be decided by the jury. In *U.S. v. Gaudin* (see § 9.05), the Supreme Court held that issues of materiality of alleged false statements were questions for the jury to decide. In *U.S. v. Klausner* (2d Cir.1996), the Second Circuit distinguished *Gaudin* finding that the "determination of materiality in the present case under § 7206(2) was purely a legal question." Other courts, however, have followed *Gaudin,* finding "no obvious of substantive distinction between the 'materiality' element of 18 U.S.C. § 1001 and the 'materiality' element of 26 U.S.C. § 7206(1)." *U.S. v. DiRico* (1st Cir.1996).

A tax preparer can be charged under either subsection of this statute. In *U.S. v. Shortt Accountancy Corp.* (9th Cir.1986), the defendant corporation was convicted of seven counts of violating section 7206(1). The corporation, through its chief operating officer, improperly structured certain investments to appear as if they occurred before a change in law. This permitted clients to receive an undeserved tax benefit.

The corporation argued on appeal that a tax preparer could not be charged under subsection one of this statute, but rather 7206(2) was the applicable offense. The accounting corporation also maintained that the actual subscriber of the return was unaware of the fraud involved and therefore did not have the requisite intent of willfully making and subscribing a false return.

The Ninth Circuit, in *Shortt*, rejected defendant's arguments, finding that section 7206(1) was not limited to taxpayers. Being a perjury statute, the court found that anyone who makes a false return could be prosecuted pursuant to this provision. The court also held that the corporation could be convicted of section 7206(1) even though the particular employee subscribing the return had no knowledge of the fraudulent scheme. To hold otherwise would permit a tax preparer to escape liability "by arranging for an innocent employee to complete the proscribed act of subscribing a false return."

CHAPTER TWELVE

CURRENCY REPORTING CRIMES AND MONEY LAUNDERING

§ 12.01 Introduction

Currency reporting crimes emanate from statutes that are of recent vintage. In an effort to monitor financial transactions, Congress enacted legislation concentrating on reporting and recordkeeping by banks. This initial act, commonly referred to as the Bank Secrecy Act, includes a requirement that financial institutions report to the government certain cash transactions.

A second major effort to use currency transaction reporting as a method to combat criminality is seen in 26 U.S.C. § 6050I. Unlike the Bank Secrecy Act, which is limited to financial institutions, section 6050I requires the reporting of certain monetary transactions by those engaged in a "trade or business." The Bank Secrecy Act and section 6050I both, however, require that parties who meet the defined class, as specified in each of these statutes, report the transaction irrespective of any criminal conduct being involved.

The Bank Secrecy Act and section 6050I include provisions prohibiting the structuring of a transaction to evade the reporting requirements.

Additionally, Congress enacted sections 1956 and 1957 of Title 18 to combat money laundering. (see § 12.07) These latter two provisions fill a gap that became apparent in initial prosecutions under the Bank Secrecy Act. Congress extended the reach of the Bank Secrecy Act and money laundering statutes in Title III of the Patriot Act, The International Money Laundering Abatement and Anti-Terrorist Financing Act of 2001.

§ 12.02 Bank Secrecy Act

Congress passed the Bank Secrecy Act in 1970. The Act was "designed to obtain financial information having 'a high degree of usefulness in criminal, tax, or regulatory investigations or proceedings.' "*California Bankers Association v. Shultz* (S.Ct.1974). The Patriot Act added an additional mission of requiring reports "in the conduct of intelligence or counterintelligence activities, including analysis to protect against international terrorism." (18 U.S.C. § 5311).

Title I of the Act, presently codified in Title 12 of the United States Code, pertains to the requirements of financial institutions to keep records, including the maintaining of records of customer identity and the microfilming of checks. Title II of the Bank Secrecy Act, presently codified in Title 31 of the United States Code, requires the reporting to the federal government of certain foreign and domestic transactions. The Act authorizes the Secretary of the Treasury to prescribe via regulation the specified bank recordkeeping and reporting requirements.

Pursuant to 31 U.S.C. § 5313 and its accompanying regulations, it is incumbent that financial institutions file reports on certain domestic transactions. Statutes also exist regarding the recordkeeping and reporting on foreign financial agency transactions (31 U.S.C. § 5314), reports on foreign currency transactions (31 U.S.C. § 5315), and reports on exporting and importing monetary instruments (31 U.S.C. § 5316).

One who causes or attempts to cause a financial institution to fail to file a report required by section 5313(a), or causes or attempts to cause a financial institution to file a report that contains a material omission or misstatement of fact, can find themselves subject to the penalties imposed under this Act. The Bank Secrecy Act also prohibits the structuring of a transaction to evade the currency reporting requirements of section 5313(a). (31 U.S.C. § 5324).

Approximately two years after the passage of the Bank Secrecy Act, an action was brought in the District Court for the Northern District of California contesting the constitutionality of the Act. Although this action's principle focus was a claimed violation of the Fourth Amendment's guarantee against unreasonable searches and seizures, plaintiffs also claimed a violation of the First, Fifth, Ninth, Tenth and Fourteenth Amendments of the Constitution. The Supreme Court, in its eventual ruling in *California Bankers Association v. Shultz* (S.Ct.1974), found that the recordkeeping requirements imposed by the regulations of the Secretary of the Treasury did not deprive the plaintiff bank of due process of law and did not invade the Fourth Amendment's guarantee against unreasonable searches and seizures.

In rejecting this constitutional challenge to the Act, the Court in *California Bankers Association* noted that the recordkeeping requirements, as imposed by the Secretary of the Treasury, did not place an unreasonable burden on banks. The Supreme Court further found that a requirement of maintenance of records did not constitute a seizure. The Court found the application of the reporting requirements to both foreign and domestic transactions to be reasonable and that the bank depositors lacked standing to challenge the Act under the Fourth and Fifth Amendment.

In the later case of *U.S. v. Miller* (S.Ct.1976), the Supreme Court held that a bank depositor had no interest protected by the Fourth Amendment in records maintained by a bank pursuant to the Bank Secrecy Act, despite the allegation that these records were obtained by the government through defective subpoenas. The Court found that defendants had no legitimate expectation of privacy in business records of the bank. The Court stated that "[t]he depositor takes the risk, in revealing his affairs to another, that the information will be conveyed by that person to the Government."

In its initial years, the Bank Secrecy Act was seldom employed by the government as a prosecutorial tool. In recent years, however, the Act has significantly influenced the banking industry and has served as a source for the prosecution of financial institutions.

The Bank Secrecy Act and its accompanying regulations impose civil and criminal penalties for noncompliance with many of the reporting requirements. Willful violations of most of the provisions found in Title 31 carry criminal penalties of up to five years imprisonment and a fine. This penalty can be enhanced up to ten years with a fine when there is a willful violation that occurs while violating another law of the United States or engaging in conduct that is part of a pattern of illegal activity involving transactions exceeding $100,000 in a twelve month period. (31 U.S.C. § 5322). The penalty for structuring transactions to evade reporting requirements also carries imprisonment of up to five years, with an additional five years possible in certain aggravated cases. (31 U.S.C. § 5324).

Willful violations of a regulation under the recordkeeping statutes found in Title 12 can result in imprisonment of up to one year and a fine. (12 U.S.C. § 1956). This can be increased up to five years imprisonment with a fine where the violation is committed in furtherance of the commission of any violation of federal law punishable by imprisonment for more than one year. (12 U.S.C. § 1957).

§ 12.03 Domestic Financial Institutions

Section 5313 concerns reports required to be filed by domestic financial institutions. A financial institution is defined in 31 U.S.C. § 5312 and in the regulations of the Secretary of the Treasury. The breadth of this term is apparent in the inclusion of businesses well beyond the typical banking association. For example, financial institutions include "a dealer in precious metals, stones, or jewels," "a pawnbroker," "a travel agency," "a telegraph company," "a business engaged in vehicle sales, including automobile, airplane, and boat sales," and "persons involved in real estate closings and settlements."

In *U.S. v. Gollott* (5th Cir.1991), defendants challenged their status as a financial institution. In upholding defendants' convictions, the Fifth Circuit examined the definition of financial institution as stated in the amended regulations. The court stated that, "[t]his language is broader than and perhaps counterintuitive to everyday understanding of what a financial institution is, but it is not vague as applied to appellants' dealings." The court decided that the jury had rationally found defendants to be a financial institution as defined by applicable regulations.

In *U.S. v. Bucey* (7th Cir.1989), the Seventh Circuit reversed a defendant's convictions premised on 31 U.S.C. §§ 5313 and 5322(b). The court found defendant Bucey, acting in his individual capacity, not to be a financial institution, where the definition of the term included the language "agency, branch, or office." The court in *Bucey* did, however, note that the term financial institution was amended in 1987 after the time of defendant's alleged violations. The amended regulation added the word "agent" prior to "agency, branch, or office."

Most circuits find that an individual may be a financial institution. In *U.S. v. Goldberg* (2d Cir.1985), the Second Circuit noted that "[t]he regulations define a financial institution in part as 'a person.' There is no indication in the statute or the regulations that a natural person cannot be considered a financial institution, and it seems strained to assume that the term 'person' was intended to exclude natural persons."

A financial institution has been defined to encompass a bank, including each of its branches. Thus, if there are multiple cash transactions at different branches of the same financial institution that meet the reporting requirements, then the bank must file a currency transaction report. *U.S. v. Giancola* (11th Cir.1986).

The terms "domestic financial agency" and "domestic financial institution" are defined in section 5312 as to "apply to an action in the United States of a financial agency or institution." In a case under a somewhat differently worded predecessor statute, the Eleventh Circuit held that even though transactions were negotiated and completed in Columbia, the defendants were a domestic financial institution where their currency exchange business deposited money in a United States bank and the bank relayed information concerning each transaction from the United States to Columbia. *U.S. v. Eisenstein* (11th Cir.1984).

§ 12.04 Recordkeeping and Reporting Requirements

The Bank Secrecy Act and its accompanying regulations specify both recordkeeping and reporting requirements. Certain records by financial institutions involving extensions of credit, transfers of currency or monetary instruments, or intents to transfer currency or monetary instruments, are subject to be retained in original, microfilm, or other form of reproduction. The threshold monetary value for this retention requirement is ten thousand dollars. In many instances, regulations found in the Code of Federal Regulations provide details of the reporting rules.

Reports on exporting and importing monetary instruments are the subject of 31 U.S.C. § 5316. Certain monetary instruments transported from the United States to a place outside this country or from outside the United States to within this country are subject to the reporting requirements. Additionally, monetary instruments received from outside the United States may be subject to these reporting requirements. In 1986 this section of the Bank Secrecy Act was amended to increase the reportable amount from five thousand dollars to ten thousand dollars.

The regulations provided by the Secretary of the Treasury pursuant to this statutory provision on reports of transportation of currency or monetary instruments contain an array of exemptions from this filing requirement. (31 C.F.R. § 103.23). For example, a federal reserve bank is not subject to this reporting requirement. Regulations also provide the procedure, including time limitations for the filing of reports. (31 C.F.R. § 103.27).

Financial institutions are required to have an anti-money laundering program that includes "the development of internal policies, procedures, and controls; the designation of a compliance officer; an ongoing employee training program; and an independent audit function to test programs." (31 U.S.C. § 5318(h)). There is also the requirement of "due diligence for United States private banking and correspondent bank accounts involving foreign persons."   This requires that "[e]ach financial institution that establishes, maintains, administers, or manages a private banking account or a correspondent account in the United States for a non-United States person, including a foreign individual visiting the United States, or a representative of a non-United States person shall establish appropriate, specific, and, where necessary, enhanced, due diligence policies, procedures, and controls that are reasonably designed to detect and report instances of money laundering through those accounts." (31 U.S.C. § 5318(I).

Other statutes also contain reporting requirements, as for example customs forms. The Supreme Court, in *U.S. v. Bajakajian* (S.Ct. 1998), held that failure to report funds on a customs currency reporting form would not subject the individual to forfeiture "of the entire $357,144 that respondent failed to declare" when the forfeiture was disproportionate to the gravity of the offense. The Court found the forfeiture to be punitive and a violation of the Excessive Fines Clause. Congress, however, in the Patriot Act, created a new bulk cash smuggling offense that criminalizes the undeclared movement of more than ten thousand dollars across U.S. borders and makes the property subject to forfeiture. (31 U.S.C. § 5332).

§ 12.05 Knowledge and Willfulness

Criminal prosecutions under the Bank Secrecy Act often require willfulness. Recent legislation removed the willfulness requirement when a structuring offense is involved.

In *Ratzlaf v. U.S.* (S.Ct.1994), the Supreme Court examined willfulness in the context of an alleged structuring offense under 31 U.S.C. § 5324. In reversing defendant's conviction, the Court held that to willfully violate "the antistructuring law, the

Government must prove that the defendant acted with knowledge that his conduct was unlawful." The Court in *Ratzlaf* stated that they were "unpersuaded ... that structuring is 'so obviously "evil" or inherently "bad" that the "willfulness" requirement is satisfied irrespective of the defendant's knowledge of the illegality of structuring.' "

In response to the *Ratzlaf* decision, Congress modified § 5324 as part of the Riegle Community Development and Regulatory Improvement Act of 1994. The modified statute omits the term willfully. By placing penalty provisions directly in § 5324, the mens rea for the structuring statute is now met when the government shows that the defendant intended to evade the reporting requirement.

In *U.S. v. Bank of New England, N.A.* (1st Cir.1987), the First Circuit found that a trial court's collective knowledge instruction was proper where a bank had a structure similar to that of a large corporation. The court stated that "[c]orporations compartmentalize knowledge, subdividing the elements of specific duties and operations into smaller components. The aggregate of those components constitutes the corporation's knowledge of a potential operation." (see § 2.03).

§ 12.06 Section 6050I

Section 6050I of the Internal Revenue Code (Title 26) was modeled after the Bank Secrecy Act. A shortcoming of the Bank Secrecy Act, as being limited to financial institutions, was met by the adoption of a statute that extended currency transaction reporting to individuals engaged in a trade or business. Section 6050I, as passed in 1984, was intended to encourage the reporting of cash income in order to reduce the deficit. In reality, this section has become a tool for monitoring criminal activity.

26 U.S.C. § 6050I is applicable to trades or businesses that receive in excess of ten thousand dollars in cash. It requires the reporting of these transactions to the Internal Revenue Service. The section excludes transactions that would be reported pursuant to the Bank Secrecy Act. A provision of section 6050I prohibits the evading or assisting in the structuring of a transaction to avoid the reporting requirement. The Internal Revenue Service's form for complying with section 6050I is found in Form 8300.

Section 6050I and Form 8300 have proved controversial in the legal community. Because the statute applies to all trades or businesses, the question has arisen as to the section's applicability to payments received by attorneys.

In *U.S. v. Goldberger & Dubin, P.C.* (2d Cir.1991), the Second Circuit found that section 6050I did not conflict with the United States Constitution. Analogizing to cases reported under the Bank Secrecy Act, the court found no Fourth or Fifth Amendment violation. The court noted that the reporting requirements targeted transactions without regard to the underlying purpose and irrespective of any criminality involved in the transaction.

The *Goldberger* court also dismissed defense arguments that section 6050I was a deprivation of the right to counsel under the Sixth Amendment. The court found the section less intrusive than the recent Supreme Court decisions that permitted forfeiture of attorney fees. The Second Circuit stated that section 6050I did not preclude clients from their choice of counsel, "they need only pay counsel in some other manner than with cash."

Equally unpersuasive to the *Goldberger* court was appellant's contention that section 6050I conflicted with the attorney-client privilege. "Absent special circumstances," the court found that client identity and fee information were not privileged matters. (see § 22.01). Since the practice of law is considered a "trade or business" for purposes of the income tax laws and the Sherman Act, *Goldberger* found that absent a specific congressional intent to exclude attorneys, section 6050I applied to lawyers.

In *U.S. v. Sindel* (8th Cir.1995), the Eighth Circuit examined when the attorney-client privilege would protect client identity and fee information. "Special circumstances" exceptions were found to include "the legal advice exception," "the last link exception," and the "confidential communications exception." "After examining Sindel's *in camera* testimony about client's special circumstances," the court found the release of information with respect to one client, could not be accomplished without revealing "confidential communication." According to the court, "special circumstances," however, did not exist with respect to a second client.

It is necessary for the government to use the procedural process correctly when seeking to obtain information from an attorney about their client. In *U.S. v. Gertner* (1st Cir.1995), the First Circuit did not address the applicability of § 6050I to attorneys, finding that summons enforcement should be denied in that the government failed to adhere to the proper procedure for the service of John Doe summonses (see § 17.04).

§ 12.07 Money Laundering

Sections 1956 and 1957 of title 18, the money laundering statutes, emanate from the Anti–Drug Abuse Act of 1986. Specifically 18 U.S.C. § 1956 concentrates on financial transactions involving proceeds of unlawful activity. It does, however, criminalize transactions involving proceeds of unlawful activity "knowing that the transaction is designed in whole or in part ... to avoid a transaction reporting requirement under State or Federal Law ...". Section 1957 pertains to those who knowingly engage or attempt to engage in monetary transactions involving "criminally derived property that is of a value greater than ten thousand dollars and is derived from specified unlawful activity."

Both sections 1956 and 1957 focus on transactions involving tainted funds. Often drug related activity is prosecuted through the use of these money laundering offenses. In recent years, white collar criminality has also produced charges under sections 1956 and 1957. This is perhaps in part a result of the simplicity in proving a section 1956 and 1957 offense and the severe penalty accompanying these charges. A case that may have been limited to fraud charges may now find money laundering charges added to the indictment. *U.S. v. Powers* (5th Cir. 1999). It is necessary, however, that "money laundering must be a crime distinct from the crime by which the money is obtained. The money laundering statute is not simply the addition of a further penalty to a criminal deed; it is a prohibition of processing the fruits of a crime or of a completed phase of an ongoing offense." *U.S. v. Abuhouran* (3rd Cir. 1998).

Section 1956(a)(1) pertains to domestic money laundering. In contrast, section 1956(a)(2) involves international money laundering. The third form of money laundering, found in 1956(a)(3) "is designed for government sting operations using money 'represented to be' the proceeds of unlawful activity, but which is, in fact, government property." *U.S. v. Manarite*, (9th Cir. 1995).

The basic elements of an offense under 1956(a)(1) are that "(1) the defendant took part in a financial transaction; (2) the defendant knew that the property involved in the transaction involved the proceeds of illegal activity; (3) that the property involved was in fact the proceeds of that illegal activity; and (4) the defendant knew that the transaction was designed in whole or in part to conceal or disguise the nature, source, location, ownership, or control of the illegal proceeds." *U.S. v. Ruiz-Castro* (10th Cir. 1996).

Property being the proceeds of illegal activity is met by being a "specified unlawful activity," a term that is a component of all subsections of this offense. The array of conduct included in the definition of "specified unlawful activity" allows the statute to have enormous breadth. For example, "specified unlawful activity" includes an offense under 18 U.S.C. § 1030, the computer fraud statute. (see § 15.02).

CHAPTER THIRTEEN

BANKRUPTCY CRIMES

§ 13.01 Introduction

Statutes pertaining to bankruptcy crimes are, for the most part, found in sections 151 through 157 of Title 18. General criminal statutes also have been employed in the prosecution of criminal conduct related to bankruptcies.

Historically 18 U.S.C. § 152 served as the key bankruptcy crime statute for the prosecution of bankruptcy fraud. This statute concentrates on the concealment of assets, false oaths, and bribery and extortion conduct occurring in connection with a bankruptcy.

Section 153 pertains to embezzlement by a trustee, officer, or their agent. A penalty of up to five years imprisonment and fine can be imposed against a trustee, custodian, marshal, or other officer who "knowingly and fraudulently appropriates" to their "own use, embezzles, spends, or transfers any property or secrets or destroys a document" in their charge that is from the debtor's estate.

A custodian, trustee, marshal, or other officer of the court, who "knowingly purchases, directly or indirectly, any property of the estate of which he is such an officer in a case under Title 11" is subject to a fine and a forfeiture of the office held by the individual. Section 154 not only contains this adverse interest statute, but also imposes the same penalty when an officer refuses a court direction permitting parties in interest a reasonable opportunity to inspect documents or refuses a United States Trustee a reasonable opportunity to inspect documents.

Section 155 prohibits a party in interest from knowingly and fraudulently agreeing with another party in interest to the fixing of a fee or other compensation from the assets of the estate. A violation of this latter provision can result in imprisonment of up to one year and a fine.

Section 156, a new bankruptcy fraud provision, penalizes a bankruptcy petition preparer "if a bankruptcy case or related proceeding is dismissed because of a knowing attempt" by the preparer to disregard the bankruptcy statutes and rules. The bankruptcy petition preparer, defined as "a person, other than the debtor's attorney or an employee of such attorney, who prepares for compensation a document for filing" faces up to one year imprisonment and a fine for the knowing disregard of a bankruptcy law or rule.

Section 157, also a new bankruptcy fraud provision, is modeled after the mail fraud statute. Like mail fraud, it authorizes a penalty of up to five years imprisonment and a fine against individuals who devise or intend to devise a scheme or artifice to defraud. The execution of the scheme can be through filing a bankruptcy petition, bankruptcy document, or the making of a "false or fraudulent representation, claim, or promise concerning or in relation" to a bankruptcy proceeding. In *U.S. v. Lee* (E.D. Pa. 2000), a district court ruled that this statute should not be given the breadth that has been afforded to other fraud statutes, such as the mail and securities fraud statutes.

Despite the existence of specific bankruptcy crime statutes, prosecutors have on occasion bypassed these statutes and proceeded with actions under general criminal statutes. Most often, bankruptcy crimes are charged in conjunction with charges using general criminal offenses found in Title 18. For example, agreements by two or more individuals to commit a bankruptcy offense have been prosecuted under both section 152 and the general conspiracy statute. (18 U.S.C. § 371). When there is a scheme to defraud coupled with a mailing in furtherance of the scheme, mail fraud has been included by prosecutors. (18 U.S.C. § 1341). Prosecutors have also included charges of wire fraud, tax evasion, and perjury in bankruptcy fraud cases.

In addition to these general criminal provisions, when there is a pattern of racketeering involving fraud connected with a case under Title 11, the offense may be the subject of a RICO prosecution. To proceed with a RICO charge it is, of course, necessary for the government to prove all the elements of this offense (see chap. 8). As a predicate act of RICO, bankruptcy fraud can be pursued in both criminal and civil RICO actions.

§ 13.02 Bankruptcy Fraud

Historically prosecutors used section 152 of Title 18 to prosecute bankruptcy fraud. The essence of this statute is to provide criminality when the debtor or others associated with the bankruptcy attempt to avoid the required distribution of non-exempt assets to creditors as provided for by the Bankruptcy Code.

The statute contains a variety of fraudulent acts upon which a criminal prosecution can be premised. Most notable among the listing is the general concealment provision. Under this aspect of the statute, criminality is imposed when one "knowingly and fraudulently conceals from the custodian, trustee, marshal, or other officer of the court charged with the control or custody of property, or from creditors in any case under Title 11, any property belonging to the estate of a debtor."

In addition to this general prohibition against concealment, section 152 specifically prohibits the knowing and fraudulent (2) making of a false oath or account, (3) making of a false declaration, (4) presenting of a false proof of claim, (5) receiving any material amount of property from a debtor, after the filing of a case under Title 11, (6) giving, offering, receiving, or attempts to obtain any money, property, or advantage for acting or forbearing to act in a bankruptcy case, (7) transferring or concealing of property in contemplation of a Title 11 case, (8) concealing, destroying, or falsifying documents relating to property or financial affairs of a debtor after or in contemplation of the filing of a Title 11 case, and (9) withholding recorded information relating to the property or financial affairs of the debtor, from an officer, after the filing of a Title 11 case. Thus, this act provides criminality to acts of concealment, false oaths, and bribery that occur in relation to a bankruptcy.

To sustain a conviction under the general concealment clause of section 152, the government must prove beyond a reasonable doubt that the accused (1) knowingly and fraudulently, (2) concealed from an officer or the creditors, (3) in a Title 11 case, (4) property belonging to the estate of the debtor. To sustain a conviction under the false oath clause of section 152, the government must prove beyond a reasonable doubt that the accused (1) knowingly and fraudulently, (2) made a false oath or account, (3) that was material, (4) in relation to a Title 11 case. A violation of section 152 is a felony and can result in a penalty of up to five years imprisonment and a fine.

§ 13.03 Concealment and False Oath

Concealment, in a variety of ways, can form the basis of a prosecution under section 152. Secreting, falsifying, and mutilating of property or information have been found to be evidence of concealment. Mere omission of an asset on a bankruptcy schedule does not, however, indicate conclusively the existence of concealment.

In *Coghlan v. U.S.* (8th Cir.1945), the Eighth Circuit discussed the circumstances of when a failure to schedule property would constitute a concealment. The court noted that although omission of assets from a schedule indicates concealment, taken alone this is inconclusive. "The conduct of the bankrupt, the relative extent of the omission, the character of the asset itself, and the reasons given for the difference between financial statements of the business and the bankruptcy schedules are the other circumstances in every case." When these circumstances explain the omission, the element of concealment is lacking. The court in *Coghlan* noted, however, that facts supporting a continued concealment consummate the offense.

The knowing and fraudulent filing of a false account or schedule of assets under oath, also can form the basis of a prosecution under the false oath provision of section 152. *Goetz v. U.S.* (7th Cir.1932). Actions premised upon the false oath provision of section 152 have been held as not requiring all of the elements of a perjury charge. *U.S. v. Lynch* (7th Cir.1950).

Some courts, however, examine the false oath in the context of perjury law. Thus, literally true, but unresponsive answers to questions cannot form a perjury charge when the examiner is put on notice to ask additional questions to clarify the answers provided. *Bronston v. U.S.* (S.Ct.1973) (see § 10.04). Perjury, however, is established if in the context in which the statement is made, it is materially untrue. Thus, a false oath prosecution can be upheld despite the existence of statements that are literally true in isolation. *U.S. v. Schafrick* (2d Cir.1989).

Actions involving false oaths and accounts require the government to prove materiality. Materiality has been defined as referring "not only to the main fact which is the subject of inquiry, but also to any fact or circumstance which tends to corroborate or strengthen the proof adduced to establish the main fact." *Metheany v. U.S.* (9th Cir.1966). Materiality does not require the government to prove that creditors were harmed by the false statement.

Matters "pertinent to the extent and nature of [a] bankrupt's assets, including the history of a bankrupt's financial transactions," have been found material. Statements designed to secure adjudication by a particular bankruptcy court have been found to be material. *U.S. v. O'Donnell*(9th Cir.1976). Failing to disclose prior bankruptcies has been found to be material in that this information can "impede an investigation into a debtor's financial affairs." *U.S. v. Lindholm* (9th Cir.1994). Additionally, statements aimed at obtaining a particular status before a court, such as *in forma pauperis*, have been held to be material. *U.S. v. Yagow* (8th Cir.1992).

In *U.S. v. Phillips* (9th Cir.1979), the Ninth Circuit found misstatements in a bankruptcy petition material, and as included in the indictment, these false statements were properly read to the jury. The statements were a false social security number, false prior addresses, and failure to give past names by which the accused had been known. The court stated that the false social security number and fabrication of prior addresses may have misled creditors as to the petitioner's identity and financial background. The failure to provide prior names can obstruct attempts to acquire a full credit history and hinder the determination of assessing one's eligibility for bankruptcy.

Crucial to a bankruptcy fraud prosecution is a bankruptcy proceeding. Provisions within section 152 permit prosecutions to be premised upon concealment in contemplation of a bankruptcy case. A defendant's belief in the invalidity of a bankruptcy proceeding does not negate the bankruptcy fraud. *U.S. v. Beery* (10th Cir.1982).

It is necessary that the actions of concealment or false oath relate to the bankruptcy. In an action premised upon the false statement provision within section 152, the Eighth Circuit held that the "in relation to" requirement should be interpreted broadly. The court found that statements made in cases arising from a central bankruptcy proceeding would be "in or in relation to any case under Title 11." *U.S. v. Yagow* (8th Cir.1992).

§ 13.04 Knowingly and Fraudulently

Section 152 requires that the defendant act knowingly and fraudulently. This intent requirement mandates proof by the government that the accused acted willfully as opposed to through mistake, excusable neglect, or inadvertence. A defendant who acts with willful blindness can be found to have acted knowingly and fraudulently. Most often this element is proved through circumstantial evidence. A jury may infer intent from the evidence presented. In *U.S. v. Gellene* (7th Cir. 1999), the Seventh Circuit permitted an "intent to deceive" to suffice in meeting the "fraudulent" element of the statute.

In *U.S. v. Goodstein* (7th Cir.1989), the Seventh Circuit upheld convictions, including a violation of section 152, against an attorney with experience in bankruptcy matters who practiced for over forty years. The court found that the jury could have concluded that the defendant fraudulently intended to evade the requirements of the bankruptcy laws. In assessing this jury determination, the appellate tribunal noted that the defendant was a "knowledgeable businessman and lawyer." The court found that this "extensive legal background and integral role in" these bankruptcy affairs indicated that a failure to notify the bankruptcy court and creditors of a transfer was not something done inadvertently.

Where the accused, in a bankruptcy fraud action alleging concealment, lacked knowledge of the bankruptcy order for relief or the appointment of a receiver, a court reversed the defendant's convictions. The defendant in *U.S. v. Guiliano* (2d Cir.1981), was neither the owner or an officer of the debtor. As a salesperson, the court found that he was not required to be familiar with the financial condition of the company. Although it was possible to speculate that when the business closed the accused should have realized that a bankruptcy would follow, mere conjecture was insufficient to meet the knowledge requirement.

With respect to one count, the Second Circuit in *Guiliano* was satisfied that there was evidence to support a jury inference of the defendant's knowledge of the bankruptcy order for relief or the appointment of a trustee. This count accused the defendant of fraudulently concealing certain equipment from the bankruptcy trustee. According to the court, there was evidence that the defendant had been requested to remove this equipment and sell it for as much cash as possible. Upon removal of these items, the defendant knew of the company's financial crisis. The court noted that the defendant also worked closely with another individual after the bankruptcy order for relief and appointment of a trustee. Although the *Guiliano* court found evidence inferring knowledge, this count was reversed and remanded for a retrial in that there was a risk that the jury was influenced in its disposition of this count by improper evidence and by allegations of a reversed RICO count.

CHAPTER FOURTEEN
ENVIRONMENTAL CRIMES

§ 14.01 Introduction

Like so many of the white collar crime areas, the environmental sector also demonstrates an overlap between civil and criminal law. A person violating a federal environmental statute is often subject to civil proceedings, criminal prosecution, or dual civil and criminal actions (see chap. 18).

There exists a wealth of environmental statutes throughout the United States Code. Many of the environmental related Acts contain provisions that criminalize conduct for noncompliance. There is, however, no single comprehensive set of environmental crimes found within the United States Code.

In recent years there has been an increasing number of federal prosecutions for environmental offenses. Typically environmental violations are investigated by the Environmental Protection Agency (EPA). Most often federal criminal prosecutions arise when the EPA refers the matter to the Department of Justice. In 1982, the Department of Justice established a separate environmental crimes unit for the prosecution of these offenses.

The prosecution of environmental crimes is not limited to the indictment of individuals for alleged violations. A significant number of prosecutions have

205

concentrated on the corporate entity. Principles of corporate criminal liability, as well as personal criminal liability in the corporate setting, play a factor in the environmental arena. Prosecutions under the Occupational Health and Safety Act (OSHA) and the Federal Food, Drug, and Cosmetic Act (FDA) have examined principles of corporate criminal liability (see § 2.06).

Water, air, and energy are among the array of environmental areas that have incorporated criminal provisions for enforcement of specific Acts. With respect to water, one observes criminal penalties for noncompliance in Acts such as the Rivers and Harbors Appropriations Act (33 U.S.C. § 401 et seq.), Safe Drinking Water Act (42 U.S.C. § 300f et seq.), and the Water Pollution Control Act (Clean Water Act) (33 U.S.C. § 1251 et seq.). Criminal penalties are provided for in the Clean Air Act (42 U.S.C. § 7401 et seq.), the Resource Conservation and Recovery Act of 1976 (Solid Waste Disposal Act) (RCRA) (42 U.S.C. § 6901 et seq.), the Toxic Substances Control Act (TSCA) (15 U.S.C. § 2601 et seq.), the Federal Insecticide, Fungicide, and Rodenticide Act (FIFRA) (7 U.S.C. § 136 et seq.), the Atomic Energy Act (42 U.S.C. § 2011 et seq.), and the Comprehensive Environmental Response, Compensation, and Liability Act of 1980 (CERCLA) (42 U.S.C. § 9601 et seq.). These are, however, by no means an exhaustive list of the federal environmental Acts that contain criminal enforcement provisions. Scattered throughout federal law are environmental statutes that use criminal sanctions for the purposes of enforcement. Many states have also incorporated environmental crimes statutes as part of their laws.

Federal prosecutions related to environmental crimes have not always been limited to the specific provisions found within an environmental Act. On occasion the government will prosecute under general criminal provisions or add general criminal provisions as additional counts against a defendant. For example, prosecutors have included conspiracy charges, pursuant to 18 U.S.C. § 371, when there are two or more offenders who agree to commit a specific offense and an overt act is performed in furtherance of the conspiracy. (see chap. 3). A false reporting of a material fact to a government agency can result in a prosecution under the false statements statute. (18 U.S.C. § 1001). (see chap. 9). Environmental crime prosecutions have also added charges of mail fraud when there is a scheme to defraud and a mailing in furtherance of that scheme. (18 U.S.C. § 1341) (see chap. 4).

§ 14.02 Mens Rea

Most environmental offenses emanate from a violation of regulatory statutes. It is common for defendants to concentrate their defense on arguing the level of intent necessary for proving a violation of the applicable statute.

Courts have not always ruled consistently when examining the issue of intent as it pertains to an environmental statute. For example, the Sixth Circuit in *U.S. v. Wulff* (6th Cir.1985), found that a felony provision of the Migratory Bird Treaty Act (MBTA), that did not require proof of scienter, violated due process. The court found that because the felony was a "crime unknown to the common law" which carried a substantial penalty, the government was required to prove that the defendant acted with some degree of scienter. In contrast, the Third Circuit in *U.S. v. Engler* (3d Cir.1986), found that the absence of a scienter requirement, in the strict liability provisions of a felony under the MBTA, did "not offend the requirements of due process."

Most environmental crimes require proof of the defendant acting knowingly. Courts usually permit knowledge to be inferred from the surrounding circumstances. In *U.S. v. International Minerals & Chemical Corp.* (S.Ct.1971), the Supreme Court held that "where ... dangerous or deleterious devices or products or obnoxious waste materials are involved, the probability of regulation is so great that anyone who is aware that he is in possession of them or dealing with them must be presumed to be aware of the regulation."

Knowledge also can be found when there is a deliberate avoidance to learn all the facts. A willful blindness instruction, however, is only proper when the defendant claims a lack of guilty knowledge and the evidence at trial supports an inference of deliberate ignorance. *U.S. v. Pacific Hide & Fur Depot, Inc.* (9th Cir.1985).

Most courts interpreting the term knowledge in the context of environmental statutes have held that there is no requirement that a defendant know the specific law being violated. For example, in examining knowledge in the context of the Comprehensive Environmental Response, Compensation, and Liability Act (CERCLA), a Sixth Circuit Court held that " ... knowledge as used in such regulatory statutes means knowledge that one is doing the statutorily prescribed acts, not knowledge that the statutes or potential health hazards exist." *U.S. v. Buckley* (6th Cir.1991).

§ 14.03 Refuse Act

The Rivers and Harbors Appropriations Act of 1899, (33 U.S.C. § 401 et seq.), has been one source of prosecution of environmental crimes. The Act, a codification of prior statutes, includes section 13 which forbids "the deposit" of all kinds of "refuse matter" into navigable rivers "other than that flowing from streets and sewers and passing therefrom in a liquid state." (33 U.S.C. § 407).

This Refuse Act provides criminal penalties for the improper discharge into navigable or tributary waters of the United States. The government can charge each separate act of discharging or depositing refuse as a separate count. The number of acts chargeable "cannot be deduced from the mere size or length of time of a discharge without more, unless discontinuity of the flow or change in composition or other evidence indicates that certain action necessarily were taken to further the discharging or depositing of refuse." *U.S. v. Allied Chemical Corp.* (E.D.Va.1976).

Refuse has been defined as "all foreign substances and pollutants apart from those 'flowing from streets and sewers and passing therefrom in a liquid state' into the watercourse." *U.S. v. Standard Oil Co.* (S.Ct.1966). In *U.S. v. Standard Oil Co.,* the Supreme Court held that commercially valuable gasoline discharged into a navigable river could come within the definition of "refuse" under the Rivers and Harbors Act.

Most courts find this Act to be a strict liability statute. *U.S. v. White Fuel Corp.* (1st Cir.1974). One court noted that depositing refuse in navigable waters is malum prohibitum, within the category of public welfare offenses, and therefore a statute of strict liability. "The public is injured just as much by unintentional pollution as it is by deliberate pollution, and it would have been entirely reasonable for Congress to attack both." *U.S. v. U.S. Steel Corp.* (N.D.Ind.1970). The Supreme Court reserved for future determination, the question of what scienter requirement is imposed by this Act. *U.S. v. Standard Oil Co.* (S.Ct.1966).

§ 14.04 Water Pollution Control Act

The Federal Water Pollution Control Act, commonly referred to as the Clean Water Act, (33 U.S.C. § 1251 et seq.), objective "is to restore and maintain the chemical, physical, and biological integrity of the Nation's waters." The Act prohibits the discharge of pollutants into navigable waters unless authorized. The Act provides for the adoption of effluent limitations for the control of pollution and permits selected point source discharges. (33 U.S.C. § 1311).

Criminal penalties exist for negligent violations of these discharge limits, with increased penalties provided for knowing violations. Repeat offenses also carry increased penalties. When the actions place another individual in "imminent danger of death or serious bodily injury" there is a possible penalty of imprisonment of up to fifteen years and fine. The fine may be increased when the knowing endangerment is by a corporation. (33 U.S.C. § 1319(c)). In *U.S. v.*

Borowski (1st Cir. 1992), the First Circuit held that a knowingly endangerment prosecution could not "be premised upon danger that occurs before the pollutant reaches a publicly-owned sewer or treatment works."

Although most prosecutions are for violations of specific discharge limits, defendants who had failed to apply for a permit, were held to be criminally liable despite the fact that effluent standards were not promulgated against them. The Third Circuit noted that it was necessary to provide flexibility to the government for industries not yet considered threats to the environment. To hold otherwise, the court stated, would permit these industries to escape liability merely because the government had not established effluent limitations. The absence of effluent limitations does not nullify the basic prohibition against the discharge of pollutants. It merely places the burden on those discharging pollutants to apply for and to obtain a permit. *U.S. v. Frezzo Brothers, Inc.* (E.D.Pa.1978).

In *U.S. v. Hanousek* (9th Cir. 1999), the defendant was charged with negligently "discharging a harmful quantity of oil into a navigable water of the United States." The Ninth Circuit rejected defendant's arguments that "gross negligence" should be required to meet this particular Clean Water Act statute. The court stated that 33 U.S.C. § 1319 (c)(1)(A) can be met with a showing of ordinary negligence.

Responsible corporate officers are statutorily included as "persons" that are subject to criminal penalties under this Act. (33 U.S.C. § 1319 (c)(6)). In interpreting the responsible corporate officer provisions in the Clean Water Act, the court in *U.S. v. Iverson* (9th Cir. 1998) stated that "a person is a 'responsible corporate officer' if the person has authority to exercise control over the corporation's activity that is causing the discharges." The Ninth Circuit noted that "[t]here is no requirement that the officer in fact exercise such authority or that the corporation expressly vest a duty in the officer to oversee the activity." The inclusion of a provision regarding a responsible corporate officer does not serve to limit the prosecution of individuals who violate the act. *U.S. v. Brittain* (10th Cir.1991).

Applicable discharges must be reported by "any person in charge." Corporations are included as a "person" under the Act. 33 U.S.C. § 1321(a)(7). "Further, the knowledge of the employees is the knowledge of the corporation."*Apex Oil Co. v. U.S.* (8th Cir.1976).

§ 14.05 Resource Conservation and Recovery Act (RCRA)

Congress enacted the Resource Conservation and Recovery Act (RCRA) to provide a national system for the safe management of hazardous waste and to promote a system that conserved valuable material and energy resources. This statute authorizes the EPA, through its adoption of regulations, to place controls on solid and hazardous wastes. The Act is divisible into two sections, one pertaining to non-hazardous solid waste management, and another regarding hazardous waste management. *U.S. v. White* (E.D.Wash.1991).

The RCRA enacted in 1976 has been termed a " 'cradle-to-grave' regulatory scheme for toxic materials, providing 'nationwide protection against the dangers of improper hazardous waste disposal.'" *U.S. v. Johnson & Towers, Inc.* (3d Cir.1984). Although originally the statute authorized misdemeanor penalties for the disposal of waste without a permit, later amendments increased the penalties for noncompliance to felonies. The amendments also expanded coverage to include not only the disposal of waste, but also the improper treatment and storage of waste.

The Act's criminal provisions have been found applicable to "any person" that stores, treats, or disposes of hazardous wastes. "Any person" is defined in 42 U.S.C. § 6903(15) as meaning "an individual, trust, firm, joint stock company, corporation (including a government corporation), partnership, association, State, municipality, commission, political subdivision of a State, or an interstate body and shall include each department, agency, and instrumentality of the United States." Courts have not limited the provisions of the RCRA only to those who are owners or operators of facilities. *U.S. v. Johnson & Towers, Inc.* (3d Cir.1984). Further, federal employees working at a federal facility have not been precluded from prosecution under this statute. In *U.S. v. Dee* (4th Cir.1990), the Fourth Circuit found that sovereign immunity did not immunize federal employees from prosecution for criminal acts that violated the RCRA.

Criminality under the RCRA is found in section 6928(d) and (e) of Title 42. Where subsection (d) provides for penalties when one "knowingly," commits certain acts specified by the statute, subsection (e) increases the penalty for a knowing endangerment in committing a violation. The terms "knowing" and "knowingly," as used throughout this statute, have been the focal point of many appellate decisions. Only recently has the government proceeded with prosecution under the knowing endangerment aspect of this statute. The Tenth Circuit found the "serious bodily injury" provision of this statute not to be unconstitutionally vague when it was applied to a corporate defendant whose employees were alleged to have suffered "psychoorganic syndrome," which may cause impairment to mental facilities. *U.S. v. Protex Industries, Inc.* (10th Cir.1989).

Despite the requirement for a "knowing" violation, courts do not require that the government prove that a defendant know they are violating specific provisions of the RCRA. Being a public welfare offense, "it is completely fair and reasonable to charge those who choose to operate in such areas with knowledge of the regulatory provisions." *U.S. v. Hayes International Corp.* (11th Cir.1986). Courts have, therefore, rejected a defense premised upon ignorance of the law. This position is consistent with the knowing requirement of most other environmental crime statutes. For example, although knowledge is an element for a violation of the Clean Air Act, the "statute requires knowledge only of the emissions themselves, not knowledge of the statute or of the hazards that emissions pose." *U.S. v. Buckley* (6th Cir.1991).

Courts, however, have not ruled consistently on whether knowledge of a permit is required. One court found that although the term "knowingly" is omitted in subsection (2)(A) of the statute, its inclusion in subsection (2)(B) implies that there must be knowledge of the requirement of a permit. In *U.S. v. Johnson & Towers* (3d Cir.1984), the Third Circuit held that, "[i]t is unlikely that Congress could have intended to subject to criminal prosecution those persons who acted when no permit had been obtained irrespective of their knowledge (under subsection (A)), but not those persons who acted in violation of the terms of a permit unless that action was knowing (subsection (B))." The court in *Johnson & Towers, Inc.* concluded that either the word "knowingly" was inadvertently omitted from subsection (A), or that "knowingly" as introducing subsection (2) applies to (B).

Many courts, however, have rejected the view taken in *U.S. v. Johnson & Towers,* (3d Cir.1984), finding that there is no requirement of knowledge of a lack of a permit for conviction under subsection (A) of this statute. As noted by the Ninth Circuit, "[t]he statute makes a clear distinction between non-permit holders and permit holders, requiring in subsection (B) that the latter knowingly violate a material condition or requirement of the permit. To read the word 'knowingly' at the beginning of section (2) into subsection (A) would be to eviscerate this distinction." *U.S. v. Hoflin* (9th Cir.1989). In rejecting the view taken by the court in *Johnson & Towers, Inc.*, the Sixth Circuit noted that "[t]he 'knowingly' which begins section 6928(d)(2) cannot be read as extending to the subsections without rendering nugatory the word 'knowing' contained in subsections 6928(d)(2)(B) and (C)." *U.S. v. Dean* (6th Cir.1992).

Although the extent to which "knowingly" modifies terms within the statute remains to be resolved by the United States Supreme Court, there is a clear consensus among the circuits that knowledge of the statutory provision is not mandated. The government must, however, prove that the defendant knew the general hazardous character of the waste material being handled. *U.S. v. Dee* (4th Cir.1990).

One appellate court has specifically refused to apply a responsible corporate officer doctrine to establish knowledge. In *U.S. v. MacDonald & Watson Waste Oil Company* (1st Cir.1991), the First Circuit held that proof of a defendant being a responsible corporate officer would be insufficient to show the required knowledge for conviction under the RCRA. The court stated that "[s]imply because a responsible corporate officer believed that on a prior occasion illegal transportation occurred, he did not necessarily possess knowledge of the violation charged. In a crime having knowledge as an express element, a mere showing of official responsibility under *Dotterweich* and *Park* is not an adequate substitute for direct or circumstantial proof of knowledge."

CHAPTER FIFTEEN
COMPUTER CRIMES

§ 15.01 Overview

Although computer offenses have not been extensively prosecuted by the federal government, one can predict an increase in prosecutions with the development and use of technology. Prior to 1984, computer criminal offenses were subject to prosecution under existing statutes that had no computer emphasis. For example, computer improprieties were on occasion prosecuted pursuant to the federal wire fraud statute. (18 U.S.C. § 1343) (see § 4.08). Today there exists specific legislation to criminalize illegal computer activities.

In 1984, Congress enacted a criminal statute (the Counterfeit Access Device and Computer Fraud and Abuse Act of 1984) that exclusively focused on computer offenses. This statute, 18 U.S.C. § 1030, concentrated on improper computer access as opposed to other improprieties, such as, computer use. This statute was amended in 1986 (the Computer Fraud and Abuse Act of 1986) to cure some of the deficiencies evident in the initial legislation. More recent amendments also modify the language of the statute. The statute is no longer restricted to crimes related to computer access.

In the "Uniting and Strengthening America by providing Appropriate Tools Required to Intercept and Obstruct Terrorism Act of 2001(USA PATRIOT

ACT)," Congress made additional changes to the computer fraud act. For example, computer fraud is now listed a specified unlawful activity of money laundering and the statute now has extraterritorial application.

Despite the existence of section 1030 in the federal criminal code, computer crimes are still facing prosecution under other statutory offenses. For example, prosecutions may be predicated upon charges of copyright infringement (17 U.S.C. § 506), conspiracy (18 U.S.C. § 371), wire fraud (18 U.S.C. § 1343), illegal transportation of stolen property (18 U.S.C. § 2314), illegal interception devices and equipment (18 U.S.C. § 2512), and unlawful access to stored communications (18 U.S.C. § 2701).

§ 15.02 Section 1030

Section 1030 contains seven variants of conduct that are subject to prosecution. As opposed to a consistent mens rea and jurisdictional predicate, each of the seven subsections specifies its own requisite jurisdiction and mens rea. Likewise, the penalties for some of these varying forms of improper computer conduct differ. In addition to imprisonment, the statute also provides for imposition of a fine.

Subsection (a)(1) basically criminalizes the conduct of one who "having knowingly accessed a computer without authorization or exceeding authorized access," thereby obtained confidential national security information "with reason to believe that such information so obtained could be used to the injury of the United States, or to the advantage of any foreign nation willfully" attempts to or communicates it to someone "not entitled to receive it, or willfully" "fails to deliver it to the officer or employee of the United States entitled to receive it." This electronic espionage provision permits imprisonment of up to ten years. Additionally, a repeat offender is subjected to imprisonment of up to twenty years.

Subsection (a)(2) pertains to one who "intentionally accesses a computer, without authorization or exceeds authorized access, and thereby obtains" financial information of a financial institution or a card issuer, "information from a department or agency of the United States," or "information from a protected computer if the conduct involved an interstate or foreign communication." This conduct is punishable by imprisonment of up to one year. The statute provides for an increase to five years if the offense is committed for private or commercial gain, "in furtherance of a criminal or tortious act in violation of the Constitution" or federal or state laws, or "the value of the information exceeds five thousand dollars." The statute also provides for an increase to ten years for the repeat offender.

Subsection (a)(3) of this statute pertains to browsing in a government computer. It applies to those who access "intentionally, without authorization to access a nonpublic computer" of a federal department or agency, said computer being exclusively for government use or the conduct "affects" the government's use of the computer. The penalty for commission of this offense is one year, but may be increased to ten years for the repeat offender.

Subsection (a)(4) concentrates on theft from protected computers. It applies to one who "knowingly and with intent to defraud, accesses a protected computer without authorization or exceeds authorized access," furthering the fraud and obtaining anything of value. An exception is provided when the object of the fraud is the computer and the value of such use does not exceed five thousand dollars in any one year period. The statute, in subsection (e), explicitly defines a "protected computer." In addition to computers used by the government and financial institutions, the term "protected computer" also includes computers "used in interstate or foreign commerce or communication." This offense is punishable with up to five years of imprisonment, with an additional five years possible for the repeat offender.

Subsection (a)(5) is divided into three parts. Subsection (a)(5)(A)(i) pertains to one who "knowingly causes a transmission of a program, information, code or command, and as a result of such conduct intentionally causes damage without authorization to a protected computer." Subsection (a)(5)(A)(ii) criminalizes the intentional access of "a protected computer without authorization, and as a result of such conduct recklessly causes damage." Finally, Subsection (a)(5)(A)(iii) criminalizes conduct of those who "intentionally" access a "protected computer without authorization, and as a result of such conduct, causes damage." Subsection (a)(5)(B) provides the effects that need to be caused or attempted to be caused by the conduct in subsections (i), (ii), and (iii). For example it includes "physical injury to any person" or "a threat to public health or safety."

Subsection (a)(5)(A)(i) carries a penalty of up to ten years imprisonment with an additional ten years possible for the repeat offender. It can also be increased to a twenty year sentence when the "offender knowingly and recklessly causes or attempts to cause serious bodily injury" resulting from the conduct in (a)(5)(A)(i), and may be increased to a life sentence "if the offender knowingly and recklessly causes or attempts to cause death from conduct in violation of (a)(5)(A)(i)." Subsection (a)(5)(A)(ii) carries a penalty of up to five years imprisonment with an additional ten years possible for the repeat offender. Finally (a)(5)(A)(iii) provides for a one year term of imprisonment that may be increased to ten years in the case of a repeat offender.

Subsection (a)(6) of this statute criminalizes interstate trafficking of passwords. The government must show that the defendant "knowingly and with intent to defraud traffics" "in any password or similar information." The trafficking must affect "interstate commerce or foreign commerce," or the computer must be used by or for the federal government. This provision carries imprisonment of not more than one year with the possibility of ten years imposed for the repeat offender.

The final subsection (a)(7), originally added as part of the National Information Infrastructure Protection Act of 1996 (Economic Espionage Act of 1996, Title II), criminalizes the conduct of one who "with intent to extort from any person any money or other thing of value, transmits in interstate or foreign commerce any communication containing any threat to cause damage to a protected computer."

This provision carries imprisonment of up to five years, with repeat offenders facing the possibility of ten years.

Often conduct relating to accessing a computer may qualify under more than one provision of the statute. The statute also provides for civil actions by those who are damaged as a result of a violation of the statute.

Aspects of a prior version of section 1030 were the subject of appellate review in the case of *U.S. v. Morris* (2d Cir.1991). The Second Circuit was faced with the issue of whether the intent requirement in then subsection (a)(5) applied only to accessing information or also to preventing the authorized use of the computer's information and thereby causing loss. Defendant Robert Morris, a graduate student at Cornell University had transmitted a "worm into INTERNET, which is a group of national networks that connect university, governmental, and military computers around the country." In transmitting this worm, Morris had underestimated the damaging effect.

The court in *Morris* found that "[d]espite some isolated language in the legislative history that arguably suggests a scienter component for the 'damages' phrase of section 1030(a)(5)(A), the wording, structure, and purpose of the subsection, examined in comparison with its predecessor provision persuade us that the 'intentionally' standard applies only to the 'accesses' phrase of section 1030(a)(5)(A), and not to its 'damages' phrase." The court also rejected defendant's argument that the statute only covered those who lacked access to any federal interest computer. The court noted that "Congress did not intend an individual's authorized access to one federal interest computer to protect him from prosecution, no matter what other federal interest computers he accesses."

In *U.S. v. Sablan* (9th Cir.1996), the Ninth Circuit found that it was constitutional to omit a mens rea for the damages element of the offense in that the defendant "must have had a wrongful intent in accessing the computer in order to be convicted under the statute." Later amendments to the statute provide a mens rea for the damages clause in the amended (a)(5)(A)(i) and (ii). There is no mens rea, however, for the damages clause in (a)(5)(A)(iii).

Merely browsing is a government computer is not sufficient for a charge under section 1030(a)(4). In *U.S. v. Czubinski* (1st Cir. 1997), the First Circuit reversed convictions for wire fraud and computer fraud that were premised upon the defendant's alleged browsing in an Internal Revenue Computer. The court found that the government failed to show that the defendant had received "anything of value." The First Circuit court held that viewing information "about friends, acquaintances, and political rivals" in an IRS computer does not merit a computer fraud conviction where there is no evidence showing "that he printed out, recorded, or used the information he browsed."

PART THREE
PROCEDURAL AND EVIDENTIARY ISSUES

CHAPTER SIXTEEN
GRAND JURY INVESTIGATIONS

§ 16.01 Investigative Advantages

Federal investigations of white collar crime commonly involve use of the powers of the grand jury in addition to (or often, in lieu of) traditional police investigative authority. The grand jury offers various advantages over police investigations as a result of six structural elements of the grand jury process: (1) use of the court's subpoena authority, (2) lay participation, (3) closed proceedings, (4) immunity grants, (5) grand jury secrecy, and (6) the role of the prosecutor in leading the investigation. The sixth feature—the role of the prosecutor—is the prerequisite that leads the government to take advantage of the others. The prosecutor serves as the primary legal advisor to the grand jury, deciding initially which witnesses will be called before the grand jury (although the grand jury can request the issuance of additional subpoenas), questioning those witnesses (although the grand jurors can pose additional questions), and exercising absolute dominion over the granting of immunity.

The grand jury process allows federal prosecutors to accomplish several investigative objectives that

224

cannot be achieved through an investigation by federal law enforcement officers. These include: (1) compelling witnesses and suspects to appear and testify (subject to their exercise of evidentiary privileges) through the use of the court's subpoena authority (failure to comply subjects the subpoenaed person to contempt sanctions); (2) requiring those persons (who generally could not be arrested and subjected to custodial interrogation by law enforcement officers) to respond to questions posed by the prosecutor in a setting in which the only other persons present are the grand jurors and grand jury personnel (the witness' counsel, in particular, not being present); (3) requiring those persons to testify under oath, thereby making them subject to the penalties of perjury for falsehoods; (4) providing these grand jury witnesses assurance through grand jury secrecy requirements that their testimony will not be divulged to the target of the investigation (or others) except under limited conditions; (5) compelling the production of documents without revealing with any specificity the possible criminal activity under investigation (in contrast to the search warrant process, which is what law enforcement officers would have to use to obtain documents); (6) compelling the production of documents without having the "probable cause" grounding needed for a search warrant; (7) precluding witness reliance upon the self-incrimination privilege to refuse to provide testimony or documents by supplanting that privilege with a grant of immunity (a grant that can be made only to persons subject to a legal obligation to testify and which therefore is not available to law enforcement officers to compel responses in their interrogations); (8) providing the prosecutor with a protective cloak of grand jury secrecy, which facilitates keeping the target in the dark and avoiding the glare of publicity while the investigation is onjoing; and (9) providing the prosecution with the symbolic shield of grand juror participation in responding to claims that its investigations are motivated by partisan influences or are designed to harass.

The value of these "advantages" varies with the activities and the persons being investigated. In some instances they may be superfluous and in others, a theoretical "advantage" (e.g. grand jury secrecy) may actually be a hindrance. The grand jury investigative process also tends to be expensive, time consuming, and logistically cumbersome as compared to police investigations. Hence the process is useful primarily where investigators will face one or more of the following tasks: unraveling a complex criminal structure; obtaining information from witnesses reluctant to cooperate (or reluctant to appear to be cooperating voluntarily); gaining information from lower level participants where the prosecutor is willing to relinquish their prosecution in return for their cooperation; obtaining information buried in extensive business records; controlling the information revealed about the investigation while the investigation is ongoing; and countering the likely claims of the target that the investigation is being used for the purpose of harassment or political manipulation.

§ 16.02 Rule 17 Subpoenas

Federal grand jury subpoenas are issued pursuant to Fed.R.Crim.P. 17, which governs subpoenas to compel testimony (the subpoena ad testificandum) and to compel the production of documents and other physical items (the subpoena duces tecum) issued in connection with any type of proceeding governed by the Federal Rules of Criminal Procedure. Rule 17 provides that the clerk "must issue a blank subpoena * * * to the party requesting it," and in the grand jury proceeding, that "party" is the prosecutor (the legal advisor to the grand jury) acting on its behalf. The prosecutor fills in the name of the witness, who is commanded to "attend and give testimony" before the grand jury at a time and place designated by the prosecutor. Pursuant to USAM § 9–11.150 (discussed in § 19.05), an "Advice of Rights Form" is attached to the subpoena. It includes a brief, very general description of the subject matter of the grand jury's investigation, usually by reference either to the generic character of the offenses under investigation (e.g., "tax offenses") or the general character of the transactions under investigation (e.g., "zoning in Baltimore County").

Where the prosecutor also seeks documents from the witness, the subpoena, as provided in Rule 17(c), will "order the witness to produce any books, papers, documents, or other objects [as] the subpoena designates." Ordinarily, the documents demanded will be described in an attachment to the subpoena. Documents may be described by type (e.g., all "invoices"), by general subject matter (e.g., all "records of purchases"), or by relationship to a specific activity (e.g., all documents that "relate to the setting of prices" for a particular item). The description usually will refer to a specific time period (e.g., "invoices for 1996–97"), unless the characterization is by reference to an event that implicitly limits the time frame. The subpoena will direct that the documents be produced before the grand jury, but prosecutors often give the party the option of simply delivering the documents to the prosecutor. This tends to be more convenient as the documents will be screened initially by the prosecutor's staff, and often only a summary will be presented to the grand jury.

§ 16.03 The Fourth Amendment's Overbreadth Prohibition

In *Boyd v. U.S.* (S.Ct.1886), the Supreme Court concluded that a court order to produce a document constituted a search under the Fourth Amendment. The order in question directed an importer to either produce the invoice for an item that the government alleged to have been illegally imported, or be bound by the government's allegation of what would be shown by the invoice. While the order was not a subpoena duces tecum, as the subpoenaed party was not subject to contempt for failure to produce the document, the consequences of failing to produce were severe and the Supreme Court treated the order as the equivalent of a subpoena duces tecum. The Court acknowledged that a court order directing the recipient to produce a document "lacked certain aggravating incidents of actual search and seizure, such as forcible entry into a man's house and searching among his papers," but stressed that it nonetheless "accomplish[ed] the substantial object of those acts in forcing from a party evidence against himself." Accordingly, a "compulsory production of a man's private papers" would be treated as "within the scope of the Fourth Amendment to the constitution, in all cases in which a search and seizure would be." Moreover, this particular "search and seizure, or what is equivalent thereto," was unreasonable within the meaning of that Amendment because the court order was seeking to compel the defendants to give what was, in effect, self-incriminatory testimony (see § 20.01).

Only twenty years after *Boyd* was decided, in *Hale v. Henkel* (S.Ct.1906), the Supreme Court dramatically modified *Boyd's* Fourth Amendment analysis. *Hale* basically rejected *Boyd's* interpretation of that Amendment's reasonableness requirement, although it reaffirmed the applicability of the Fourth Amendment to a "compulsory production of a man's private papers." The *Hale* majority initially held that *Boyd* had erred in reading together the Fourth and Fifth Amendment protections. The Fifth Amendment provided a completely separate source of protection against compelled production of documents (see § 20.01), which did not apply in *Hale* since the challenged grand jury subpoena was directed to corporate documents and corporations do not have the benefit of the self-incrimination privilege (see § 20.09). However, the Court continued, the corporation was entitled to the protection of the Fourth Amendment, and "an order for the production of books and papers" could still constitute "an unreasonable search and seizure." In defining what constitutes unreasonableness in this context, *Hale* utilized a standard that would have sustained the *Boyd* order for a single, obviously relevant document as a "reasonable search." The key issue, the Court noted, was whether the subpoena duces tecum was "far too sweeping in its terms to be regarded as reasonable." The subpoena in *Hale* failed in this regard as it required production of virtually "all the books, papers, and documents found in the offices" of the subpoenaed corporation. Such a broad request, the Court noted, was capable of preventing the corporation from carrying on its business. While the government might have need for many of these documents, it would have to make some showing of that need before it could "justify an order for the production of such a mass of papers."

In the area of police searches, the Fourth Amendment generally requires that the search be based on probable cause. *Hale* imposed no such requirement, insisting only that the search not be overbroad. The Supreme Court did not explain in *Hale* why overbreadth is the only concern of Fourth Amendment reasonableness in the context of a subpoena duces tecum. One possibility is that the subpoena does not require a probability showing because it is a less invasive form of "search." The *Hale* Court acknowledged that the execution of a subpoena did not present the usual physical attributes of the search. The service of the subpoena involved "no element of trespass or force," nor was it "secret and intrusive." The subpoena could not be "finally enforced except after challenge, and a judgment of the court upon the challenge." These qualities led Justice McKenna in dissent to conclude that the Fourth Amendment simply was not implicated. The majority arguably reasoned that there was a "search" for Fourth Amendment purposes, but its less invasive character meant that it did not have to meet the requirements commonly associated with the "warrant clause" of the Fourth Amendment (i.e., the clause providing that "no warrants shall issue but upon probable cause supported by oath and affirmation and particularly describing the place to be searched and the persons or things to be seized"). Rather, under the Fourth Amendment's first clause (guaranteeing the "right of the people to be secure in their persons, houses, papers, and effects against unreasonable searches"), it was sufficient that the subpoena not be overbroad in its reach.

Support for the above analysis is found in *Oklahoma Press Publishing Co. v. Walling* (S.Ct.1946), involving subpoenas duces tecum issued by an administrative agency. The Court there noted that "these cases present no question of actual search and seizure," as they involved no attempt by government officials "to enter petitioners' premises against their will, to search them or to seize or examine their books." To avoid "misconceptions," a distinction must be drawn between the "so called 'figurative' or 'constructive' searches" of subpoenas and "cases of actual search and seizure." As to the former, the Fourth Amendment "if applicable," did no more than "guard against abuse only by way of too much indefiniteness or breadth" in the subpoena. The interests to be protected were "not identical with those protected against invasion by actual search and seizure" but arose out of the right of persons to be free from "officious examination [that] can be expensive, so much so that it eats up men's substance," and thereby "become[s] persecution when carried beyond reason."

§ 16.04 Applying the Overbreadth Prohibition

Post-*Hale* cases applying the constitutional prohibition against overly broad subpoenas duces tecum frequently start out by noting that the stated standard proscribing breadth "far too sweeping * * * to be regarded as reasonable" necessarily requires a fact-specific judgment, with each ruling tied to the circumstances of the individual case. At the same time, the courts have sought, with limited success, to develop some general criteria to guide that judgment. Initially, the subpoena poses difficulties only if it has sufficient breadth to suggest either that compliance will be burdensome or that the subpoena's scope may not have been shaped to the purposes of the inquiry. If it has that breadth, the court then will turn to the three "components" of reasonableness developed by the lower federal courts: "(1) the subpoena may command only the production of things relevant to the investigation being pursued; (2) specification of things to be produced must be made with reasonable particularity; and (3) production of records covering only a reasonable period of time may be required." *U.S. v. Gurule* (10th Cir.1970). The second component in the above formulation is commonly described as having "two prongs": first, "particularity of description" so that the subpoenaed party "know[s] what he is being asked to produce' " and second, "particularity of breadth" so that the subpoenaed party "is not harassed or oppressed to the point that he experiences an unreasonable business detriment."

While many courts have treated the elements of relevancy, particularity of description, particularity as to breadth, and limited time period as separate requirements of reasonableness, with a deficiency as to any one invalidating the subpoena, it is clear that these elements are interrelated. Greater particularity as to breadth, by narrowing the range of documents to be produced, will extend the time period into which the subpoena may reach. On the other hand, as a subpoena reaches farther into the past, a court is more likely to require a stronger showing of relevancy. So too, the significance of the burden of production will be weighed against the strength of the showing as to relevancy and the reasonableness of the time period.

While the subpoenaed party bears the ultimate burden of establishing that a challenged subpoena is unreasonable, many courts insist that the government make an initial showing of relevancy since it alone knows the precise nature of the grand jury inquiry. Ordinarily, this showing requires no more than a general description of the relationship of the material sought to the subject matter of the investigation. Moreover, the government generally is thought to be entitled to considerable leeway on the issue of relevancy. Courts recognize that "some exploration or fishing necessarily is inherent" since the grand jury will not ordinarily have a "catalog of what books and papers exist" nor "any basis for knowing what their character or contents immediately are." *Schwimmer v. U.S.* (8th. Cir. 1956).

§ 16.05 Other Fourth Amendment Objections

Where a subpoena is not "too sweeping," are there other Fourth Amendment grounds for challenging the subpoena? In the companion cases of *U.S. v. Dionisio* (S.Ct.1973), and *U.S. v. Mara* (S.Ct.1973), the Supreme Court rejected one such possibility, which rested on treating the subpoena directing a person to appear before the grand jury as the equivalent of a "seizure" of the person. Both cases involved grand jury subpoenas directing witnesses to produce identification evidence (voice and handwriting exemplars). The lower court, looking to the analogy of a court order allowing police to take persons into custody to obtain such exemplars, concluded that the Fourth Amendment required the government to show (1) some reasonable suspicion justifying the selection of these persons to provide the exemplars, and (2) that the request for the exemplars was relevant to the subject of the grand jury's inquiry and was not excessive in light of that inquiry. The Supreme Court held that the Fourth Amendment did not apply and neither showing should be required.

The *Dionisio* majority concluded that the lower court's analogy to police-detention cases was flawed because "a subpoena to appear before a grand jury is not a 'seizure' in the Fourth Amendment sense." There was a dramatic difference between the "compulsion exerted" by a subpoena and an "arrest or even an investigative stop." The "latter is abrupt, is effected with force of the threat of it and often in demeaning circumstances, * * * [while the] subpoena is served in the same manner as other legal process; it involves no stigma whatever * * * and it remains at all times under the control and supervision of a court." Admittedly, appearing before a grand jury could be both "inconvenient" and "burdensome," but these were simply "personal sacrifices" inherent in the "historically grounded obligation of every person to appear and give evidence before the grand jury." The subpoena's directive to give identification evidence did not alter the nature of that burden because the taking of voice or handwriting exemplars did not in itself involve a search; both procedures related only to physical characteristics "constantly exposed to the public" and thus were to be distinguished, for example, from the taking of a blood sample.

Having found that the Fourth Amendment had no application to either the summons to appear or the directive to provide identification exemplars, the *Dionisio* Court concluded that there was "no justification for requiring the grand jury to satisfy even the minimal requirement of 'reasonableness' imposed by the [lower court]." The grand jury "could exercise its 'broad investigative powers' on the basis of 'tips, rumors, evidence offered by the prosecutor, or [the jurors'] own personal knowledge,'" and it should not be required to explain the basis for each of its subpoenas. To "saddle a grand jury with minitrials and preliminary showings would assuredly impede its investigation and frustrate the public's interest in the fair and expeditious administration of the criminal laws."

U.S. v. Calandra (S.Ct.1974), rejects still another possible Fourth Amendment objection to grand jury procedures. Under *Calandra*, a grand jury witness cannot successfully challenge being subpoenaed to testify, or being asked particular questions, because the government was led to the witness or to its questions by a search that violated the Fourth Amendment. The Supreme Court in *Calandra* refused to extend the Fourth Amendment's exclusionary rule to prohibit the use before the grand jury of the fruits of an illegal search. The Court reasoned that sufficient deterrence against unconstitutional searches was provided by the prohibition against use of the fruits of such a search at trial. Due to a special provision in Title III of the Omnibus Crime Control and Safe Streets Act of 1968, 18 U.S.C. § 2515, the fruits of illegal electronic surveillance are treated differently. That Act prohibits the government from using conversations intercepted by illegal electronic surveillance, or information derived from those conversations, in a grand jury proceeding. Accordingly, a grand jury witness can object to government questioning based upon information obtained from an illegal wiretap. *Gelbard v. U.S.* (S.Ct.1972).

§ 16.06 Rule 17(c) Objections

Rule 17(c), governing the subpoena duces tecum, provides that the court "may quash or modify the subpoena if compliance would be unreasonable or oppressive." *U.S. v. R. Enterprises* (S.Ct.1991), provides the leading interpretation of that provision as applied to a grand jury subpoena. The Supreme Court there rejected the contention that a grand jury subpoena was not "reasonable" under 17(c) unless it met the same standards applied to a subpoena duces tecum directing production of documents for use at trial. In the trial context, the moving party must show that the document subpoenaed is relevant, admissible, and adequately specified, and the subpoenaed party argued that the government here had failed to make the first two showings and could not do so. The government responded, and the Court agreed, that there was no need for a government showing as to relevancy and admissibility. The requirement of evidentiary admissibility made no sense as to the grand jury, as it had long been held that the grand jury's "operation generally is unrestrained by the technical procedural and evidentiary rules governing the conduct of criminal trials." Requiring a preliminary showing as to relevancy, "would invite procedural delays and detours while courts evaluate the relevancy * * * of [the] documents sought," exactly the kind of disruptive "minitrial" warned against in *Dionisio* (see § 16.05). So too, a mandated preliminary showing, by requiring the government to "explain in too much detail the particular reasons underlying a subpoena," could very well "compromise 'the indispensable secrecy of grand jury proceedings' " and "afford the targets of the investigation far more information abut the grand jury's internal workings * * * than the Federal Rules of Criminal Procedure appear to contemplate."

Turning to the fashioning of an appropriate Rule 17(c) standard for the unique setting of the grand jury, the Court noted that several considerations had to be balanced. Initially, it had to be recognized that "the investigatory powers of the grand jury are * * * not unlimited," that the grand jury cannot, for example, "engage in arbitrary fishing expeditions" or "select targets of investigation out of malice or an intent to harass." Fashioning a procedure to enforce such limits, however, required consideration of conflicting elements in the grand jury process. On the one hand, the decision as to the appropriate charge "is routinely not made until after the grand jury has concluded its investigation," and "one simply cannot know in advance whether information sought during the investigation will be relevant and admissible in the prosecution for a particular offense." On the other hand, the party to whom the subpoena is directed "faces a difficult situation" in challenging the improper use of a subpoena. Grand juries ordinarily "do not announce publicly the subjects of their investigations," and the subpoenaed party therefore "may have no conception of the Government's purpose in seeking production of the requested information." Thus, what was needed was a Rule 17(c) standard of reasonableness that "gives due weight to the difficult position of subpoena recipients but does not impair the strong governmental interests in affording grand juries wide latitude, avoiding minitrials on peripheral matters, and preserving a necessary level of secrecy."

Several general guidelines, the Court noted, gave substance to such a standard. Initially "the law presumes, absent a strong showing to the contrary, that a grand jury acts within the legitimate scope of its authority." Consequently, "a grand jury subpoena issued through normal channels is presumed to be reasonable, and the burden of showing unreasonableness must be on the recipient who seeks to avoid compliance." In this case, that party "did not challenge the subpoena as being too indefinite, nor did [it] claim that compliance would be overly burdensome." The challenge was strictly on relevancy grounds and for such a challenge, the presumption of regularity produced the following standard: "[T]he motion to quash must be denied unless the district court determines that there is no reasonable possibility that the category of materials the Government seeks will produce information relevant to the general subject of the grand jury's investigation."

Recognizing that the above standard imposed an "unenviable task" upon the party raising a relevancy objection, the Court noted that the district court had authority to ease that task through appropriate procedures. Because a subpoenaed party who does not even know the general subject matter of the grand jury's investigation is "unlikely" to make the necessary showing "no matter how valid that party's claim," a district court "may be justified in a case where unreasonableness is alleged in requiring the Government to reveal the general subject of the grand jury's investigation before requiring the challenging party to carry its burden of persuasion." The district court, however, in fashioning appropriate procedures for this purpose would also have to take account of "the strong governmental interests in maintaining secrecy, preserving investigatory flexibility, and avoiding procedural delays." One possibility, the Court noted, was to require the government simply to "reveal the subject of the investigation to the trial court *in camera*, so the court may determine whether the motion to quash has a reasonable prospect for success before it discloses the subject matter to the challenging party."

A three-justice concurrence in *R. Enterprise* maintained that the subpoenaed party might succeed on a showing less demanding than the Court's "no-reasonable-possibility" standard where that party also could show that either (1) responding to the subpoena would be particularly burdensome due to the volume and location of the subpoenaed documents, (2) the "subpoena would intrude significantly on * * * privacy interests or call for the disclosure of trade secrets or other confidential matter," or (3) that "compliance would have First Amendment implications." So far, however, only the third situation has resulted in a reshaping of standards by the lower courts (see § 16.07).

§ 16.07 "Chilling Effect" Objections

Grand jury witnesses have argued in various contexts that even though the testimony or documents demanded of them clearly would be relevant, the grand jury should be required to show a compelling need for that information where the impact of its inquiry is to chill the exercise of a constitutionality protected right. The Supreme Court's ruling in *Branzburg v. Hayes* (S.Ct.1972) often is viewed as standing against such a requirement, at least with respect to a chilling impact upon First Amendment rights. *Branzburg* rejected the contention that newspaper reporters could not be compelled to reveal to state grand juries the identity of their confidential sources (who were apparent participants in drug offenses) unless the prosecution first established a compelling need for obtaining that information from the reporters. The Court majority questioned the potential adverse impact of such disclosures upon a reporter's ability to obtain confidential sources, and concluded that any resulting impact upon the capacity of the press to gather and report news was more than offset by the interest of the public in criminal investigation, as reflected in the traditional investigative authority of the grand jury.

How far *Branzburg* should be taken is unclear. Noting that *Branzburg* was concerned with the press function of news gathering, which has never been placed at the core of First Amendment rights, several courts have held that the government should bear a special burden of justification where the disclosure required by a subpoena bears upon the direct exercise of a First Amendment right. These courts typically speak of requiring the government to show that the information sought by the subpoena is "substantially related" to a "compelling government interest." *Branzburg*, however, is viewed as having established that the government interest in investigating crime is per se a "compelling interest," so that standard is automatically met by a government showing of a substantial relationship to a grand jury's investigation, absent factors strongly suggesting that the grand jury investigation was initiated in bad faith. *National Commodity and Barter Association v. U.S.* (10th Cir.1991). To establish that the information sought is "substantially related" to the grand jury's investigation, the prosecution ordinarily must offer an explanation as to how the information sought relates to the subject of the investigation. This explanation must establish a linkage somewhat more substantial than the *R. Enterprises* standard of a "reasonable possibility" of relevancy, but it may fall far short of establishing a critical need for the information.

Other courts have rejected entirely the contention that the government must ordinarily make a special showing to sustain a subpoena that has the potential for chilling the exercise of First Amendment rights. The Fourth Circuit adopted that position upon remand in the *R. Enterprises* case, considering there a First Amendment claim (not presented to the Supreme Court) that compliance with the challenged subpoena would chill the petitioner's continued operations in the distribution of sexually explicit magazines. *In re Grand Jury 87–3 Subpoena Duces*

Tecum (4th Cir.1992). It reasoned that *Branzburg,* in recognizing the sufficiency of the district court's capacity to respond to a "bad faith exercise of grand jury powers," rejected the need to impose any special burden on the government. Consistent with this reading of *Branzburg,* First Amendment interests are adequately protected by the district court applying, "with special sensitivity where values of expression are potentially implicated," the standards of *R. Enterprises,* keeping in mind the "traditional rule," as set forth in *R. Enterprises,* that "grand juries are not licensed to engage in arbitrary fishing expeditions, nor may they select targets out of malice or an intent to harass."

A "chilling effect" argument also has been raised where the grand jury requires the testimony of an attorney, asking questions concerning client identity or the source of fee payments (matters generally not within the attorney-client privilege, see § 22.04). Finding that the attorney-client privilege provides adequate protection of the lawyer-client relationship, the lower courts generally have refused to require a special governmental showing of need to compel the attorney to testify as to matters not within the privilege. Indeed, the Second Circuit has held that no such showing was needed even where the attorney was currently representing the target of the grand jury investigation on a related criminal charge and the act of testifying before the grand jury could conceivably lead to the attorney's disqualification as defense counsel on that charge. *In re Grand Jury Subpoena Served Upon Doe* (2d Cir.1986) (en banc). Other circuites have noted, however, that the district court has sufficient discretionary authority to quash such a subpoena where compliance could have an overly chilling impact upon the defendant's right to counsel on a pending criminal charge. See *In re Grand Subpoena for Attorney Representing Criminal Defendant (Reyes-Requena)* (5th Cir.1990) (district court had discretion to quash as oppressive subpoena requiring attorney to appear and testify as to fee payment where appearance was demanded on same day as defendant's scheduled bail hearing and government offered no justification for the timing).

§ 16.08 Subpoena Misuse Objections

Blair v. U.S. (S.Ct.1919) generally is viewed as barring a subpoenaed party from challenging the authority of the grand jury to indict for (and therefore investigate) the activities that are the subject of its inquiry. In *Blair*, the witness claimed that the transaction under investigation was beyond the grand jury's investigative authority because the applicable federal criminal statute was unconstitutional. The Supreme Court initially noted that consideration of the constitutionality of the statute at this point, prior to any indictment, would be contrary to the long-established practice of "refrain[ing] from passing upon the constitutionality of an act of Congress unless obliged to do so." It then proceeded, however, to speak in quite general terms of a witness' lack of capacity to challenge the "authority * * * of the grand jury," provided the jury had "de facto existence and organization." The Court treated the position of the grand jury witness as analogous to that of the trial witness. Neither could raise objections of incompetency or irrelevancy, for those matters were of "no concern" to a witness, as opposed to a party. For the same reasons, witnesses also should not be allowed "to take exception to the jurisdiction of the grand jury or the court over the particular subject matter that is under investigation." The grand jury operates as a "grand inquest," which requires broad investigative powers. It must have authority, in particular, "to investigate the facts in order to determine the question of whether the facts show a case within [its] jurisdiction." The witness could not be allowed "to set limits to the investigation that the grand jury may conduct."

A long line of cases, in contrast to *Blair*, recognize the right of the subpoenaed party to challenge a subpoena on the ground that it is being used for a purpose inconsistent with the grant of subpoena authority to a grand jury. Since such a "misuse" of the subpoena is deemed contrary to Rule 17, and since the relief sought is quashing the subpoena (rather than dismissing the indictment), these rulings, which largely predate *U.S. v. Williams* (see § 16.10), are deemed consistent with the limitations *Williams* placed on the exercise of federal court supervisory authority with respect to grand juries. Recognized instances of subpoena misuse include: (1) employment of the grand jury subpoena primarily to elicit evidence for use in a pending or future civil action; (2) employment of the grand jury subpoena "for the sole or dominating purpose of preparing an already pending indictment for trial;" (3) employment of the grand jury process to further independent investigations by police or prosecutor rather than to produce evidence for grand jury use; and (4) calling a witness for the purpose of "harassment," with "harassment" described as encompassing various objectives other than producing relevant evidence, such as burdening the witness with repeated appearances or seeking to punish the witness by forcing the witness into a situation where she will refuse to answer (or lie) and be held for contempt (or perjury).

A common thread running through the judicial treatment of misuse objections is that "a presumption of regularity" attaches to the grand jury proceeding and the objecting party bears a substantial burden in seeking to overcome that presumption. It clearly is not sufficient simply to show that the use of the grand jury process has (or will) benefit the government with respect to civil discovery, criminal discovery on a pending indictment, or some other alleged improper purpose. Courts have stressed that misuse exists only if the "primary" prosecutorial purpose in the use of the subpoena is improper; the prosecutor will not be enjoined from carrying forward a legitimate grand jury investigation simply because one byproduct may be the production of evidence useful in other proceedings in which the government has some interest. To gain an evidentiary hearing on a claim of alleged misuse, the objecting party ordinarily must at least point to surrounding circumstances "highly suggestive" of improper purpose.

Even where the surrounding circumstances strongly suggest improper use to obtain civil discovery or discovery on a pending criminal indictment, courts have expressed a reluctance to judge the dominant purpose of the investigation while it is still ongoing. The objecting party, it is noted, should not be allowed to "break up the play before it was started and then claim the government was offsides." *U.S. v. Doe (Ellsberg)* (1st Cir.1972). A preferable remedy, they note, is to allow the investigation to continue to its completion and then judge its purpose if the government should attempt to utilize the fruits of its alleged misuse in another proceeding. Where the alleged improper purpose is the development of evidence for a civil proceeding, the Rule 6(e) motion needed to disclose the grand jury material to civil attorneys ordinarily will provide the objecting party with an opportunity to challenge the purpose of the investigation after it has been completed (see § 18.06). Where the alleged improper purpose is gaining additional information for use in a trial on a pending indictment, the judge presiding at that trial can determine whether to require an inquiry into the dominant purpose of the post-indictment grand jury investigation when (and if) the government makes use in its prosecution of the fruits of that allegedly tainted investigation.

§ 16.09 Challenging Secrecy Violations

Rule 6(e)(2) of the Federal Rules of Criminal Procedure sets forth the general secrecy requirements of federal grand jury proceedings. It provides that the grand jurors, grand jury personnel, government attorneys, and personnel assisting government attorneys may not disclose "a matter occurring before the grand jury." Rule 6(e)(2) further provides that no obligation of secrecy may be imposed on any person "except in accordance with this Rule." Rule 6(e)(3) recognizes several "exceptions" to the general rule of secrecy imposed by Rule 6(e)(2)(see § 18.06).

Individuals or entities who have furnished information to the grand jury, or whose activities are the subject of the grand jury investigation, often seek to challenge a disclosure by government personnel that the government acknowledges but justifies as consistent with Rules 6(e)(2) and 6(e)(3). As discussed in § 18.06, such persons may challenge proposed court orders that would authorize disclosure to third persons or other governmental units under Rule 6(e)(3)(E)(i) (disclosure "preliminary to or in connection with a judicial proceeding"). So too, as noted in § 18.05, subjects of an investigation may seek relief with respect to disclosures that government personnel have made without a court order—i.e., where the government claims that the disclosures either were not covered by Rule 6(e)(2) because they did not include "matter occurring before the grand jury" or fit within the Rule 6(e)(3) exceptions that authorize limited disclosures without a court order. In both of the above situations, no question exists as to who disclosed (or intends to disclose) what information to whom, and the primary issue is whether the disclosure meets the standards of Rule 6(e)(3) or is outside the coverage of Rule 6(e)(2).

A quite different type of challenge is presented where the individual or entity claims that there have been "leaks" of grand jury matter to the media. Here, the issue ordinarily is not whether the alleged disclosures to the media by persons clearly subject to the Rule 6(e)(2) secrecy requirements (in particular, government attorneys and assisting personnel) would fall within the exceptions recognized in Rule 6(e)(3), or otherwise would be justified under Rule 6(e)(2) (they clearly would not), but whether those persons actually did leak grand jury matter, and, if so, what is an appropriate remedy.

Rule 6(e)(7) provides that "a knowing violation of Rule 6 may be punished as a contempt of court." A few lower court opinions suggest that this provision refers only to criminal (and not civil) contempt, and, of course, whether criminal contempt sanctions should be pursued lies in the discretion of the supervisory court, which is responsible for enforcing Rule 6's secrecy provisions. The Fourth Circuit has held that the Rule 6(e)(7) provision refers as well to civil contempt, but that it does not create a private cause of action to seek a civil contempt sanction. *Finn v. Schiller* (4th Cir.1996). Under either of these readings of Rule 6(e)(7), neither the witness whose testimony is leaked, nor the person who is the subject of the information leaked, has a cause of action for which relief can be demanded. Such individuals or entities may notify the court of the alleged violation and urge it to hold an evidentiary hearing for the purpose of determining whether imposition of criminal contempt (or civil contempt) is appropriate, but the court has discretion to pursue the alternative route of referring the matter to the Department of Justice's Office of Professional Responsibility for internal investigation and the possible imposition of internal sanctions. *Matter of Grand Jury Investigation* (90–30–2) (E.D.Mich.1990).

Other courts have concluded that Rule (e)(7) authorizes a civil contempt remedy, and that enables the victim of the alleged secrecy violation to pursue a civil action for relief, to obtain an evidentiary hearing upon establishing a prima facie case, and to gain a civil contempt order if a knowing violation is established. *Barry v. U.S.* (D.C.Cir.1989). A few courts also have suggested that the contempt sanction specified in Rule 6(e)(7) might not be the exclusive remedy. Thus, if leaks persist and their source cannot be identified, a court could quash a subpoena on behalf of a witness who would suffer prejudice if her testimony were leaked. Since courts have agreed that whatever relief is available should not "unnecessarily interfere with the grand jury process," such relief would be rare, and arguably a court should never be compelled to go so far as to dismiss the grand jury and terminate the investigation because of continued leaks. *Barry v. U.S.*.

These courts rarely have had to rule definitively on the appropriate remedy because of the complainant's almost insurmountable hurdle of establishing that there was a leak. Initially, to establish the grounding even for an evidentiary hearing, the complaining party must make a prima facie showing that there has been an unauthorized disclosure. This requires showing both that the information disclosed probably was within the protection of grand jury secrecy (i.e., was "grand jury matter," see § 18.05, rather than, for example, information acquired by government agents through their own investigative efforts) and that the disclosure was likely to have come from government personnel, the grand jurors, or grand jury personnel, rather than from a person not sworn to secrecy under Rule 6(e)(2) (in particular, a witness). Thus, newspaper articles that refer only to the general character of the investigation (rather than grand jury testimony or grand jury actions) ordinarily will be insufficient, and even articles that refer specifically to grand jury matter (e.g., a witness having refused to testify on self-incrimination grounds) may be insufficient because it may reflect speculation by the journalist or information furnished by the witness or someone with whom the witness shared that information. *In re Grand Jury Investigation (Lance)* (5th Cir.1980).

Should a prima facie case be established, the government will be required to respond at an evidentiary hearing. The leading appellate opinions provide little guidance as to the scope of that hearing. Typically, the government will seek to rely on affidavits stating that all relevant government personnel deny any disclosure on their part. Courts may be wary of requiring the government even to disclose on the record the names of all such personnel on the ground that it would provide the subject of the investigation with discovery of internal grand jury operations. *U.S. v. Eisenberg* (5th Cir.1983). Although journalists can be called as witnesses and questioned as to their source, they are most unlikely to respond even though that information will not be privileged under federal law. *Branzburg v. Hayes* (see § 16.07).

Although claims of secrecy violations usually are directed at disclosures, persons who are the subject of an investigation have also raised objections to prosecutorial efforts to preclude witnesses from discussing their testimony with those persons. Since Rule 6(e)(2) does not include the witness in the list of persons sworn to secrecy, and further provides that "no obligation of secrecy may be imposed on any person except in accordance with this Rule," most lower courts have concluded that the Rule prohibits the imposition of a requirement of secrecy upon a witness. However, several federal lower courts have concluded that their "inherent authority to maintain the integrity of grand jury proceedings" would allow them to impose an obligation of secrecy upon a witness, on a prosecution showing that disclosure by the witness would substantially impede the grand jury's capacity to investigate. These courts read Rule 6(e)(2) as only prohibiting the extension to witnesses of the obligation of secrecy imposed by that Rule.

Congress has separately addressed the witness-secrecy issue in dealing with certain types of "third-party subpoenas" – subpoenas directing commercial service providers (e.g., banks, and e-mail providers) to produce the records of customers who are the subjects of grand jury investigations. The service provider's authority to notify the customer of the subpoena is particularly significant because the service provider ordinarily has little interest in challenging the subpoena, and without notification, the customer will not be in a position to challenge. Accordingly, Congress has enacted a statutory obligation of customer notification as to certain types of third-party source providers (although in the Financial Privacy Act, that obligation does not apply to grand jury subpoenas, in contrast to other subpoenas, such as administrative agency subpoenas). At the same time, Congress has authorized court orders prohibiting the third party from notifying the customer for a specified time period upon a government showing of "reason to believe" that notification at this point will endanger another, produce flight, result in "the destruction or tampering with evidence", or "otherwise seriously jeopardiz[e] an investigation." 18 U.S.C. § 3413 (applicable to subpoenas to financial institutions).

§ 16.10 Target Standing

Although a subpoena recipient ordinarily is not precluded from informing a target that the subpoena demands documents relating to the target, a target receiving that information may not be in a position to challenge the subpoena. Initially, any challenge by the target must be brought prior to the recipient's production of the documents in compliance with the subpoena. Secondly, and more significantly, the target will not have standing to present all of the objections that a subpoenaed party may raise. Thus, *U.S. v. Miller* (S.Ct. 1976) held that a customer lacks standing to challenge on Fourth Amendment grounds a subpoena directing a third party service provider (there, a bank) to disclose its records of the customer's transactions. Although some of the records were originally created by the customer, in giving control over the records to the service provider, the customer assumed the risk of disclosure by the provider. In general, as in *Miller,* the target of the grand jury investigation has no standing to object to a subpoena directing a third party to produce information relating to the target. Certain misuses of grand jury authority, however, will directly impact the rights of the target, and here the target may challenge the third-party. Thus, a target may challenge a grand jury's misuse of the subpoena to enhance the prosecutor's criminal discovery on an indictment pending against the target, or to gain discovery for a civil action to be brought against the target. So too, an employer/target was held to have standing to object to subpoenas issued to its employees where it alleged that the government's design was to harass the employer by repeatedly calling its employees to testify.

§ 16.11 Indictment Challenges Based on Prosecutorial Misconduct

Challenges to an indictment based on alleged prosecutorial misconduct during the course of the grand jury proceedings must overcome four major hurdles. First, there is the practical problem of establishing that the misconduct occurred. The best source for determining what happened before the grand jury usually is the transcript of the grand jury proceedings, but under Rule (6)(e)(3)(E)(ii), that transcript can be obtained by the defendant only upon showing "that a ground may exist to dismiss the indictment because of a matter that occurred before the grand jury." Federal courts generally hold that disclosure will not be permitted under this provision unless the defense first makes a preliminary showing, from the sources available to it, of specific likely misconduct that might justify dismissal.

Second, the range of "misconduct" that can provide a grounding for challenging an indictment is quite narrow. In *U.S. v. Williams* (S.Ct.1992), the Supreme Court concluded that "as a general matter at least," federal courts lack the authority to independently prescribe standards of appropriate prosecutorial conduct before the grand jury and to then dismiss indictments because of the prosecutor's failure to abide by those standards. Stressing the grand jury's "functional independence from the judicial branch," *the Williams* Court concluded that federal courts generally lack authority to utilize their supervisory power to dismiss indictments unless they do so "as a means of enforcing or vindicating legally compelled standards of prosecutorial conduct before the grand jury," as established in statutes, the Federal Rules of Criminal Procedure, or constitutional prohibitions. Accordingly, *Williams* held, a federal court could not dismiss an indictment because the prosecutor failed to present before the grand jury known exculpatory evidence, as there was no statute, court rule, or constitutional provision that required the prosecutor to present such evidence to the grand jury.

The *Williams* Court cited examples of "those few, clear rules which were carefully drafted and approved by the Court and Congress to ensure the integrity of the grand jury" and therefore could be enforced by a dismissal of an indictment. They consisted largely of the provisions of Rule 6 and a series of limited statutory prohibitions (such as the prohibition against presenting unlawful wiretap evidence before the grand jury and the prohibition against subornation of perjury). Those provisions do not encompass much of what would be viewed as prosecutorial misconduct in many states (e.g. inflammatory remarks about the witness or target, expressions of personal opinion as to the target's guilt, and misstatements of the law). As for constitutional violations, the Supreme Court has not yet identified any action by the prosecutor that would constitute a violation of due process or the defendant's Fifth Amendment right to be prosecuted by indictment.

Third, should defendant establish prosecutorial misconduct violating the constitution, a statute, or Federal Rule 6, dismissal of the indictment still may not be obtained if that violation constituted a "harmless error." In *Bank of Nova Scotia v. U.S.* (S.Ct.1988), the Supreme Court held that "dismissal of the indictment is appropriate only if it established that the violation substantially influenced the grand jury's decision to indict or if there is 'grave doubt' that the decision to indict was free from the substantial influence of such violations." Since the *Bank of Nova Scotia* Court noted that that case did not present any constitutional error on the part of the prosecutor, arguably the harmless error standard applicable to prosecutorial constitutional error at trial would also apply where prosecutorial misconduct constituted constitutional error in the grand jury setting. Under that standard, dismissal would be required unless the court is convinced "beyond a reasonable" doubt that the constitutional error "did not contribute" to the grand jury's decision to indict. *Chapman v. California* (S.Ct.1967). Of course, as *Bank of Nova Scotia* noted, prosecutorial misconduct that does not relate to the presentation of the prosecution's case before the grand jury almost always constitutes harmless error under either standard, because only in the most unusual circumstances will it have contributed to the grand jury's decision to indict. Thus, the Court noted that the Rule (6)(e) secrecy violations raised there (disclosing grand jury matter to third parties and imposing secrecy obligations upon witnesses), clearly constituted harmless error because they simply "could not have affected the charging decision."

Finally, even should the defense establish a prosecutorial violation of a court rule or statute that seems likely to have affected the grand jury's decision, *U.S. v. Mechanik* (S.Ct.1986) suggests that no relief is available if the challenge is being considered after the defendant was convicted at trial. In *Mechanik*, the defense learned of a Rule 6(d) violation (the presence of unauthorized persons—here multiple witness—before the grand jury) during the middle of the trial, and the trial court postponed consideration of defense's subsequent challenge to the indictment until the trial ended. The Supreme Court in *Mechanik* held that at that point, with the defendant already convicted, the misconduct before the grand jury had become a moot issue. Even if the Rule 6(d) violation might have influence the grand jury on its finding of the probable cause needed to indict, the "petit jury's subsequent guilty verdict" rendered that irrelevant because that verdict "not only means that there was probable cause to believe that the defendants were guilty as charged, but that they are in fact guilty as charged beyond a reasonable doubt." Thus, the "petit jury's verdict rendered harmless any conceivable error in the charging decision that might have flowed from the [Rule 6(d)] violation".

Federal lower courts have disagreed as to how broadly *Mechanik* should be read. Reasoning that *Mechanik* was "carefully crafted along very narrow lines" and involved misconduct that "at worst, was [a] technical [violation]," the Tenth Circuit holds postconviction review available for allegations of misconduct suggesting the prosecutor "attempted to unfairly sway the grand jury or to otherwise affect the accusatory process" and misconduct that "transgressed the defendant's right to fundamental fairness." *U.S. v. Taylor* (10th Cir.1986). Other circuits have rejected such a narrow reading. They acknowledge that *Mechanik* does not extend to misconduct which denies fundamental fairness and thereby presents a constitutional claim, but see it as extending to the full range of nonconstitutional improprieties that might justify dismissal if considered prior to conviction.

§ 16.12 Assistance of Counsel

The Supreme Court has twice indicated that a grand jury witness does not have a constitutional right to the assistance of counsel while testifying before a grand jury. In *In re Groban* (S.Ct.1957), a case holding that a witness in a fire marshall's investigative proceeding did not have a constitutional right to the assistance of counsel, the Court drew an analogy to grand jury proceedings and stated: "A witness before a grand jury cannot insist, as a matter of constitutional right, in being represented by counsel." In *U.S. v. Mandujano*, discussed in § 19.06, the plurality opinion rejected the defendant's contention that, as a putative defendant called before the grand jury, he should have been told not simply that "he could have a lawyer outside the room with whom he could consult", but that counsel would be appointed to assist him if he was indigent. The plurality reasoned that, since "no criminal proceedings had been instituted," the "Sixth Amendment right to counsel had not come into play." That Amendment, which provides the usual constitutional grounding for requiring appointed counsel for the indigent, describes that right as one of the "accused", and the Court had previously held that a person does not become an "accused" until subjected to "adversary judicial proceedings", which does not include grand jury proceedings. *Miranda v. Arizona* recognized a Fifth Amendment right of the indigent arrestee (also not an "accused") to insist upon receiving the advice of an appointed counsel when subjected to custodial interrogation, but the

Mandujano plurality, for reasons set forth in § 19.06, concluded that *Miranda* did not extend to the grand jury setting.

Though the government has no constitutional obligation to provide counsel for persons subpoenaed to appear before the grand jury, due process might well be violated should it bar subpoenaed persons from consulting with retained counsel prior to complying with the subpoena. That issue is unlikely to arise, however, as the longstanding federal practice is to facilitate consultation even at the point where the witness appears before the grand jury. Federal Rule 6(d) operates to preclude counsel's presence within the grand jury room as it allows for the presence only of the witness, the jurors, the prosecutor, and needed grand jury personnel. However, the federal practice, is to allow the witness to interrupt her testimony and consult with retained counsel located in the anteroom. Indeed, the notification of rights attached to the subpoena (see § 19.06) states: "If you have retained counsel, the grand jury will permit you a reasonable opportunity to step outside the grand jury to consult with counsel if you desire."

When counsel represents more than one witness in a grand jury proceeding, more than one target or subject of the investigation, or a combination of witnesses and non-witness targets or subjects, the government may move to bar such representation as presenting an actual or potential conflict of interest. The Supreme Court has recognized the authority of a trial court to preclude joint representation of criminal defendants, in the interest of both protecting the defendant's right to effective assistance of counsel and preserving the "appearance of fairness" in legal proceedings, even where the defendants are willing to "waive" their right to conflict-free counsel. *Wheat v. U.S.* (S.Ct.1988). Lower courts have assumed that the same authority exists with respect to the grand jury setting—especially since the participants here cannot rely on any Sixth Amendment right to counsel of choice, but must rely, at best, on an due process right not to have the government arbitrarily interfere in the participant's efforts to obtain legal advice.

Wheat recognized the right of the trial judge to preclude multiple representation not only where an actual conflict existed (i.e. where the clients' current positions make action favoring one harmful to the other), but also where there exists a "serious potential for conflict." The latter situation encompasses many of the settings in which the government has challenged multiple representation, such as the representation of a target and witnesses who might testify against the target, the representation of targets who had different levels of culpability in the activities under investigation, and the representation of the corporate employer and the employee whose actions can give rise to the corporation's liability. The government has also challenged multiple representation of same-level targets or subjects who adopt a "united front" position of all refusing to testify on self-incrimination grounds. It occasionally has been argued that disqualification should be ordered in such cases because the united front threatens the effectiveness of the grand jury's investigation. The few federal courts considering such an argument have found this contention unpersuasive, but disqualification in such cases commonly can be reached under the *Wheat* standard (particularly where the government might well grant concessions to one person willing to testify against the others, and the joint representation thereby keeps each client from obtaining conflict-free advice as to whether she should be that person).

CHAPTER SEVENTEEN
ADMINISTRATIVE AGENCY INVESTIGATIONS

§ 17.01 Administrative Subpoenas

Most federal administrative agencies have been authorized by Congress to issue administrative subpoenas (also called "summonses") to compel testimony and the production of documents. While that authority has been given to the agencies only to facilitate their investigation of activities that may violate the various regulatory statutes that are within their enforcement domain, its use for that purpose can readily have a direct bearing on criminal prosecutions, particularly as to white collar crime. Violations of those regulatory statutes may constitute crimes as well as civil wrongs, and even when that is not the case, the circumstances surrounding a violation may suggest that a non-regulatory crime has been committed. Of course, the agency may not itself initiate criminal enforcement, but it may deliver the evidence it has collected to the appropriate prosecuting official, along with the agency recommendation for prosecution (see § 18.02). Should further investigation be desired, the prosecutor may utilize the expertise of the agenc~ investigators already familiar with the case ⁺ grand jury's subsequent investigation (se⸱ Should a prosecution eventually b⸢ evidence collected by the agency ⸱ criminal trial.

Unlike grand jury subpoenas, an administrative subpoena is not process of the district court. To enforce it, the agency must bring an independent civil action as authorized in the statute granting it subpoena authority. One consequence of this distinction is that a court order enforcing the subpoena is a final judgment and may be appealed in the same manner as a civil judgment (in contrast to the enforcement of the grand jury subpoena, where the party directed to comply ordinarily can gain review only by being held in contempt and then appealing that order).

The administrative subpoena, like the grand jury subpoena, is subject to the subpoenaed party's testimonial privileges. The individual may rely on the self-incrimination privilege, the lawyer-client privilege, and other privileges recognized in federal courts to refuse to provide particular documents or to answer specific questions put to the witness while testifying before an agency examiner. The subpoenaed party also may raise in the enforcement proceeding several other challenges, the most significant of which are discussed below.

In several areas of federal regulation, Congress has granted to the Department of Justice subpoena authority similar to that granted to administrative agencies. These subpoenas are commonly described as "administrative subpoenas", and they are subject to roughly the same challenges as the subpoenas issued by administrative agencies.

§ 17.02 Fourth Amendment Overbreadth

In its initial response to broad administrative ubpoenas duces tecum, the Supreme Court warned

against administrative "fishing expeditions" and
suggested that Fourth Amendment principles limited
the agency to compelling production only where it
had "some ground * * * for supposing" the
documents subpoenaed contained information
relevant to a violation of the statute the agency was
charged with enforcing. *FTC v. American Tobacco
Co.* (S.Ct.1924). That view was flatly rejected,
however, in *Oklahoma Press Publishing Co., v.
Walling* (S.Ct.1946), and *U.S. v. Morton Salt Co.*
(S.Ct.1950). *Oklahoma Press* distinguished
subpoenas duces tecum from traditional searches (see
§ 16.03), and concluded that "the Fourth
[Amendment], if applicable, at the most guards
against abuse only by way of too much indefiniteness
or breadth in the things required to be 'particularly
described', if also the inquiry is one the demanding
agency is authorized by law to make and the
materials specified are relevant." That was the "gist"
the Court noted, of the Fourth Amendment
requirement of "reasonableness." In *Morton Salt*, the
Court specifically acknowledged that the *Oklahoma
Press* standard allowed for some "fishing
expeditions." The administrative agency, the Court
noted, had been given by Congress "the power of
inquisition". This was a power "more analogous to
the grand jury" than to that of a court which issues
a subpoena in a specific "case or controversy", and it
therefore allowed the agency to "investigate merely
on suspicion that the law is being violated, or even
just because it wants assurance that it is not."

The standard set forth in *Oklahoma Press*, as
explained in *Morton Salt*, is very much like the
overbreadth doctrine applied to grand jury subpoenas
duces tecum (see § 16.03). *Oklahoma Press* did cite as

separate elements the requirements that the investigation be within the scope of the agency authority as granted by Congress and that the documents requested be "relevant" to the investigation. The former requirement basically insists that the subject matter be within the agency's jurisdiction. Its practical significance is limited by the well established standard of review that gives to the agency the opportunity to explore the potential coverage of its mandate, and therefore allows it to investigate for the very purpose of deciding whether or not the particular activity falls within its bailiwick. *Endicott Johnson Corp. v. Perkins* (S.Ct.1943). As for relevancy, that is a factor considered in any event in applying the overbreadth standard (see § 16.04).

§ 17.03 The *Powell* Prerequisites

In *U.S. v. Powell* (S.Ct.1964), the Supreme Court set forth four prerequisites for district court enforcement of an Internal Revenue Service summons. The statutory provision on enforcement noted simply that the district court was given "jurisdiction by appropriate process" to enforce the summons, but the Court found guidance as to what must be shown to merit enforcement in the statutory provisions governing IRS investigations and the IRS summons. "Reading the statutes as we do," the Court noted, "the Commissioner * * * must show that the investigation will be conducted pursuant to a legitimate purpose, that the inquiry may be relevant to the purpose, that the information sought is not already within the commissioner's possession, and that the administrative steps required by the Code have been followed—in particular, that the 'Secretary or his delegate,' after investigation, has determined the further examination to be necessary and has notified the taxpayer in writing to that effect."

Although *Powell* was speaking only of the IRS summons, the four prerequisites announced there—legitimate purpose, relevancy, lack of current possession, and adherence to agency procedures for issuance—have been applied by lower courts to administrative subpoenas generally. Lower court opinions interpreting the four *Powell* prerequisites have focused primarily on challenges to the government's allegation of a legitimate purpose (see § 17.04), but they have also lent additional content to the other prerequisites.

In seeking enforcement of a subpoena, the agency will present a statement as to the purpose of the investigation. That statement typically refers to the investigation of possible violations of designated statutory provisions (or the agency rules and regulations adopted thereunder) by specified individuals or entities in the course of activities that may be described in a fairly general fashion. Relevancy is then determined by assessing the possible relationship of the documents requested to this subject of investigation. The relevancy requirement is met, according to a frequently quoted standard, if the subpoenaed documents "might throw light" upon the subject of the investigation. *Foster v. U.S.* (2nd Cir.1959). However, a somewhat stronger standard of relevance may be imposed where the burden of producing the subpoenaed material is substantial, or the subpoena seeks personal financial information. (*In re Administrative Subpoena John Doe, D.P.M.* (6th Cir.2001) (stronger showing for personal financial records not needed, however, where party could easily transfer assets from business account to personal account).

The third *Powell* prerequisite, that the information sought must not already be within the possession of the government, has been considered primarily in the context of a IRS summons calling for the production of records previously examined by IRS agents. Courts have held that the prerequisite of "possession" means actual physical possession, and is not satisfied by previous knowledge of the contents.

The content of the fourth prerequisite, compliance with administrative procedures for issuance of the subpoena, varies with the statutes applicable to the particular agency and the rules adopted thereunder. One common requirement is that the administrative subpoena be issued with the approval of a person in a specified position within the agency—the requirement to which the *Powell* Court referred. In the case of the IRS, where the subpoena is issued to a third party record-keeper, § 7609(a) of the Internal Revenue Code requires the IRS to provide notice to the taxpayer, who may then intervene. The Fifth Circuit has suggested that violation of § 7609(a) does not necessarily bar enforcement of the summons (as where, for example, the taxpayer learned of the summons without a § 7609(a) notice and subsequently was allowed to intervene). *U.S. v. Texas Heart Institute* (5th Cir.1985). On the other hand, the First Circuit has held indispensable compliance with the authorization requirement of § 7609(f), which allows a special third party record-keeper summons that does not identify the taxpayer-target (a "John Doe" summons) only if issued by a judicial officer after a showing of reasonable basis. *U.S. v.*

Gertner (1st Cir.1995). That provision, the First Circuit argued, provides a protection that cannot be supplied by an after-the-fact determination that the John Doe summons would have issued if it had been properly presented to a court. Compare *U.S. v. Ritchie* (6th Cir.1994) (suggesting a contrary conclusion).

§ 17.04 Legitimate Purpose Challenges

In discussing the prerequisites for enforcement, the *Powell* Court noted that a "court may not permit its process to be abused" and that "such an abuse would take place if the summons had been issued for an improper purpose, such as to harass the taxpayer or to put pressure on him to settle a collateral dispute, or for any other purpose reflecting on the good faith of the particular investigation." This language is sometimes described as permitting a "bad faith" challenge to the subpoena that stands apart from the *Powell* prerequisites, but it actually does no more than recognize one possible ground for challenging the agency's allegation of legitimate purpose.

Challenges to purpose typically allege improper motivation and typically are grounded on one of the two bad-faith illustrations offered in *Powell*. A purpose of harassment is often tied to a claim that the investigation is indicative, i.e. the investigation was designed to punish a person who exercised his rights. While vindictiveness clearly is improper, that does not mean that an agency cannot shift to a more adversary stance in response to the exercise of a right. *U.S. v. Texas Heart Institute* (5th Cir.1985) (where statute of limitations for civil actions is about to run and taxpayer will not voluntarily extend it, bad faith is not shown by informing taxpayer that case will be transferred to the Criminal Investigation Division, not subject to the same statute of limitations). In *SEC v. Wheeling–Pittsburgh Steel Corp.* (3d Cir.1981), the Third Circuit recognized that improper motivation need not spring from the agency, but could also be the product of third party influence, there the alleged political coercion imposed by a competitor and a legislator.

The *Powell* Court noted that "the burden of showing an abuse of the court's process is on the taxpayer." Most lower courts have held that the government bears the initial burden of demonstrating a lawful purpose by submission of the agency's formal order of investigation (where used), or the affidavit of the responsible agency official, setting forth a purpose that is within the agency's statutory domain. The subpoenaed party then has the burden of asserting and proving that the subpoena is actually motivated by an improper purpose. In *U.S. v. Gertner* (1st Cir.1995), the First Circuit suggested that perhaps the burden on a subpoenaed party should be only to "create a substantial question in the court's mind regarding the validity of the government's purpose," and then the ultimate burden of proof should shift back to the government as the plaintiff in the enforcement action. Under either view, the subpoenaed party faces a significant burden, as it does not have an automatic right to discovery, enforcement proceedings being summary in nature.   Federal Rules of Civil Procedure, Rule 81. To even obtain a hearing on the purpose issue, the subpoenaed party must be able to point to specific events that clearly suggest an improper purpose. See *U.S. v. Millman* (2d.Cir.1985) (burden met by showing possible grounds for a vindictive purpose and agent actions and statements suggesting vindictiveness).

§ 17.05 Third-Party Subpoenas

As in the case of grand jury subpoenas (see § 16.10), administrative subpoenas are often directed to service providers for records relating to the use of their services by customers. Of course, there will be no opportunity for the customer to challenge the subpoena if the customer is not made aware of the subpoena. Absent the command of a statute or administrative regulation, the agency issuing the subpoena has no obligation to give notice of the subpoena to the customer. See *S.E.C. v. Jerry T. O'Brien, Inc.* (S.Ct. 1984). Congress has imposed such an obligation, however, as to third-party subpoenas directed at certain types of records (e.g., financial records under the Right to Financial Privacy Act, and stored electronic communications under the Electronic Communications Privacy Act) and as to particular agencies (e.g., the Internal Revenue Service under 28 U.S.C. § 7609, discussed in § 17.03). At the same time, it has included in some of these statutes, provisions for a court-ordered delay of government notification (supplemented by a prohibition of notification by the third-party service provider), upon a government showing of a reason to believe that the notification would jeopardize the investigation. See § 16.09.

Having received notification prior to compliance, the customer can challenge the subpoena, but any such objection must satisfy the standing requirements for the particular objection. Thus, *U.S. v. Miller* (S.Ct.1976) held that a customer could not raise a Fourth Amendment challenge to a subpoena requiring disclosure of bank records as those records were not the customer's property.   Provisions requiring customer notification typically also establish standing by providing for a timely customer challenge. The challenges they authorize, however, are largely limited to relevancy and legitimacy grounds, thus providing a parallel to the key prongs of the *Powell* objection. Similarly, the notification provision will require the government to set forth "with reasonable specificity, the nature of the law enforcement inquiry" that supports the subpoena, see 12 U.S.C.A. § 3405 (RFPA), which provides a starting point for examining any customer challenge to relevancy and legitimacy.

§ 17.06 Criminal Referrals and Continuing Investigations

In *U.S. v. LaSalle National Bank* (S.Ct.1978), the Supreme Court considered the extent to which an IRS summons could be employed to obtain evidence for use in a criminal prosecution. The Court noted that the IRS statutory scheme has "interrelated criminal and civil elements," and in authorizing investigations, Congress had not sought to compartmentalize investigations of actions that could have both civil and criminal consequences. Accordingly, the IRS could utilize its summons to investigate possible tax fraud even when it was apparent that the evidence uncovered could lead to a criminal prosecution. On the other hand, Congress had refrained from giving the IRS summons authority "for purely criminal investigations," as to do so would have "broaden[ed] the Justice Department's right of criminal litigation discovery" and "infring[ed] on the role of the grand jury as a principal tool of criminal accusation." As a practical matter, such an invasion of discovery limits and the grand jury's role was most likely to occur when the IRS summons was used after a case had been referred to the DOJ for criminal prosecution. With referral, the IRS lost its capacity to settle the civil case, but it was expected to cooperate with DOJ in its resolution of civil liability, and there was no "information barrier" that would keep a continuing IRS investigation from stretching its cooperation to include providing discovery for the criminal prosecution. Accordingly, a prophylactic standard would be adopted prohibiting any post-referral use of the IRS summons. To ensure that this standard was not circumvented, the Court also recognized a challenge based on a purposeful delay in referral for the sole purpose of collecting evidence for criminal prosecution. This objection, however, had to be based upon the "institutional posture" of the IRS, rather than the motivation of the individual agent. A subpoenaed party opposing enforcement on this ground would have to show "delay in submitting a recommendation to the Justice Department when there is an institutional commitment to make the referral", thereby evidencing that the IRS was acting "merely * * * to gather additional evidence for the prosecution."

In 1982, Congress amended the statutory provision on IRS summonses (Internal Revenue Code § 7602) by adding subsections (b) and (c). Subsection (b) states that the purposes for which the IRS summons may be used "include the purpose of inquiring into any offense connected with the administration or enforcement of the internal revenue laws." Subsection (c) then provides that "no summons may be issued * * *, and the Secretary may not begin an action * * * to enforce any summons, with respect to any person if a Justice Department referral is in effect with respect to such person." Lower courts have disagreed as to whether this legislation establishes a single bright-line cutoff of actual referral and thereby rejects any claim of institutional bad faith in delaying referral. Compare *Hintze v. IRS* (4th Cir.1989), with *Scotty's Contracting and Stone, Inc. v. U.S.* (6th Cir.2003).

Lower courts have refused to extend the rationale of *LaSalle National Bank* to preclude post-referral issuance of administrative subpoenas by administrative agencies other than the IRS. In some instances, the agency statute specifically gives it the authority to investigate both criminal and civil violations, and in others, important enforcement responsibilities require that the agency be allowed to continue its civil investigation and bring it to a prompt close even while the DOJ is acting on the agency's referral and pursuing a criminal investigation. *SEC v. Dresser Industries* (D.C.Cir.1980) (noting that "unlike the IRS, which can postpone collection of taxes for the duration of parallel criminal proceedings without seriously impairing the public, the *SEC* must often act quickly, lest the false or incomplete statements of corporations mislead investors and infect the markets"). Also, because an agency's subpoena authority will be no broader than that of a grand jury, the courts see no potential for broadening the prosecution's "discovery rights" so long as the criminal investigation is still before the federal grand jury (i.e., the referral has not yet resulted in an indictment), as the grand jury could give the prosecution access to the same material. So too, while agency investigations may not be subject to secrecy provisions of the type imposed in the grand jury investigations, the courts do not see that as undercutting the independence or effectiveness of the grand jury investigation. Indeed, where the agency has the authority to investigate both civil and criminal violations, courts have even upheld a "joint investigation" strategy that selects the post-referral agency summons over the grand jury subpoena to obtain evidence both agency and grand jury desire, with the agency then sharing its evidence with the grand jury. *U.S. v. Educational Development Corp.* (3d Cir.1989).

§ 17.07 Staff Misconduct

In *Powell*, the Supreme Court noted: "[I]t is the court's process which is invoked to enforce the administrative summons and a court may not permit its process to be abused." While the *Powell* Court made that statement in the course of discussing the district court's authority to refuse to enforce a subpoena issued for an improper purpose, several lower courts have held that it also supports refusing to enforce a subpoena that is the product of flagrant staff misconduct. Illustrative is *SEC v. ESM Government Securities, Inc.* (5th Cir.1981), where ESM alleged that an SEC investigator deceived ESM in gaining access to its records (the investigator pretended to be interested only in gaining a basic education on the government securities market, while ESM was actually his investigative target), and that the information he obtained through that deception led to the issuance of the challenged subpoena. The Fifth Circuit concluded that if ESM's allegations were true—that the "SEC intentionally or knowingly mislead ESM about the purposes of its review of ESM's files", that "ESM [was] in fact mislead," and that the subpoena as to the particular documents requested was "a result of the SEC's allegedly improper access"—then enforcement of the subpoena as to those documents would be denied "as an abuse of process." The Fifth Circuit reasoned that "fraud, deceit, or trickery" by government agents could constitute "grounds for refusing enforcement," as the district court's obligation in "determining whether to enforce * * * [is to] evaluate the seriousness of the violation [by the staff] under all the circumstances, including the government's good faith and the degree of harm imposed by the unlawful conduct."

Staff misconduct has also served as the grounding for defense challenges to the government's use in the criminal prosecution of evidence obtained through that misconduct. Insofar as the staff's misconduct lies simply on its violation of agency regulations, that will not justify suppression of the evidence. In *U.S. v. Caceres* (S.Ct.1979), the Supreme Court rejected a judicial suppression remedy for such "internal" standards, noting that such a remedy could have "a serious deterrent impact" on agency formulation of additional standards. On the other hand, insofar as the misconduct constitutes deception that may be characterized as having undermined a consensual relinquishment of Fourth Amendment rights, suppression can be founded on the exclusionary rule of the Fourth Amendment. In general, courts here have required an affirmative misrepresentation of compliance with internal regulations which leads the target to falsely assume that investigation is no more serious than a routine civil inquiry. See *U.S. v. McKee* (6th Cir.1999) (reviewing IRS cases, and noting alternative reliance on the due process clause to bar government use of all fruits of the deception).

§ 17.08 The Role of Counsel

Unlike the grand jury witness, the witness subpoenaed to testify in an agency proceeding may be accompanied by counsel. Indeed, that right is recognized in the Administrative Procedures Act [APA § 6(a), 5 U.S.C. § 555(b)] as well as many agency regulations dealing specifically with investigations. Very often those agency regulations also will define the role of counsel. Thus, Rule 203.7 of the SEC's Rules Relating to Investigation states that the witness' right to counsel is a right to have the attorney "(1) advise such person before, during and after the conclusion of such examination, (2) question such person briefly at the conclusion of the examination to clarify any of the answers such person has given, and (3) make summary notes during such examination solely for the use of such person." 17 C.F.R. 203.7(c). The objective of such provisions is to preclude counsel from converting the agency's taking of testimony into a trial, with counsel offering objections and arguments, and requiring the staff examiner to explain the basis and relevance of each and every question.

In some instances, agency regulations seek to deter multiple representation by the same counsel. Thus, SEC Rule 203.7(c) allows counsel to make summary notes solely for the use of the witness counsel is then representing. Also, SEC Rule 203.7(b) provides that "all witnesses shall be sequestered, and unless permitted in the discretion of the officer conducting the investigation, no witness or the counsel accompanying any such witness shall be permitted to be present during the examination of any other witness called in such proceeding." 17 C.F.R § 203.7(b). While such provisions do not absolutely prohibit multiple representation, they can take away from a witness whose counsel has appeared with a previous witness the assistance of that counsel of choice during the witness' appearance before an examiner. However, that potential has been narrowed substantially by the D.C. Circuit's ruling that use of a sequestration provision to exclude the witness' counsel of choice contravenes the Administrative Procedure Act's guarantee of counsel unless the exclusion is based on "concrete evidence" that the agency investigation will be "obstructed or impeded" by the same counsel appearing with more than one witness. *Professional Reactor Operator Society v. U.S. Nuclear Regulatory Commission* (D.C.Cir.1991).

CHAPTER EIGHTEEN
PARALLEL PROCEEDINGS

§ 18.01 Introduction

With violations of regulatory statutes and administrative rules so often also creating criminal liability, administrative agency proceedings (both investigations and enforcement actions) may readily overlap in subject matter with criminal proceedings (both investigations and prosecutions). So too, with white collar offenses frequently also constituting common law torts and violations of statutes creating private causes of action (e.g. civil RICO), civil actions may readily overlap in subject matter with criminal proceedings. Where the civil or administrative proceedings and the criminal proceedings appear likely to produce such an overlap, they are commonly described as "parallel proceedings." Whether brought simultaneously or seriatim, parallel criminal and civil/administrative proceedings require the participants in those proceedings to give consideration to the bearing of one proceeding upon the other. That is especially true for the "dual target"—i.e., the person who is or anticipates being a defendant in a criminal prosecution (or at least the target of a criminal investigation) and who is or anticipates being a defendant in a civil or administrative proceeding (or at least the target of an administrative agency investigation).

Where the dual target must respond first in a civil suit or an administrative proceeding, consideration must be given to whether that response will be available to the prosecutor in the parallel criminal proceeding (see § 18.02), and if so, what benefits will that give to the prosecutor. Depending upon the nature of the dual target's response, a prosecutor could gain from that response: (1) incriminating evidence or leads to incriminating evidence; (2) recorded statements that can be used to impeach the target and the target's witnesses should they vary from those statements in their testimony in the criminal case, and that can provide, in any event, a useful springboard at an early date for preparing cross-examination; and (3) notice of the target's likely defense well in advance and in far greater depth than the notice that could be obtained through criminal discovery. Should these benefits for the prosecutor be likely, the dual target may seek to delay being required to respond until after the criminal proceeding reaches a conclusion (see § 18.03). If that should fail, the dual target may consider exercising the privilege against self-incrimination to limit the content of the response (see § 18.04).

Where the dual target must respond first in a criminal investigation, a major potential peril of cross-proceeding discovery is that opponents in a subsequent civil action or administrative proceeding will be able to obtain the product of the government's criminal investigation. Of special significance here is the reach of grand jury secrecy (see § 18.05) and the conditions under which materials covered by grand jury secrecy can be transferred to potential opponents in parallel civil and administrative actions (see §§ 18.06, 18.07). When required to respond initially to a criminal prosecution, the dual target must consider not only the cross-proceeding discovery that will be given to opponents in any subsequent parallel civil or agency actions by going to trial, but also the possibility that the prosecution could end in a guilty verdict that will bar the target from contesting critical issues in those other proceedings (see § 18.08).

§ 18.02 Prosecution Discovery From Parallel Proceedings

What is disclosed at trial in a civil proceeding is open to the public, including, of course, the prosecutor. As for the documents recording disclosures made in civil discovery (e.g., deposition transcripts, interrogatories), these too ordinarily are public documents, freely open to inspection after being filed with the clerk. And even where local rule allows the documents of discovery not to be filed, an opposing party would be free to deliver that material to the prosecutor, and if the opposing party resisted a prosecutorial request, the grand jury could subpoena that material.

Under Rule 26(c)(6) of the Federal Rules of Civil Procedure, the district court may issue an order that discovery material remain under seal where such an order would serve to "secure the just, speedy, and inexpensive determination" of the suit by "encouraging full disclosure of all relevant evidence." *Martindell v. ITT* (2d Cir.1979). The Second Circuit in *Martindell* held that where such a protective order was issued because critical witnesses otherwise would have relied on their self-incrimination privilege to refuse to provide deposition testimony, the order prevailed over a grand jury subpoena for the record of their deposition testimony. However, three other circuits have rejected this view, concluding that the grand jury subpoena always "trumps a district court's protective order." In re *Grand Jury Subpoena Served on Meserve & Hughes* (9th Cir.1995). They reason, inter alia, that: (1) the grand jury has need for such deposition testimony even if it can gain the witness' testimony by granting immunity because it must determine whether the immunized testimony is truthful, and (2) allowing the protective order to prevail over the subpoena constitutes, in effect, a judicial grant of immunity as to that deposition testimony, which is contrary to executive branch authority to control immunity grants (see § 19.12). Two other circuits have taken what has been described as a "middle position": a grand jury subpoena will not invariably trump a protective order, but there is a strong (albeit rebuttable) presumption that the grand jury subpoena will prevail. Under this position, to preclude disclosure, the subpoenaed party must "sho[w] the existence of exceptional circumstances that clearly favor enforcing the protective order against the grand jury subpoena." *In re Grand Jury* (3d Cir.2002).

Statutes governing agency investigations commonly treat information acquired through agency investigative subpoenas as "confidential," rather than as matter of public record. However, they also allow for disclosures in the public interest, which clearly encompasses disclosure to a prosecuting authority. Indeed, agency regulations often encourage staff to inform the Department of Justice or U.S. Attorney's office of agency investigations with criminal implications long before a formal referral is made. A notable exception is § 6103 of Internal Revenue Code, which restricts IRS disclosure of information collected in tax administration and enforcement, giving the greatest protection to "taxpayer return information" (tax returns and other information furnished by the taxpayer). Where taxpayer return information appears to relate to criminal activity, it may be disclosed to federal prosecutors, but that requires an "ex parte order [issued] by a federal district court or magistrate" upon a finding that: "(i) there is reasonable cause to believe, based upon information believed to be reliable, that a specific criminal act has been committed, (ii) there is reasonable cause to believe that the return or the return information is or may be relevant to a matter relating to the commission of such act, and (iii) the return or return information is sought exclusively for use in a Federal criminal investigation or proceeding concerning such act, and the information sought to be disclosed cannot reasonably be obtained, under the circumstances, from another source."

§ 18.03 Delaying the Parallel Civil or Administrative Proceeding

In *U.S. v. Kordel* (S.Ct.1970), the Supreme Court rejected the defendants' contention that they had been denied due process by a sequence of events that included the government's initial filing of an in rem action against two food products produced by the corporation of which they were officers, notification shortly thereafter that the FDA was recommending their criminal prosecution, denial of their request to stay the civil action or extend their time for answering interrogatories until after the disposition of the anticipated criminal proceedings, and the subsequent use in the criminal prosecution of their answers to those interrogatories. Though recognizing that individuals who are the targets of parallel civil and criminal proceedings face certain perils when required to respond to the civil action in advance of the criminal proceeding (although compulsory incrimination was not one of these perils, since they could exercise the privilege against self-incrimination in the civil action), the Court concluded that there was no constitutional mandate that dual targets be relieved of those perils by the issuance of a stay of the discovery in the civil proceeding. To mandate an automatic stay of the civil proceedings "would stultify enforcement of Federal law" by requiring government agencies "invariably to choose either to forego recommendation of criminal prosecution once it seeks civil relief or to defer civil proceedings pending ultimate outcome of a criminal trial."

The *Kordel* Court held open, however, the possibility that certain circumstances might produce a due process violation either in denying a stay or in allowing the government to use in a criminal case the fruits of its civil discovery. It noted: "We do not deal here with a case where the Government has brought a civil action solely to obtain evidence for its criminal prosecution or has failed to advise the defendant in its civil proceeding that it contemplates his criminal prosecution; nor with a case where the defendant is without counsel or reasonably fears prejudice from adverse pretrial publicity or other unfair injury; nor with any other special circumstances that might suggest the unconstitutionality or even the impropriety of this criminal pros[

Although a stay may not b[
mandated, the federal distr[
Fed.R.Civ.P. 26(c), has discretion.. .
does an administrative agency. In determining
whether to grant a stay requested by a dual target,
courts and agencies tend to apply a balancing test,
weighing (1) the harm that will be suffered by the
moving party from the failure to grant the stay, (2)
the interest of the opposing party in proceeding
expeditiously (including any prejudice it might suffer
through the delay), (3) the concerns of interested
persons who are not a party to the litigation
(including, in particular, the "public interest"), and
(4) the interests of the court in maximizing judicial
efficiency.

Courts have noted that the "strongest case" for
deferring civil proceedings comes when the parallel
criminal proceeding has reached the indictment
stage. At that point, the likely period of deferment is
more predictable and ordinarily shorter than the
deferment granted during an ongoing criminal
investigation. Because the prosecutor cannot use the
grand jury to gather further evidence once the
indictment is issued (see § 16.08), there is greater
concern that the prosecutor will use the civil
proceeding (at least where the government is a party)
to gain discovery not available through the Rules of
Criminal Procedure. Also, with the government
having made a firm commitment to prosecute, the
defendant is under greater pressure to accept the
adverse consequences (even a default) that may
accompany reliance on the self-incrimination
privilege (see § 18.04), rather than risk giving the

prosecution valuable discovery through her presentation in the civil case. Even with these considerations working in favor of a post-indictment deferment, however, the stay will not be granted if the alleged civil violations are ongoing and threaten continued injury to the public.

The defense may prefer to go forward with the civil action, rather than seek a stay, when the government is the opposing party and the defense concludes that the civil discovery process will produce more benefit than harm as a result of what it will learn about the case the government is likely to present in the criminal prosecution. Here, it is the government who often will be seeking to stay the civil case. Courts have tended to grant such requests on the ground that administrative policy gives priority to the public interest in law enforcement. Where the criminal defendant brought the civil action against the government, there often is concern that the action was brought simply to obtain such discovery.

§ 18.04 Asserting the Self–Incrimination Privilege

A person may claim the privilege against self-incrimination in a civil case or administrative proceeding if the person's testimony realistically could provide the government with a link in the chain of evidence needed to prosecute for a crime (see § 19.02). In the civil case, the privilege may be claimed not only as to questions posed at trial or in depositions, but also as to interrogatories, requests for admissions, and subpoenas to produce documents (see § 20.02). The privilege is not available to entities (see § 20.07), so the entity that is the defendant or plaintiff in a civil action cannot rely on the privilege to refuse to answer interrogatories. Should the officer of the entity designated to answer them refuse on the ground that the answers would tend to incriminate the officer personally, the burden lies on the entity to find some other agent who can provide the answers. Where the exercise of the privilege by all knowledgeable witnesses places the entity in a position where it cannot establish its claim (as a plaintiff) or present a defense (as a defendant), it may seek a stay (or a protective order that convinces the witnesses to testify), but if such relief is unavailable, it simply must bear the consequences. See *Afro-Lecon, Inc. v. U.S.* (Fed.Cir.1987) (stay should not have been denied simply because entity was plaintiff, where it could not produce the accounting needed to sustain its claim because key witnesses were exercising the self-incrimination privilege).

The exercise of the privilege by a civil plaintiff or defendant is not without costs. If the party claiming the privilege thereby finds herself unable to present evidence supporting her side of the case, the consequence is likely to be a summary judgment. Moreover, courts may take remedial action because the party claiming the privilege has disadvantaged the opposing party by depriving that party of a useful source of evidence. Since an individual has a right to claim the privilege and since litigants do not have a right to discovery of privileged materials, courts have emphasized that any such remedy should be aimed at repairing the disadvantage rather than punishing the exercise of the privilege. *SEC v. Graystone Nash Inc.* (3d Cir.1994). Ordinarily, the entry of a dismissal or a default judgment would be viewed as punishment, but it may be justified in extreme cases, as where the exercise of the privilege results in a wholesale denial of discovery. Older cases suggest that a dismissal is always appropriate where the plaintiff exercises the privilege to restrict discovery as the plaintiff should be viewed as "automatically waiving" the privilege in seeking judicial relief. The prevailing view, however, is to tailor the remedy to the impact of the exercise of the privilege.

One common response to the exercise of the privilege, in both civil and administrative actions, is to bar the admission of particular evidence where the party's exercise of the privilege kept from the opposing party the means of challenging that evidence. *Gutierrez-Rodriguez v. Cartagena* (1st Cir.1989). Another common response is to allow the finder of fact to draw an adverse inference as to the information not received (see § 19.09). Thus, where a defendant in a civil case exercises the privilege in responding to interrogatories, the plaintiff can ask the jury to assume that the answer not given would have been that most unfavorable to the defendant. Ordinarily, when a non-party witness invokes the privilege, no adverse inference may be drawn. However, where the witness is so closely connected to the party as to be "within its control" (e.g., officers of an entity) and has particular knowledge of its activities, an adverse inference may be drawn against that party.

§ 18.05 Grand Jury Matter

Insofar as information obtained by the prosecution during a criminal investigation is governed by the Rule 6(e)(2) provision on grand jury secrecy (see § 16.09), the prosecution can only share that information with potential litigants in parallel proceedings where the conditions prescribed in 6(e)(3) are met (see §§ 18.06, 18.07). When the information is not governed by Rule 6(e)(2), the prosecution ordinarily is free to share the information if it deems sharing to be in the public interest (which will almost invariably be the case where the criminal process has reached its end and the information would be useful to other government offices in bringing a parallel civil or administrative action).

Rule 6(e)(2) applies to a "matter occurring before the grand jury." That phrase is a term of art, not to be construed literally as encompassing only events that have taken place before the grand jury. *In re: Sealed Case No. 99-3091* (D.C. Cir.1999) ("matter before the grand jury" extends to "anticipated testimony" and "strategy and direction" of grand jury presentations, though not the "internal deliberations of prosecutors"). Thus, "grand jury matter" will include an office interview given by a subpoenaed witness in lieu of a grand jury appearance, a prosecution memorandum describing documents or testimony that was presented to the grand jury, and an expert's report to the prosecutor that served as the basis for the experts' final conclusion, which alone was given to the grand jury.

On the other hand Rule 6(e)(2) does not apply to material generated independently of the grand jury even though similar material was later presented to the grand jury. Thus, where FBI agents independently obtain through interviews with possible witnesses information that is relevant both to an ongoing grand jury investigation and an administrative investigation, they may disclose that information to the administrative agency even though the persons interviewed subsequently testified before the grand jury (and presumably conveyed the same information in that testimony). *In re Grand Jury Subpoena (U.S. v. Under Seal)* (4th Cir.1990). So too, where the prosecutor learns of the existence of a document through sources independent of the grand jury, and desires to acquire that document in a fashion that will permit sharing it with an administrative agency without having to meet the requirements of Rule 6(e)(3), the prosecutor may achieve that end by obtaining the document through process other than a grand jury subpoena (e.g., by use of a search warrant or by requesting that the agency utilize its own subpoena power to obtain the document). *U.S. v. Educational Development Network*, discussed in § 17.05.

Even where documents were obtained by grand jury subpoena and were presented to the grand jury, they may not be treated as grand jury matter in all possible disclosure situations. Consider, for example, the situation in which the document in question was preexisting (i.e., it was not prepared for the purpose of complying with the subpoena), the prosecutor did not return the document to the subpoenaed party after presenting it to the grand jury, a civil litigant or government agency was aware of the document and sought to obtain it from the subpoenaed party, that party then responded that the document had been subpoenaed by the grand jury and was currently in the possession of the prosecutor, and the civil litigant or government agency then sought to obtain the document from the prosecutor. A handful of federal court decisions have adopted a standard that would require the third party in such a situation to seek court ordered disclosure under Rule 6(e)(3), as they view the government's disclosure to a third party of any document presented to the grand jury as an otherwise prohibited disclosure of "matter occurring before the grand jury." However, most federal courts have adapted standards that would hold disclosure in this type of situation not to fall within Rule 6(e)(2), under at least some circumstances. *U.S. v. Dynavac* (9th Cir.1993) (surveying different positions).

§ 18.06 The "Preliminary To" Requirement

Rule 6(e)(3) sets forth several exceptions to the basic secrecy requirement of Rule 6(e)(2) (see § 16.09). Each exception authorizes disclosure of grand jury matter to persons who were not present during the grand jury proceeding. Most of these exceptions relate to disclosure to implement criminal law enforcement, as in (1) disclosure to U.S. Attorneys and other DOJ attorneys for use in enforcing federal criminal law; (2) disclosure to assisting personnel, including agency personnel designated by the prosecutor as needed to assist in the grand jury's criminal investigation (with such personnel specifically prohibited from "utilizing that grand jury material for any purpose other than assisting the attorney for the government in the performance of such attorney's duty to enforce federal criminal law"); (3) disclosure to another grand jury; and (4) disclosure to a state prosecuting official for the purpose of enforcing state criminal law. The only Rule 6(e)(3) exception possibly authorizing disclosure to a prospective litigant in a parallel civil or administrative action is found in subdivision (6)(e)(3)(E)(i)—providing for court-ordered disclosure "preliminary to or in connection with a judicial proceeding."

Where the parallel proceeding is a civil action, and is already underway, it will meet the "in connection with" portion of the Rule (6)(e)(3)(E)(i) standard. Where the civil action has not yet been filed, but is readily anticipated, that is sufficient to meet the "preliminary to" standard. The major hurdle arises where the proceeding first anticipated is an administrative proceeding, for Rule (6)(e)(3)(E)(i) refers only to a "judicial" proceeding. As the Supreme Court noted in *U.S. v. Baggot* (S.Ct.1983), this limitation "reflects a judgment that not every beneficial purpose, or even every valid government purpose, is an appropriate reason for breaching grand jury secrecy." Rather, only "uses related fairly directly to some identifiable litigation" in a court were thought to merit such a breach.

Baggot held that disclosure to the IRS for use in an IRS audit of civil tax liability did not fall within the "preliminary to" requirement since the IRS's calculation and collection of any amount determined by it to be due did not require judicial intervention. The mere possibility that the taxpayer might challenge the agency's non-judicial means of enforcing its determination would not make the agency proceeding "preliminary to a judicial proceeding." On the other side, where an administrative proceeding requires a judicial determination for enforcement (as in attorney disbarment), disclosure to assist the agency in its proceeding generally is treated as within the "preliminary to" requirement. Indeed, courts here have held that the same is true where judicial review is not mandatory, but still plays "a significant role" in the "operation of the regulatory/statutory scheme." *In re Grand Jury 89–4–72* (6th Cir.1991). Of course, as to any administrative proceeding, the agency investigation may be at such a preliminary stage, far removed from a substantial likelihood of a finding that would require judicial enforcement, that disclosure could not yet be viewed as preliminary to a judicial proceeding. *Baggot* specifically left open what was needed in this regard, although noting that the possibility the individual might consent to the agency's proposed sanction should not be sufficient to negate the anticipated judicial proceeding.

§ 18.07 Particularized Need

Disclosure under Rule (6)(e)(3)(E)(i) also requires that the party seeking disclosure establish a "particularized need"—i.e., establish that "the need for disclosure is greater than the need for continued secrecy, and that th[e] request is structured to cover only material so needed." *Douglas Oil Co. of California v. Petrol Stops Northwest* (S.Ct.1979). The Supreme Court and the circuit courts have pointed to a variety of factors that should be weighed by a district court in the balancing required by the particularized need standard.

Initially, the court should look to the status of the investigation that produced the requested grand jury material. The need for secrecy clearly is greatest while the grand jury is still gathering evidence and considering whether to indict. Once the grand jury is finished with the matter, the need for secrecy declines and the movant's burden in establishing a particularized need declines. As the Supreme Court noted in *Douglas Oil*, however, the value of grand jury secrecy is only "reduced," not "eliminated," by the termination of the investigation, for consideration must be given to the long term impact of disclosure, extending beyond the particular case. Frequent authorization of disclosure will undercut the effectiveness of the promise of secrecy in gaining the cooperation of grand jury witnesses.

Another factor weighed is whether the third party seeks disclosure that might subject grand jury witnesses to "retribution or social stigma." One of the considerations that the Supreme Court found to weigh against disclosure to a participant in a civil antitrust suit was that witnesses in an antitrust investigation often are employees of the target companies, or their customers, competitors or suppliers, and might face discharge or other forms of retaliation if their testimony were disclosed to their employers. *U.S. v. Procter & Gamble* (S.Ct.1958). On the other hand, if there already has been substantial disclosure of the grand jury materials to the investigated companies (as where the companies were indicted and gained the witness's statements in the course of criminal discovery), disclosure to the other parties in the parallel civil suit is less likely to cause concern.

Another important consideration is the narrowness of the disclosure requested. Under a standard of "particularized" need, a request for broad disclosure will almost certainly work against the petitioner, as it did in *Procter & Gamble,* where the Court characterized the rejected request as seeking "wholesale discovery." As the Supreme Court has noted, the "typical showing of particularized need arises when a civil litigant seeks to use the grand jury transcript at the trial to impeach a witness, to refresh his recollection, to test his credibility and the like." The disclosure there "can be limited to those portions of a particular witness' testimony that bear upon his * * * direct testimony at trial." *Douglas Oil.* In addition, such requests are less likely to be based on a speculative judgment as to need, while the use involved serves the important interest of ensuring that the factfinder is not misled. In assessing need even as to fairly limited disclosure, however, the court also must take into consideration the availability of alternative means (such as civil discovery) that might produce the same information. The fact that disclosure will avoid the significant expense and delay of the alternative means is not in itself sufficient to establish the requisite need.

Where the request for disclosure comes from a governmental agency pursuing an administrative or civil claim, many courts have required a somewhat lesser showing of particularized need. The Supreme Court has rejected the contention that a government agency can justify disclosure simply by showing the relevancy of the requested material, but it has also said that the balancing process may be somewhat different for disclosure to government bodies as opposed to private parties. The Court has noted in particular that "the district court may weigh the public interest, if any, served by disclosure to a government body—along with the requisite particularized need—in determining whether the need for disclosure is greater than the need for continued secrecy." *Illinois v. Abbot & Associates* (S.Ct.1983). Thus, where the contemplated disclosure was to civil attorneys within the government for the purpose of deciding whether to file a civil action, the district court could properly take into account the likelihood that the disclosure would "sav[e] the Government, the potential defendants, and witnesses, the pains of costly and time consuming depositions and interrogatories which might later have turned out to be wasted if the Government decided not to file a civil action after all." *U.S. v. John Doe, Inc. I* (S.Ct.1987). Accordingly too, while the governmental agency's capacity to obtain the same information through its own investigative authority is a consideration weighing against the need for disclosure, that factor cannot be treated as a per se bar against authorizing disclosure. Indeed, that authority may strengthen the case for disclosure as it responds to another concern noted by the Court—that the use of grand jury materials by other government agencies not "threaten to subvert the limitations applied outside the grand jury context on the Government's powers of discovery and investigation." *John Doe, Inc. I.*

§ 18.08 Collateral Estoppel

A defendant who goes to trial in a criminal case must consider the dual perils of disclosure and collateral estoppel as they relate to subsequent parallel civil and administrative actions. The trial puts on the public record the prosecution's case and the defendant's defense, making them available to prospective opponents in the parallel proceedings. Information that was protected by grand jury secrecy becomes available to all when the prosecution presents that information through its witnesses and documents at trial.

Of course, the prosecution's evidence may fail to convince the criminal jury, but that does not necessarily mean that it will fail to convince the finder of fact when duplicated (or improved upon) in the parallel proceeding, where there is a lower standard of proof. Even if the parallel civil proceeding involves precisely the same issue and is brought by the government, that lower proof standard means the acquitted defendant cannot use the doctrine of collateral estoppel. *U.S. v. One Assortment of 89 Firearms* (S.Ct.1984). On the other hand, should the defendant be convicted by trial or by guilty plea, in the subsequent civil or administrative action, collateral estoppel will treat that conviction as conclusive as to any issue determined by the criminal case. In some instances, this will mean that the only issue left to be resolved in the civil action is that of damages.

A criminal conviction based on a plea of *nolo contendere*, however, is treated differently. Although a plea of *nolo contendere* supports a conviction, it technically is not an admission of guilt (defendant saying, in effect, "I do not contest"). Accordingly, a defendant who has pleaded *nolo contendere* is not estopped from denying in a subsequent civil proceeding the facts on which the criminal charge was based, and the conviction based on a *nolo* plea is not evidence that the defendant committed the crime. *Hudson v. U.S.* (S.Ct.1926).

For a criminal defendant more concerned about the consequences of anticipated parallel proceedings than the consequences of a conviction (often the case for an entity), the preferred strategy may be to enter a plea of *nolo contendere* rather than provide discovery and risk both a conviction and collateral estoppel by contesting guilt at trial. The *nolo contendere* plea, however, can be entered only with the approval of the district court. Moreover, Rule 11(b) of the Federal Rules of Criminal Procedure directs the court to accept such a plea only after giving due consideration to "the parties' views and the public interest in the effective administration of justice." The plea is more likely to be accepted where the government does not object, but that lack of objection may require negotiated concessions by the defendant relating to restitution and other remedial orders.

CHAPTER NINETEEN
THE SELF–INCRIMINATION PRIVILEGE: TESTIMONY

§ 19.01 Applicability of the Privilege

The Fifth Amendment's self-incrimination clause provides that "no person * * * shall be compelled in any criminal case to be a witness against himself." It was not until more than a century after the Amendment's adoption that the Supreme Court, in *Counselman v. Hitchcock* (S.Ct.1892), put to rest the possibility that this Fifth Amendment privilege was available only to a defendant refusing to be compelled to testify in the defendant's own criminal case. *Counselman* held that the "criminal case" phrasing refers to the eventual use of the testimony, not the nature of the proceeding in which the testimony is compelled. The Fifth Amendment, *Counselman* concluded, applies to a subpoenaed witness "in any proceeding" where compelled to give testimony that could be used against the witness in a subsequent criminal case. Since the prohibition is against the compulsion, the witness could object at the point of compulsion, even though it could not be said with certainty that the witness later would be prosecuted, and that the testimony sought in the current proceeding would then be introduced, making the individual "a witness against himself." A realistic potential for such use was sufficient and that potential could exist in any type of proceeding in which a witness was compelled to testify. Thus, the privilege became available not only to the grand jury witness (the precise issue in *Counselman*), but also to persons compelled by subpoena to testify in civil suits and in administrative proceedings (see §§ 17.01, 18.04). In *Chavez v. Martinez* (S.Ct.2003), four justices characterized the rulings making the privilege available to witnesses in noncriminal proceedings as establishing a "prophylactic rule" and two others described those rulings as establishing "complementary protection" that went beyond the "core guarantee," but all the justices accepted the continuing validity of those rulings.

§ 19.02 Potential for Incrimination

The Fifth Amendment privilege is available, of course, only if the compelled testimony carries the potential of later being used against the witness as a defendant in a criminal case. This requires a content that potentially would be harmful to a criminal defendant. Although that covers a great deal, it is not without limits. Thus, the Supreme Court has noted that content is incriminating only as it relates to criminal liability, *Ullman v. U.S.* (S.Ct.1956) (civil disabilities and social stigma, no matter how severe, are not sufficient), and that the potential incriminating character must relate to the witness' own criminal liability, not the criminal liability of others, *Rogers v. U.S.* (S.Ct.1951). Moreover, the potential for criminal incrimination must be "real and appreciable," not "imaginary and unsubstantial." *Brown v. Walker* (S.Ct.1896).

A witness' assertion of the privilege does not, in itself, establish that the witness' testimony would have this potentially incriminating quality. As *Hoffman v. U.S.* (S.Ct.1951), stressed, "it is for the court to say whether [the witness'] silence is justified, and to require him to answer 'if it clearly appears to the court that he is mistaken.'" *Hoffman* also indicated, however, that courts are to give the witness every benefit of the doubt in reviewing an assertion of the privilege. "The privilege," the Court noted, applies "not only to answers that would in themselves support a conviction but likewise * * * those which would furnish a link in the chain of evidence needed to prosecute the claimant." The witness must have "reasonable cause" to believe that his testimony would have this potential, but he cannot be expected to "prove * * * [that] hazard in the sense in which a claim is usually required to be established in court," as that would "compel * * * [the witness] to surrender the very protection which the privilege is designed to guarantee." Accordingly, to sustain the witness' claim, "it need only be evident from the implications of the question, in the setting in which it is asked, that a responsive answer to the question or an explanation of why it cannot be answered might be dangerous because injurious disclosure could result."

The *Hoffman* case also provides a fine illustration of the need for the court to look to all surrounding circumstances and to imagine the worst in the witness' possible responses in determining whether there is a "real and appreciable" possibility that the witness' testimony will furnish that "link in the chain of evidence" sufficient to make it incriminating. The Supreme Court there ruled that the district court had erred in holding the privilege inapplicable to questions concerning the witness' current occupation and his contacts with a person who was a fugitive witness. Since the lower court was aware that the grand jury was investigating racketeering, it should have recognized that questions concerning Hoffman's current occupation might require answers relating to violations of various gambling laws. It also should have recognized that the answers to questions concerning Hoffman's contacts with the fugitive witness could have referred to efforts to hide that witness, which would be criminal.

Although *Hoffman* suggests that witness claims of the privilege will usually be sustained without requiring any specific explanation of the possibilities for incrimination, special settings may impose that burden upon the witness. One such setting is the questioning of the witness regarding criminal acts for which the witness already has been convicted (assuming that the conviction is "final", so the double jeopardy will bar any reprosecution for that offense). Here, the usual assumption is that the individual "no longer has the privilege against self-incrimination as he can no longer be incriminated by his testimony about the crime." *Reina v. U.S.* (S.Ct.1960). However, as illustrated by *Malloy v. Hogan* (S.Ct.1964), the privilege may be available even as to such questioning under some circumstances. *Malloy* found error in a lower court's rejection of a self-incrimination claim by a witness who had pled guilty to a gambling charge and was now being asked about the circumstances surrounding his arrest and plea. The Court noted that the questions were obviously designed to determine the identity of the witness' employer, and "if this person were still engaged in unlawful activity, disclosure of his identity might furnish a link in a chain of evidence sufficient to connect the [witness] with a more recent crime for which he still might be prosecuted."

In re Morganroth (6th Cir. 1983) presented another setting in which a court may assume that the self-incrimination claim is not based on a realistic threat. The witness there had previously testified in separate proceedings about the same transactions that were the subject of the current questions. The district court held that the privilege did not apply to questions identical to those asked earlier, and the Sixth Circuit affirmed, concluding that the witness had failed to furnish sufficient information to establish a reasonably grounded risk of incrimination. Both the questions propounded and the witness' answers to these questions in the earlier proceedings had an entirely "innocent" content, and the Sixth Circuit rejected the witness' claim that the risk of incrimination per se existed because answers truthful in light of his current memory of events could be inconsistent with his earlier testimony, and thus lead to a perjury prosecution. To require no more to sustain an assertion of the privilege, the court reasoned, would give every witness who had happened to testify previously on an overlapping subject matter the capacity, no matter how innocuous the questions asked, to become, in effect, the "final arbiter" of the validity of his self-incrimination claim.

§ 19.03 Incrimination Under the Laws of Another Sovereign

For many years, American courts took the position that the self-incrimination privilege protected only against incrimination under the laws of the sovereign which was compelling the witness' testimony. Thus, if a witness in a federal proceeding was granted immunity against federal prosecution, he could not refuse to testify on the ground that his answers might be incriminating under the laws of a state or a foreign nation. In *Murphy v. Waterfront Commission* (S.Ct.1964), the Supreme Court rejected this "separate sovereign" doctrine as applied to state and federal incrimination. Noting that the doctrine would allow a witness to be "whipsawed into incriminating himself under both state and federal law," the Court concluded that the "policies and purposes" of the Fifth Amendment require that the privilege protect "a state witness against incrimination under federal as well as state law and a federal witness against incrimination under state as well as federal law."

As *Murphy* noted, where a witness in a federal proceeding claims potential state incrimination, the federal government has the authority to grant the witness immunity that extends to state proceedings, which permits it to compel the witness' testimony. As for the states, *Murphy* held that where a state granted immunity to a witness, the federal government would be prohibited from making any use of the testimony given under that immunity, so that the state immunity, like the federal, would operate upon both sovereigns (see § 19.11). In contrast, neither the federal government nor the states have the authority to grant immunity against foreign prosecution. Elimination of the dual sovereignty doctrine as applied to foreign prosecutions would place the state and federal systems in a position where they could not supplant the privilege and compel the testimony with a grant of immunity. This consideration was noted in *U.S. v. Balysys* (S.Ct.1998), where the Court held that incrimination under the laws of a foreign country was beyond the protection of the self-incrimination clause. The reference to "any criminal case" in the Fifth Amendment, the Court reasoned, extended only to prosecutions in jurisdictions subject to that Amendment (the federal government and the states, via the Fourteenth Amendment), and not to foreign nations.

§ 19.04 Compelling the Grand Jury Target to Appear

The self-incrimination privilege has long been held to prohibit the prosecution from forcing a defendant to take the stand as a witness at his own trial and to then invoke the privilege as to specific questions; the defendant's privilege protects him from even being called to testify. Should the prosecutor similarly be prohibited from forcing the "target" of an investigation to appear before the grand jury, or is the Fifth Amendment satisfied by simply allowing the target-witness, like any other witness, to refuse to respond to individual questions where his answer might be incriminating? Federal courts have concluded that the target should be treated no differently than any other witness. "The obligation to appear," the Supreme Court has noted, "is no different for a person who may himself be the subject of the grand jury inquiry." *U.S. v. Dionisio*

(S.Ct.1973). The defendant's right of silence grew out of the early common law rule on the incompetency of parties to testify, which had bearing only on the trial.

Internal Justice Department guideline provide a series of standards relating to subpoenaing targets. A target is defined as "a person as to whom the prosecutor or grand jury has substantial evidence linking him or her to the commission of a crime, and who, in the judgment of the prosecutor, is a putative defendant." A target who refuses to appear voluntarily may be subpoenaed, but only with the approval of both the grand jury and the federal prosecutor. In deciding whether to subpoena the target, consideration is to be given both to the importance of the target's anticipated testimony and the availability of alternative sources of information. If the target is subpoenaed, but then gives advance notice of an intention to claim the privilege, the target "ordinarily should be excused from testifying." The grand jury and prosecutor can jointly insist upon appearance, however, where justified by consideration of the importance of the testimony and the possible inapplicability of the privilege. Also, while not constitutionally compelled to do so (see § 19.06), federal prosecutors are directed to advise witnesses who are known targets of their target status.

§ 19.05 Invocation of the Privilege

A witness in any type of proceeding ordinarily must invoke the privilege on a question by question basis. A blanket objection is not satisfactory, although a court may terminate questioning along a certain line when the witness indicates that he intends to assert the privilege as to all questions relating to that particular topic. Above all, the witness must refuse to testify and note that his refusal is based on the privilege. The witness bears the responsibility for recognizing that the privilege would apply to his testimony and invoking it by refusing to give that testimony. Should the witness simply testify, the privilege is lost as to that testimony (and often more, see § 19.08), even though his failure to assert the privilege may have been the product of ignorance or confusion regarding the existence and application of the privilege. This consequence occasionally has been described as a product of "waiver," but the Supreme Court has recognized that it is not sustained by the traditional standard for waiver of constitutional rights (requiring a "knowing and intelligent" relinquishment of the right). *Garner v. U.S.* (S.Ct.1976). Rather, the invoke-or-forfeit standard rests on an analysis of the element of compulsion that was summarized by Justice Frankfurter in an oft-quoted passage from his dissent in *U.S. v. Monia* (S.Ct.1943): "The Amendment speaks of compulsion. It does not preclude a witness from testifying voluntarily in matters which may incriminate him. If, therefore, he desires the protection of the privilege, he must claim it or, he will not be considered to have been 'compelled' within the meaning of the Amendment."

§ 19.06 Advice as to Right

In *Miranda v. Arizona* (S.Ct.1966), the Supreme Court held that the Fifth Amendment bars admission of a statement obtained by police through custodial interrogation of a suspect where the police have failed to advise the suspect of various rights relating to the self-incrimination privilege. The *Miranda* mandated advice, which has come to be known as the "*Miranda* warnings," includes informing the suspect of the right to "remain silent." In *U.S. v. Mandujano* (S.Ct.1976), the defendant argued that the rationale of *Miranda*, rather than that of *Monia*, should govern the testimony of a grand jury witness who was a "putative defendant," in that the witness was being questioned about an event for which the government already had probable cause to charge him. In the absence of appropriate warnings, Mandujano argued, his failure to invoke the privilege was irrelevant, and his grand jury testimony should be viewed as compelled (as in *Miranda*) rather than as voluntary (as in *Monia*). Because Mandujano had committed perjury in his grand jury testimony (which would not be excused even if his testimony had been compelled), the Supreme Court was able to affirm his perjury conviction without ruling on whether a "putative defendant" called before a grand jury has to be advised of his right to assert the privilege. However, six justices did speak to the need for self-incrimination warnings.

Chief Justice Burger's plurality opinion, speaking for four members of the Court, flatly rejected extension of *Miranda* to the grand jury setting. *Miranda*, he noted, applied only to the special setting of custodial interrogation. The position of a subpoenaed grand jury witness could hardly be compared to that of the arrestee subjected to police questioning in the "hostile" and "isolated" setting of the police station. See also *Minnesota v. Murphy* (S.Ct.1984) (Court majority notes: "We have never held that [*Miranda* warnings] must be given to a grand jury witness").

Chief Justice Burger added that since Mandujano had been advised of his right to exercise the privilege against self-incrimination, there was no need to decide whether even that limited advice—less complete than the full set of *Miranda* warnings—was constitutionally required. However, the Chief Justice also stated that a grand jury witness' exercise of the privilege, whether or not a prospective defendant, should be governed by the compulsion analysis of *Monia*, and that analysis does not *require* that any warning be given (although judges, as a practical matter of practice, often will advise a hearing or trial witness of the right to exercise the privilege when the question posed clearly appears to call for incriminating information). Justice Brennan, joined by Justice Marshall, viewed the Chief Justice's reliance upon *Monia* as indicating no warning would be needed and expressed disagreement with that position.

Justice Brennan's opinion in *Mandujano* did not stop with requiring warnings as to the privilege alone. In his view, the Fifth Amendment also required the prosecution to inform a witness who was a putative defendant that "he was currently subject to possible criminal prosecution for the commission of a stated crime." In *U.S. v. Washington* (S.Ct.1977), the Court rejected (over Justice Brennan's dissent) the contention that the Fifth Amendment requires some form of notification of "target" status. The witness there had been given full *Miranda*-type warnings, but had not been told that he was a primary suspect in the theft of a motorcycle as a result of his possession of the stolen motorcycle. The Court reasoned that a failure to give a potential defendant a target warning simply did not put the witness at a "constitutional disadvantage." His status as a target "neither enlarge[d] nor diminish[ed]" the scope of his constitutional protection. He "knew better than anyone else" whether his answers would be incriminating, and he also knew that anything he did say, after failing to exercise the privilege, could be used against him. The "constitutional guarantee," the Court noted, ensures "only that the witness be not *compelled* to give self-incriminating testimony."

Although the Supreme Court in *Washington* again found it unnecessary to decide whether a target witness has to be informed of the right to refuse to answer incriminating questions, that issue has largely been mooted by the Department of Justice guidelines on the questioning of grand jury witnesses. Under those guidelines, all witnesses who are either a "target" or a "subject" of the grand jury investigation are informed of several rights by a form attached to the grand jury subpoena. That form advises the witness of; (1) the general subject of investigation (e.g., "illegal gambling"); (2) the right "to refuse to answer any question if a truthful answer to the question would incriminate you"; (3) that any testimony given could be used against the witness by the grand jury or in a "subsequent legal proceeding"; and (4) that the witness will be given a reasonable opportunity to consult with retained counsel (see § 16.12). Since a "subject" is defined in the guidelines as "a person whose conduct is within the scope of the grand jury's investigation", the requirement that the advice be furnished to subjects as well as targets ensures coverage of virtually all persons in a position where possible incrimination reasonably could be anticipated. As noted in § 19.03, the Department of Justice guidelines also call for target warnings, although *Washington* made clear that such warnings are not constitutionally mandated.

§ 19.07 Separate Proceedings

When a witness testifies as to particular activities in one proceeding, that does not prohibit the witness from claiming the privilege and refusing to testify as to the same activities in another proceeding (assuming the witness' testimony would be incriminating). The privilege is "proceeding specific," so that testifying in one proceeding does not relinquish the privilege as to the same information in a second proceeding. On occasion, however, there may be a question as whether separate hearings are necessarily separate proceedings. With a lone exception, federal circuits take the position that a grand jury inquiry and a subsequent trial are separate proceedings.

§ 19.08 Scope of the Testimonial Forfeiture

When a witness testifies, he relinquishes the privilege in that proceeding not only as to his testimony, but often also as to further information on the subject of his testimony. *Rogers v. U.S.* (S.Ct.1951), is the leading case on the scope of such testimonial "forfeiture" or "waiver." The witness there testified before a grand jury that, as treasurer of the Communist Party of Denver, she had been in possession of party records, but had subsequently delivered those records to another person. She refused, however, to identify the recipient of the records, asserting that would be incriminating. A divided Supreme Court affirmed her contempt conviction, holding the privilege inapplicable. The Court noted that Rogers had already incriminated herself by admitting her party membership and past possession of the records; disclosure of her "acquaintanceship with her successor present[ed] no more than a 'mere imaginary possibility' of increasing the danger of prosecution." A witness would not be allowed to disclose a basic incriminating fact and then claim the privilege as to "details." To uphold such use of the privilege would "open the way to distortion of facts by permitting a witness to select any stopping point in her testimony."

Although *Rogers* often is described as posing great danger for the witness who answers even seemingly "innocuous questions," the decision actually is fairly limited. Lower courts have held, for example, that where a witness' initial admission related to only one element of an offense, that did not constitute a waiver as to questions that might require him to admit other elements of the offense. The fact that the second question asks for further detail as to the same event does not in itself establish that the privilege is not available. Indeed, most of the reported cases finding a forfeiture as to further information have involved, as did *Rogers*, a witness' refusal to name others in a setting suggesting that the witness actually was concerned about incriminating those persons rather than himself.

§ 19.09 Penalties and Burdens

The Fifth Amendment, the Supreme Court has noted, guarantees to the witness both the "right * * * to remain silent until he chooses to speak in the unfettered exercise of his own will, and to suffer no penalty * * * for such silence." *Malloy v. Hogan* (S.Ct.1964). *Griffin v. California* (S.Ct.1965) presents the classic illustration of the prohibition against governmental action that penalizes the exercise of the privilege. At issue there was the constitutionality of the prosecutor's adverse comment on the defendant's failure to take the stand and give testimony, thereby offering no explanation of incriminating circumstances peculiarly within his knowledge. In an earlier ruling, *Grunewald v. U.S.* (S.Ct.1957), the Court had held that a defendant who testified at trial could not be impeached by reference to the fact that he had exercised his privilege against self-incrimination when questioned about some of the same circumstances before the grand jury. But that ruling was not constitutionally based, as it rested largely on the lack of inconsistency between exercising the privilege in the earlier proceeding (thereby asserting that his answers were potentially incriminatory) and providing testimony at trial that denied guilt and offered innocent explanations for the circumstances in question. In *Griffin*, the prosecution argued that drawing an adverse inference from defendant's failure to come forward and testify on critical facts "peculiarly within the accused's knowledge" was entirely logical and something the jury would do even if the prosecution did not ask it to do so. The Court responded, however, that the critical factor was the prosecution's attempt, with the trial court's acquiescence, to use the defendant's exercise of the privilege as evidence of his guilt. That was a characteristic "of the inquisitorial system of criminal justice, which the Fifth amendment outlaws." Adverse comment on the defendant's exercise of the privilege constituted "a penalty imposed by courts for exercising a constitutional privilege," which "cuts down on the privilege by making its assertion costly," and therefore violates the self-incrimination clause itself.

Spevack v. Klein (S.Ct.1967) and its progeny provide a line of "penalty" cases of special relevance to the field of white collar crime. *Spevack* held that the state could not utilize the exercise of the privilege as the basis for disbarring a lawyer who had refused on self-incrimination grounds to produce documents subpoenaed in a state bar disciplinary proceeding. Disbarment here was being used as a penalty and therefore violated the Fifth Amendment. The Court reasoned that "in this context, 'penalty' is not restricted to fine or imprisonment," but extends to "the imposition of any sanction which makes assertion of the Fifth Amendment 'costly' ", and therefore certainly includes "the threat of disbarment," which entails "the loss of professional standing, professional reputation, and of livelihood." Relying on *Spevack*'s analysis of prohibited penalties, the Supreme Court subsequently held invalid: state statutes that required the dismissal of police officers and other government employees who refused to waive their privilege against self-incrimination in an official inquiry relating to their employment, *Gardner v. Broderick* (S.Ct.1968), and *Uniformed Sanitation Men Association v. Commissioner of Sanitation of New York* (S.Ct.1968); a state statute that required disqualification of a contractor from doing business with the state for five years should the contractor refuse to waive the privilege before a grand jury investigating transactions with the state, *Lefkowitz v. Turley* (S.Ct.1973); and a state statute that imposed a five year bar on holding office in a political party should an officeholder refuse to waive the privilege before a grand jury investigating possible misuse of his office, *Lefkowitz v Cunningham* (S.Ct.1977).

As illustrated by *Baxter v. Palmigiano* (S.Ct.1976), not all burdens resulting from the exercise of the privilege are deemed penalties and therefore prohibited by the Fifth Amendment. In *Baxter*, a prison inmate summoned before a disciplinary board on a charge of causing a disturbance was told that the charge against him involved a potential criminal violation, and that he therefore had a right to remain silent, but that the board would be entitled to draw an adverse inference from that silence in resolving the disciplinary charge. The Supreme Court held that drawing an adverse inference in this setting did not penalize the exercise of the self-incrimination privilege. Unlike *Griffin*, the inference here was not being drawn in a criminal case. Unlike, the *Spevack* line of cases, the state here did not automatically impose a sanction upon the person who exercised the privilege. A prison inmate who remained silent was not automatically found guilty of a disciplinary infraction. The disciplinary board simply was allowed to give his silence whatever "evidentiary value was * * * warranted by the facts surrounding the case." Lower courts have followed *Palmigiano* in a variety of administrative inquiries.

The *Palmigiano* Court noted that its ruling was "consistent with the prevailing rule that the Fifth Amendment does not forbid adverse inferences against parties to civil actions when they refuse to testify in response to probative evidence offered against them." *Palmigiano* has been viewed by the lower courts as also lending support for the imposition of various other adverse consequences within a civil suit that may attach to a party's invocation of the privilege (see § 18.04).

What if the state threatens to impose a penalty upon the exercise of the privilege and the individual, rather than risk that sanction, provides testimony? Exactly that happened in *Garrity v. New Jersey* (S.Ct.1967), where police officers, after being warned that they would be discharged if they did not forgo the privilege and give testimony relating to ticket-fixing, gave incriminating testimony. The Supreme Court held that testimony could not be used against them at trial because it was not given voluntarily.

§ 19.10 Immunity: Constitutional Grounding

In *Brown v. Walker* (S.Ct.1896), a sharply divided Court concluded that precluding reliance on the privilege by granting a witness immunity from criminal prosecution was entirely consistent with the purposes of the Fifth Amendment privilege, as illustrated by historical practice. That practice, the majority noted, established that the Fifth Amendment could not be "construed literally as authorizing the witness to refuse to disclose any fact which might tend to incriminate, disgrace, or expose him to unfavorable comments." The history of the Amendment made clear that the privilege's objective was only to "secure the witness against criminal prosecution." Thus, the English adopted an immunity procedure, known as providing "indemnity" against criminal prosecution, soon after the privilege against compulsory self-incrimination became firmly established, and a similar practice was followed in the colonies. So too, the self-incrimination privilege had been held inapplicable where the witness' compelled testimony would relate only to an offense as to which he had been pardoned or as to which the statute of limitations had run. Such rulings implicitly sustained the constitutionality of the immunity procedure. Since the immunity grant removed the only danger against which the privilege protected the witness, the witness could no longer claim that he was being compelled to be "a witness against himself" in a "criminal case."

§ 19.11 The Constitutionally Required Scope of the Immunity

In *Counselman v. Hitchcock* (S.Ct.1892), the Court struck down a federal immunity statute that granted protection only against the prosecution introducing the witness' immunized testimony into evidence in a subsequent prosecution of the witness. The Court stressed that the statute failed to afford protection against derivative use of the witness' testimony. Thus, the statute "could not, and would not, prevent the use of his testimony to search out other testimony to be used in evidence against him." At the conclusion of its opinion, however, the Court spoke in terms of even broader protection than prohibiting derivative use. "To be valid," it noted, an immunity grant "must afford absolute immunity against future prosecution for the offense to which the question relates." This statement was taken as indicating that a valid immunity grant must absolutely bar prosecution for any transaction noted in the witness' testimony. Accordingly, Congress adopted a new immunity statute providing for such "transactional immunity." This provision was upheld in *Brown v. Walker*, and for many years it was assumed that immunity had to be transactional. Even so, it was recognized that transactional immunity was subject to two major limitations, inherent in any type of immunity grant. First, the witness may still be prosecuted for perjury committed in the immunized testimony. Second, the immunity does not extend to an answer totally unresponsive to the question asked. Thus, the witness could not gain immunity from prosecution for all previous criminal acts by simply including a reference to these transactions in her testimony even though they had nothing to do with the subject about which she was questioned.

In *Murphy v. Waterfront Commission* (S.Ct.1964), discussed in § 19.03, the Court clearly indicated that immunity need not be as broad in scope as traditional transactional immunity. Following *Murphy*, Congress adopted a new immunity provision for federal witnesses, replacing transactional immunity with a prohibition against use and derivative use as to both federal and state prosecutions. The statute provided that "no testimony or other information compelled under the [immunity] order (or any information directly or indirectly derived from such testimony or other information) may be used against the witness in any criminal case, except a prosecution for perjury, giving a false statement, or otherwise failing to comply with the order." In *Kastigar v. U.S.* (S.Ct.1972), a divided Court upheld the new federal provision. The "broad language in *Counselman*," which suggested the need for transactional immunity, was discounted as inconsistent with the "conceptual basis" of the *Counselman* ruling. The crucial question, as *Counselman* noted, was whether the immunity granted was "coextensive with the scope of the privilege against self-incrimination." The traditional Fifth Amendment remedy of simply excluding from evidence the compelled statement and its evidentiary fruits (as exemplified by coerced confession cases) indicated that the privilege did not require an absolute bar against prosecution. A prohibition against use and derivative use satisfied the privilege by placing the witness "in substantially the same position as if * * * [the witness] had claimed his privilege."

The *Kastigar* majority rejected the argument, relied upon by the dissenters, that the bar against derivative use could not be enforced so effectively as to ensure that the witness really was placed in the same position as if he had not testified. The statute's "total prohibition on use," it noted, "provides a comprehensive safeguard, barring the use of compelled testimony as an 'investigatory lead,' and also barring the use of any evidence obtained by focusing investigation on a witness as a result of his compelled disclosures." Appropriate procedures for "taint hearings" would ensure that this prohibition was made effective. Once a defendant demonstrates that he previously testified under a grant of immunity, the prosecution must carry "the burden of showing that [its] evidence is not tainted by establishing that [it] had an independent, legitimate source for the disputed evidence." This requirement, the Court noted, would provide the immunized witness with "protection commensurate with that resulting from invoking the privilege itself."

§ 19.12 The Federal Immunity Provisions: 18 U.S.C. §§ 6000–6005

Chapter 601 of the Federal Criminal Code (18 U.S.C. §§ 6000–6005) sets forth the immunity provisions commonly relied upon in federal white collar cases. Section 6002 defines the scope of the immunity. The immunity is restricted to a witness who refuses, "on the basis of his privilege against self-incrimination, to testify or provide other information in a proceeding before or ancillary to" (1) a federal court, (2) a federal grand jury, (3) an "agency of the United States", (which covers a series of agencies, e.g., the S.E.C., specified in the definitions section, § 6001), and (4) Congressional Committees. Once granted pursuant to court order, the witness is compelled to testify and "no testimony or other information compelled under the order (or an information directly or indirectly derived from such testimony or other information) may be used against the witness in any criminal case, except in a prosecution for perjury, giving a false statement, or otherwise failing to comply with the order."

The immunity order for a witness in a grand jury or agency proceeding is issued by the district court, but that court does not assess the justification for granting immunity. Its sole function is to assure that the procedural prerequisites of § 6003 and § 6004 are met. The executive branch has the sole responsibility for determining whether or not immunity should be granted to a particular witness who otherwise would exercise the self-incrimination privilege. The basic procedural prerequisites of § 6003 (governing grand jury witnesses) are: (1) the prosecution's request for the issuance of an immunity order must have been approved by one of several high-level Justice Department officials specified in the statute; and (2) the prosecutor must state in the request that, "in his judgment," (i) the "testimony or other information * * * [sought from the witness] may be necessary to the public interest," and (ii) the witness "has refused or is likely to refuse to testify or provide other information on the basis of his privilege against self-incrimination." In the case of a witness called before an administrative agency, the agency must be one of those listed in § 6001, the agency must gain approval of the Attorney General, and it must have "in its judgment" reached the same conclusions as to the public interest and the witness' reliance on the privilege as are required for the prosecutor who seeks a § 6003 immunity order.

Once granted immunity, the witness can be ordered to respond to all questions within the scope of the immunity order. A witness refusing to respond faces contempt sanctions, absent some legal justification for refusing to respond (e.g., the attorney-client privilege). Self-incrimination is no longer a valid justification for refusing to respond, as the immunity grant supplants the privilege as to both state and federal prosecution. Witnesses sometimes claim that they fear physical retaliation by associates, but the lower courts have invariably found that a true case of duress is not presented, as the threat must be of a "palpable, imminent danger." *In re Grand Jury Proceedings of December 1989 (Freligh)* (7th Cir.1990).

The immunity order under § 6002 is proceeding specific. Thus, *Pillsbury v. Conboy* (S.Ct.1983) held that where a witness had given immunized testimony in a grand jury proceeding, and later was called to testify in a civil case and asked there whether he had testified previously as to the content of his immunized testimony, he could assert the privilege against self-incrimination. The Supreme Court majority reasoned that it need not decide whether an affirmative answer would itself be excludable in a subsequent criminal prosecution as the fruit of immunized grand jury testimony. The witness could not be compelled to testify by virtue of the earlier grant of immunity, as it did not extend to the civil proceeding. The § 6002 immunity order was not intended to serve as the basis for compelling testimony except where it makes a "duly authorized assurance of immunity at the time" (i.e., the proceeding in which the order is obtained).

§ 19.13 Prosecuting the Immunized Witness

Unlike transactional immunity, use/derivative-use immunity does not absolutely preclude later prosecuting an immunized witness for criminal activities touched upon in the immunized testimony. To sustain such a prosecution, however, the government must establish, under a preponderance of evidence standard, that the evidence upon which it relies was not derived from the defendant's immunized testimony, but came instead from a "legitimate source wholly independent of the compelled testimony." *Kastigar v. U.S.* (§ 19.11). The primary hearing on this issue—commonly called a taint hearing—" 'may be held' pre-trial, post-trial, [or] mid-trial (as the evidence is offered)," at the discretion of the trial court. *U.S. v. North* (D.C.Cir.1990). Many courts favor a pretrial hearing on the ground that the defendant should not be forced to trial unless the government can show that its evidence is not tainted. One byproduct of such a hearing is to give the defense valuable pretrial discovery that would otherwise not be available, as the government identifies each item of evidence it intends to use and cites its independent source.

Some courts have suggested that the government cannot possibly sustain its *Kastigar*-burden if the evidence shows that "but for" the immunized testimony, the government would not have come into possession of its evidence. Others suggest that a causal connection can be so attenuated—particularly where critical steps in uncovering the evidence were taken by non-governmental actors—that the evidence will be considered not to have been derived from the immunized testimony even though that testimony was the catalyst for the initiation of the process that eventually brought the evidence to the government's attention. *U.S. v. Helmsley* (2d Cir.1991). Courts generally agree that the government is most likely to meet its *Kastigar*-burden when it can show that its evidence was collected before the witness was ever given immunity. Thus, the Department of Justice's guidelines direct prosecutors to follow the practice of preparing a memorandum prior to the grant of immunity listing all evidence against the witness then known to exist and designating its source and date of receipt.   Where that evidence consists, however, of witnesses who testified before the grand jury and those witnesses subsequently learn of the defendant's immunized testimony before testifying at trial, their testimony at trial may be tainted by virtue of the immunized testimony having further shaped their memory of events. *U.S. v. North.*

Although *Kastigar* spoke primarily of immunity granting protection against the government using the compelled testimony as evidence or as an investigatory lead to other evidence, it also used broader language that several courts have read as establishing a prohibition against the government's "tactical" or "nonevidentiary" use of the compelled testimony. The theory here is that the government must be placed in the same position where it would have been if the witness (now defendant) had never testified, so all uses of the testimony are prohibited. *U.S. v. McDaniel* (8th Cir.1973). Other courts have suggested that certain "nonevidentiary" uses are so tangential to the strength of the prosecution's case as to be consistent with *Kastigar*'s protection. Thus, the prosecution should not be banned from utilizing the compelled testimony in deciding whether to indict or whether or not to offer the defendant a plea bargain. *U.S. v. Byrd* (11th Cir.1985). Because of concern about claims of possible nonevidentiary use where the trial prosecutor was familiar with the immunized testimony, prosecutors often seek to insure that the portion of the staff working on the criminal prosecution be cut off from any possible exposure to the defendant's immunized testimony.

§ 19.14 Immunity Agreements

Where the witness is willing to testify in exchange for immunity, the prosecutor may prefer to provide immunity through an agreement (whereby the witness agrees to testify in exchange for a promise of non-prosecution) rather than an immunity grant. Use of an immunity agreement, rather than statutory immunity, permits the prosecutor to tailor the scope of the immunity to the needs of the case.

Thus, a prosecutor may believe that an informal grant of transactional immunity will be more effective in gaining witness cooperation. In other situations, the immunity provided by statute may be more than the witness requires or the prosecutor is willing to give; an immunity agreement may be limited to barring prosecution only as to certain aspects of the transaction. For the witness, an immunity agreement has an advantage primarily where the agreement grants broader immunity than would be available by statute. Very often, however, the witness will go along with narrower agreement immunity because the prosecution simply will not offer statutory immunity. Federal courts have frequently upheld the use of immunity agreements, viewing them as similar in nature to plea agreements that are conditioned on the defendant providing testimony against others. *U.S. v. Pelletier* (2d Cir.1990). This means that the recalcitrant witness who wants to back away from an agreement cannot be compelled to testify, *U.S. v. Winter* (1st Cir.1981), but once the witness provides the testimony he promised to give, the government will be required to honor its side of the agreement. *Pelletier.*

Prosecutors often demand, as a prerequisite for considering a grant of immunity, that the possible cooperating witness provide a proffer of his testimony. A limited form of immunity is commonly granted as the proffer itself through a proffer agreement. Federal Rule 11(f), by incorporating Federal Rule of Evidence 410, provides that a statement made in the course of plea discussions which do not result in guilty plea may not later be admitted in evidence against the person making the statement. Although discussions of possible immunity are also likely to consider a guilty plea alternative, to ensure protection of the type provided under Rule 11(f), counsel for a potential cooperating witness commonly will insist that the prosecution agree to Rule 11(f) treatment of that person's proffer. However, the prosecutor in turn will insist on an exception allowing impeachment use of the proffer, a practice upheld as to plea discussions in *U.S. v. Mezzanatto* (S.Ct. 1995). Thus, if the potential cooperating witness is not granted immunity, but is instead prosecuted, the prosecution may not use the proffer as evidence against him in its case-in-chief, but may use the proffer to impeach him if he testifies inconsistently with his proffer at trial. Indeed, courts have upheld agreements that permit the prosecution to use the proffer as rebuttal evidence if the defendant simply presents a defense at trial that is "inconsistent" with the proffer. *U.S. v. Krilich* (7th Cir.1999) (where proffer admitted to commission of crime, a defense that went beyond challenging the general trustworthiness of the government witnesses, but sought to establish that the defendant was not present at the scene of the crime, was inconsistent with the proffer). Even if Rule 11(f) protection is fully extended to the proffer, without any exceptions, the proffer poses risks since Rule 11(f) does not preclude prosecution use of evidence derived from information contained in the proffer.

CHAPTER TWENTY
THE SELF–INCRIMINATION PRIVILEGE: DOCUMENTS

§ 20.01 *Boyd v. United States* and "Content Protection"

Boyd v. U.S. (S.Ct.1886), was the first Supreme Court case to consider the applicability of the self-incrimination privilege to compelled production of documents, and for close to a century thereafter, *Boyd* dominated Fifth Amendment analysis of the subpoena duces tecum. At issue in *Boyd* was the constitutionality of a court order requiring an importing firm organized as a partnership to produce the invoice it had received for items alleged to have been illegally imported. The Court initially concluded that the court order was the equivalent of a search and therefore was subject to the Fourth Amendment (see § 16.03). It then concluded that the search was unreasonable because it constituted a forcible compulsion that was contrary to the 5th Amendment's self-incrimination clause. Just as the Fifth Amendment prohibited "compulsory discovery by extorting the party's oath," it also prohibited discovery by "compelling the production of his private books and papers." The documentary production order was simply another form of "forcible and compulsory extortion of a man's own testimony."

It is unclear whether *Boyd's* self-incrimination analysis was intended to be limited to the compelled production of documents. As documents contain words, the compelled disclosure of their content can be viewed as more closely analogous to the compelling of testimonial utterances than compelling the disclosure of other forms of property possessed by the subpoenaed party. Also, the Court spoke of "private" papers, which would often have been authored by the owner. However, the document at issue in *Boyd* itself was not authored by the owner and was not a confidential document relating to a personal or private matter, but a business record that had been prepared by the shipper of the items in question. Moreover, the Court spoke generally of the individual's privacy interest in the possession of personal property as to which the public had no entitlement (such entitlement existing, the Court noted, only where a third-party had a superior right, as with stolen property, or the state had a superior interest, as with records required to be kept by law). Thus, the *Boyd* approach to the Fifth Amendment has been characterized by commentators as more property than privacy oriented, and the Supreme Court, later described *Boyd* as having protected the individual "from any disclosure, in the form of oral testimony, documents, or chattels sought by legal process against him as a witness." *U.S. v. White* (S.Ct.1944). Consider also *U.S. v. Hubbell* (S.Ct.2000) (Justices Thomas and Scalia, in a concurring opinion, urge the Court to consider reviving *Boyd*, a decision they view as supporting the proposition that "the Fifth Amendment privilege protects against the compelled protection not just of incriminating testimony, but of any incriminating evidence").

Starting with *Hale v. Henkel* (S.Ct.1906), decided only two decades after *Boyd*, the Supreme Court gradually developed a series of doctrines that chipped away at the broad implications of *Boyd's* property-rights/privacy analysis of Fifth Amendment protection. The Court recognized various "exceptions" to the application of the Fifth Amendment to document production, including those for entity records (see § 20.09), required records (§ 20.08), and third party production (§ 20.07).

More significantly, the Court also adopted doctrine that rejected, at least in part, a property rights or privacy analysis of the Fifth Amendment. Building upon *Boyd*, the Court had initially held that a search was unreasonable under the Fourth Amendment if it sought personal property that was not contraband or the fruits or instrumentalities of a crime (i.e., property that was "mere evidence" of a crime). However, it rejected that doctrine in the mid-1960s and a decade later upheld a search for documents of the very type involved in *Boyd*. *Andressen v. Maryland* (S.Ct.1976). So too, in a series of cases culminating in *Schmerber v. California* (S.Ct.1966), the Court held that privilege was limited to testimonial compulsion. Thus, *Schmerber* held that the compelled extraction of a blood sample was not subject to the privilege, notwithstanding the privacy and property interests obviously involved. The individual was not making a "communication" in providing blood, but was simply being made "the source of 'real' or 'physical' evidence." Communication was not necessarily limited to statements "compelled from a person's own lips"; it could take other forms as well, but those other forms must also convey "testimony"—i.e., reflect the "contents of the mind." *U.S. v. Doe* (§ 20.04).

In *Fisher v. U.S.* (S.Ct.1976), the Court majority concluded that all that remained of *Boyd* was a prohibition against compelling the production of documents, which had "long been a rule searching for a rationale." In light of *Schmerber*, the prohibition could not rest on the incriminating content of the documents, for the court order does not direct the subpoenaed party to author the requested documents, but simply to produce documents that are preexisting. Since the documents were prepared voluntarily, they "cannot be said to contain compelled testimonial evidence." The documents may contain incriminating writing, but whether the writing of the subpoenaed party or another, that writing is not a communication compelled by the subpoena. Its content is no more protected than the content of physical evidence with similar incriminating content (as in *Schmerber*). As explained in § 20.02, the *Fisher* Court did find an element of compelling testimony implicit in the act of producing the preexisting document, and where the communicative aspect of that act of production—not the contents of the document—is potentially incriminating, the privilege remains as a bar to requiring production of the document.

While *Fisher* did not overturn *Boyd*, in offering the act of production as the focal point for the application of the self-incrimination doctrine, *Fisher* certainly appeared to turn away from a rationale that looked to the "private" character of the subpoenaed documents. That rationale, advanced by Justices Brennan and Marshall in concurring opinions in *Fisher*, relies in large part on the content of the records, which the *Fisher* majority characterized as irrelevant. In *U.S. v. Doe* (S.Ct.1984), a case involving a grand jury subpoena for various business records, the lower court had sustained a claim of the privilege both upon a privacy analysis that it drew from *Boyd* and upon the act-of-production analysis of *Fisher*. Affirming solely on the latter ground, the Supreme Court criticized the lower court's alternative analysis, noting that it tied the privilege to the content of the documents and that reasoning was contrary to "the reasoning underlying this Court's holding in *Fisher*." Justice O'Connor wrote separately "to make explicit what is implicit in the analysis of [the Court's] opinion; that the Fifth Amendment provides absolutely no protection for the contents of private papers of any kind. The notion that the Fifth Amendment protects the privacy of papers originated in *Boyd v. U.S.*, but our decision in *Fisher v. U.S.*, sounded the death-knell for *Boyd*." Justice Marshall, joined by Justice Brennan, expressed disagreement, noting that the *Doe* case dealt only with business records "which implicate a lesser degree of concern for privacy interests than, for example, personal diaries."

Subsequent lower court opinions have been divided in their response to contentions that a privacy analysis can still sustain the privilege even when the act of production would not do so. Many have agreed with Justice O'Connor's analysis, concluding that the rationale of *Fisher* and *Doe* precludes self-incrimination protection of the contents of a voluntarily prepared document, no matter how personal the document. Other courts have also rejected a privacy contention, but on the ground that the papers before them did not fall in the class of "intimate papers such as private diaries and drafts of letters or essays." If the "content of papers are protected at all," they note, "it is only in rare situations, where compelled disclosure would break the heart of our sense of privacy." *In re Steinberg* (1st Cir.1988).

§ 20.02 The Act–Of–Production Doctrine

Having concluded that the application of the privilege cannot rest on the declarations contained in a preexisting voluntarily authored writing that the subpoenaed party was now compelled to produce, the *Fisher* Court looked to communicative aspects of the very act of producing the documents and concluded that such a communication could sometimes (but not always) be sufficient to invoke the privilege. The act of producing subpoenaed documents, the Court noted, "has communicative aspects of its own, wholly aside from the contents of the papers produced." Compliance with a subpoena "tacitly concedes the existence of the papers demanded and their possession or control by the [subpoenaed party]." It also would indicate that party's "belief that the papers are those described in the subpoena," and in some instances this could constitute authentication of the papers. These three elements of production—acknowledgment of existence, acknowledgment of possession or control, and potential authentication by identification—were clearly compelled, but whether they also were "testimonial" and "incriminating" would depend upon the "facts and circumstances of particular cases or classes thereof." The resolution of that question, the Court reasoned, should determine whether a

particular documentary production
Fifth Amendment challenge.

The *Fisher* Court was concerned in that
the testimonial significance of the implicit adm
as to the existence and possession of an accountan
workpapers through their compelled production.
Relying upon what came to be known as the
"foregone conclusion" standard, the *Fisher* Court
concluded:

> It is doubtful that implicitly admitting the
> existence and possession of the papers rises to the
> level of testimony within the protection of the Fifth
> Amendment. The papers belong to the accountant,
> were prepared by him, and are the kind usually
> prepared by an accountant working on the tax
> returns of his client. Surely the Government is in
> no way relying on the "truthtelling" of the
> taxpayer to prove the existence of or his access to
> the documents. The existence and location of the
> papers are a foregone conclusion and the taxpayer
> adds little or nothing to the sum total of the
> Government's information by conceding that he in
> fact has the papers. Under these circumstances by
> enforcement of the summons "no constitutional
> rights are touched. The question is not of
> testimony but of surrender."

In further explaining this forgone conclusion
analysis, the Court cited by analogy its rulings
holding the Fifth Amendment inapplicable to a court
order requiring an accused to submit a handwriting
sample. Incidental to the performance of that act, the
Court noted, the accused necessarily "admits his
ability to write and impliedly asserts that the
exemplar is his writing." But the government

obviously is not seeking this information—the "first would be a near truism and the latter self-evident"—, and therefore "nothing he has said or done is deemed to be sufficiently testimonial for purposes of the privilege." Where the existence and possession of the documents to be produced were a "foregone conclusion," the act of production was viewed by the *Fisher* Court as having the same non-testimonial character. The government in such a case obviously was not seeking the assertions of the subpoenaed party as to the facts of existence and possession, and her incidental communication as to those facts, inherent in the physical act that the government had the authority to compel, therefore would not rise to the level of compelled "testimony."

Fisher did not have before it an act of production that had a significant potential for providing authentication evidence, and therefore spoke of the foregone conclusion doctrine only as it related to establishing existence and possession of the documents. However, two later cases, *U.S. v. Doe* (S.Ct.1984) and *U.S. v. Hubbell* (S.Ct.2000), established that the foregone conclusion analysis applied as well to this potentially testimonial aspect of the act of production.

After *Fisher*, the government had two major avenues for defeating a self-incrimination claim as to the production of preexisting to documents: (1) establishing that the act of production was not testimonial because existence, possession, and authentication (to the extent applicable) are a foregone conclusion; (2) contending that the act of production, even though testimonial, does not present the realistic potential for incrimination required for the privilege to apply. The standards applied to those contentions, as established by the Supreme Court, are discussed below.

§ 20.03   The Foregone Conclusion Standard

Fisher offered only limited insight as what was needed to meet the foregone conclusion standard. The Court's reference to the accountant's workpapers as a type of document commonly prepared for taxpayers led the government to contend that the existence and location of standard business documents was always a foregone conclusion.   *U.S. v. Doe* (S.Ct.1984) appeared to reject this contention, as the documents subpoenaed there were standard business documents and the Court sustained the lower court findings that the government had failed to establish "that possession, existence, and authentication were a foregone conclusion." But the Court in *Doe* did not offer an independent analysis of this conclusion. Rather, it emphasized that two lower courts had found that the act-of-production there would present testimonial self-incrimination, that this finding rested basically on "factual issues," and that the Court had "traditionally been reluctant to disturb findings of fact in which two courts below have concurred."

In *U.S. v. Hubbell* (S.Ct.2002), however, the Court both confirmed the implicit message of *Doe* and offered a reading of *Fisher* consistent with the lower court rulings demanding that the government, to meet the foregone conclusion standard, demonstrate with "reasonable particularly that it knows of the existence and location of subpoenaed documents." The subpoena in *Hubbell* called for 11 categories (almost all broadly described) of largely business documents. The Court reasoned that, "given the breadth of the 11 categories, * * * the collection and production of the materials demanded was tantamount to answering a series of interrogatories asking a witness to disclose the existence and location of particular documents fitting broad descriptions." The government responded that this obviously "communicative aspect of production" was nontheless not sufficiently testimonial "because the existence and possession of such records by any business is a foregone conclusion." Rejecting this contention, the Court reasoned:

Whatever the scope of this "foregone conclusion" rationale, the facts of this case plainly fall outside of it. While in *Fisher*, the Government already knew that the documents were in the attorneys' possession and could independently confirm their existence and authenticity through the accountants who created them, here the Government has not shown that it had any prior knowledge of either the existence or the whereabouts of the 13,120 pages of documents ultimately produced by respondent. The Government cannot cure this deficiency through the overboard argument that a businessman such as respondent will always possess general business and tax records that fall within the broad categories described in this subpoena. The *Doe* subpoenas also sought several broad categories of general business records, yet we upheld the District Court's finding that the act of producing those records would involve testimonial self-incrimination.

Hubbell's description of *Fisher* illustrates one means of meeting the foregone conclusion standard, although its scope is not clear. *Fisher* presented two features that contributed to the foregone conclusion finding there – one fairly common and one unusual. The fairly common factor is the availability of third persons (in *Fisher*, the accountants) who can establish that the documents had been prepared and delivered to the person now being investigated. The unique factor is that the target's lawyers (who had possession of the documents), in order to establish the lawyer-client privilege (through which the self-incrimination issue was raised, see § 22.04), had to acknowledge that their client had possessed the documents and had transferred them to the lawyers in the course of seeking legal advice. In general, lower courts have not demanded such strong evidence of existence and current possession as that acknowledgment, but they have insisted that foregone conclusion evidence be case specific and, typically, that it relate to documents described in such a manner as not to require the subpoenaed party to use her special knowledge of historical fact in identifying the document (a factor emphasized by the *Hubbell* Court, as in its analogy to answering interrogatories).

§ 20.04 Potential Incrimination

The Court in *Fisher* stated that even if the act of production in that case had been testimonial, the privilege still would not apply because there had been no showing that the communicative aspects of production posed a "realistic threat of incrimination to the taxpayer." As to authentication, it noted that production would not provide the government with evidence that could be used to authenticate the subpoenaed workpapers since production by the taxpayer would "express nothing more than the taxpayer's belief that the papers are those described in the subpoena" and the taxpayer could not thereby authenticate as he "did not prepare the papers and could not vouch for their accuracy." As to existence and possession, "surely it was not illegal to seek accounting help in connection with one's tax returns or for the accountant to prepare workpapers and deliver them to the taxpayer." "At this juncture," the Court noted, it was "quite unprepared to hold that either the fact of the existence of the papers or their possession by the taxpayer" posed a sufficient threat to raise a legitimate self-incrimination claim.

In *Doe*, in contrast to *Fisher*, the lower courts had found that the production of the documents had a potential for incrimination. Indeed, the Supreme Court, in a revealing footnote, rejected the government's contention that even if the act of production there were viewed as having sufficient "testimonial aspects," any incrimination would be "so trivial" that the Fifth Amendment would not be implicated. Respondent Doe, the Court noted, had never conceded that the records subpoenaed actually existed or were within his possession. As respondent also had noted, "even if the government could obtain the documents from another source, by producing the documents, respondent would relieve the government of the need for authentication." The potential prosecution uses of respondent's act of production, the Court noted, "were sufficient to establish a valid claim of the privilege."

The *Doe* Court, in its brief comment on self-incrimination potential, did not seek to distinguish *Fisher*. Certainly the cases cannot be distinguished by the general character of the records involved: the records subpoenaed in *Doe* were standard business records (e.g., billings and cancelled checks) and the possession of such records was just as innocuous on its face as the possession of an accountant"s workpapers. The critical distinction apparently related to the possible content of the records and incriminating potential of possession in light of that content. *Doe*, of course, involved a grand jury investigation (in contrast to the administrative IRS subpoena in *Fisher*) and the government obviously was seeking to establish though the documents that the subpoenaed party had a connection to the businesses that had created the records (a connection which respondent Doe denied). Under these circumstances, the subpoenaed party had shown enough to establish a "substantial and real" possibility of incrimination. In the typical grand jury investigation, the subpoenaed party should be able to meet that standard by reference to the subject of the investigation, the relevancy of the documents, and the status of the subpoenaed party (as a target or subject of the investigation). In *Hubbell*, such factors so clearly pointed to a realistic threat of incrimination that the issue was not even raised before the Supreme Court (and, of course, the later use of documents, after immunity had been granted, had established their incriminating character).

§ 20.05 Act of Production Immunity

In *U.S. v. Doe* (S.Ct.1984), the government argued that, should the Supreme Court accept the lower court's finding that the privilege applied to the subpoena duces tecum, the Court should nonetheless order the district court to enforce the subpoena on condition that the government agree not to make use or derivative use of the act of production. Rejecting this proposal, the Court noted that the government was, in effect, offering to provide immunity for the act of production and that only could be done in accordance with the immunity statutes (see § 19.12). The Court did note, however, that the government "could have compelled respondent to produce the documents" by utilizing the federal immunity statutes, and that the use/derivative-use immunity granted thereunder could be limited to the act of production. There was no need for the immunity grant to extend to the contents of the documents as such, because the privilege was based solely on the act of production and the "immunity need be only as broad as the privilege."

Concurring in *Fisher*, Justice Marshall noted that immunity tied to the act of production would nonetheless commonly serve to "effectively shield" the contents of the subpoenaed documents, as the contents would be a direct fruit of the "immunized testimony" contained in the act of production. In contrast to Justice Marshall, the Department of Justice took the position that immunity limited to the act of production never extends derivatively to the document itself (including its contents) because *Fisher* held quite clearly that the contents were not compelled and therefore not subject to the Fifth

Amendment privilege. All that the immunity required, the D.O.J. argued, was that the documents be treated, in effect, as "manna from heaven" – i.e., no reference be made to their source. If this was done, the documents themselves could be used for any purpose, including their introduction in evidence (if otherwise authenticated).

In *U.S. v. Hubbell* (S.Ct.2002), the Supreme Court flatly rejected the D.O.J.'s argument, although it arguably did not go so far as to accept Justice Marshall's position. The government in *Hubbell* had granted the respondent Hubbell act-of-production immunity for his compliance with a subpoena calling for 11 different categories of documents, but it contended that the immunity did not impact its subsequent prosecution of Hubbell. It was not using the documents produced by respondent, but other evidence discovered through an examination of the contents of the produced documents. The Court held this showing insufficient because the government could not also show that it had not made "derivative use" of the "testimonial aspect[s] of the act-of-production itself." Indeed, the Court concluded, the prosecution in various ways had violated the derivative use prohibition.

Certain aspects of the Court's discussion of the government's derivative use focused on the special character of the subpoena in *Hubbell* and what it had required for compliance. Because of the breadth of the different categories, it was "unquestionably necessary for respondent to make extensive use of the 'contents of his own mind' in identifying the hundreds of documents responsive to the subpoena." He had, through his act of production, provided "the prosecutor with an accurate inventory of the many sources of potentially incriminating evidence sought by the subpoena," and that inventory presented the "first step in the chain of evidence that led to the prosecution." This discussion might suggest that if the testimonial aspects of the act of production do not assist in describing the background of the documents and in categorizing the documents, but simply establish their existence, the government may use the contents of the documents (assuming no reference is made to the act of production).

The *Hubbell* opinion, however, also used broader language. It noted, for example, that it was only through "respondent's truthful reply to the subpoena that the Government received the incriminating documents", and that the act of production had provided testimony as to "existence" and "whereabouts," which were not part of the government's prior knowledge. Such language suggests that the availability of the document itself (including the examination of its contents) was a derivative use, and thus the government cannot make use of documents produced under an immunity grant even where the subpoena is narrowly drawn to identify a particular document.

§ 20.06 Requiring Non–Testimonial Writings

Building upon the reasoning of *Fisher*, *Doe v. U.S.* (S.Ct.1988) recognized that even a compelled writing could be nontestimonial. The Court there held that an individual could not rely on the privilege to refuse to obey a court order directing the individual to sign a form authorizing a foreign bank to release records relating to any account held by the individual. The government's purpose, it noted, was not to have the individual, by signing the form, "relate a factual assertion or disclose information." Indeed, the form was carefully drafted so that the signing party noted that he was acting under court order and did not acknowledge the existence of any account in any particular bank. The form did not constitute evidence that the requested documents existed and offered no assistance to the government in later establishing the authenticity of any records produced by the bank in response to the form. Accordingly, the Court concluded, the signed form constituted a communication, but did not constitute "testimony" for Fifth Amendment purposes. The district court was directing the individual only to perform the act of signing a directive to the bank, not to engage in "truth telling" through the directive.

§ 20.07 Third Party Production

In both *Fisher* and *Couch v. U.S.* (S.Ct.1973), the owner of records had transferred the records to an independent professional, and it was that person who was subpoenaed to produce the records. In *Couch*, the taxpayer had delivered various financial records to her accountant for the purpose of preparing her income tax returns, and the IRS subsequently issued a summons directing the accountant to produce the papers. In *Fisher*, the IRS directed a summons to lawyers for production of accountant's workpapers that had been delivered to them by the taxpayer in seeking legal advice. In both instances, the taxpayers sought to challenge the IRS summons as invading the taxpayer's privilege against self-incrimination. They stressed their ownership of the documents and the potential incrimination that would fall upon them though the content of the documents. The Supreme Court responded that the persons compelled to produce the documents were the professionals, not the taxpayers, and the Fifth Amendment protected only those persons who themselves were "compelled" to give testimony or perform a testimonial act. The taxpayers themselves were not required "to do anything." (In *Fisher*, because of the lawyer-client privilege, see § 22.04, the lawyers were able to place before the court the taxpayer's self-incrimination contention, but the taxpayer could not raise that claim directly).

Both *Fisher* and *Couch* acknowledged that "situations might exist where constructive possession is so clear or the relinquishment of possession is so temporary and insignificant as to leave the personal compulsion upon the accused substantially intact." Lower courts have since indicated that constructive possession is a concept largely limited in application to situations in which an employer seeks to raise the privilege in response to a subpoena directed to an employee who maintains the employer's records under the supervision of the employer. Moreover, to take advantage of the concept, the employer must show that he "exercised dominion" over the records and that the employee's control was restricted. *In re Grand Jury Proceedings (Manges)* (9th Cir.1984).

§ 20.08 Required Records

Where individuals engage in a regulated business, they may be required to keep certain records and to make such records open for inspection by public officials. In *Shapiro v. U.S.* (S.Ct.1948), the Supreme Court held that the self-incrimination privilege does not provide protection against the compelled disclosure of such records as the records were created for the public benefit, with the government reserving the right to insist upon their production. The *Shapiro* Court acknowledged that "there are limits which the Government cannot constitutionally exceed in requiring the keeping of records which may be inspected * * * and may be used in prosecuting statutory violations committed by the record-keeper himself," but it had no need to consider those limits in the context of the records before it—records of commodity sales that wholesale fresh produce dealers were required to keep in the implementation of the Wartime Emergency Price Control Act. Subsequently, in *Grosso v. U.S.* (S.Ct.1968), the Court characterized three elements as necessary "premises of the [required records] doctrine."

First, "the purposes of the United States' inquiry [requiring that the records be kept] must be essentially regulatory." The government's interest in the records must arise out of a regulatory scheme rather than a criminal law enforcement objective. Thus, the doctrine could not be used to impose a reporting requirement on professional gamblers, a "group inherently suspect of criminal activities." Most states make gambling a crime, and looking to the "characteristics of the activity" and "the composition of the group to which inquires are made," the Court could not say that Congress was dealing here with "an essentially non-criminal and regulatory area." *Grosso v. U.S.*

Second, the information that is to be obtained by the government by "requiring the preservation of records" must be of a kind which the regulatory party has customarily kept. This reduces the burden placed upon the record keeper and often supports the regulatory relevance of the record. "[T]hird, the records themselves must have assumed 'public aspects' which render them at least analogous to public documents." This characteristic was said to exist in *Shapiro* because the "transaction which it [the required record] recorded was one in which petitioner could lawfully engage solely by virtue of the license granted to him under the statute."

§ 20.9 The Entity Exception

Hale v. Henkel (S.Ct.1906) not only reconstructed *Boyd's* Fourth Amendment analysis (see § 16.03), but also added a major exception to the application of its Fifth Amendment analysis. *Hale* held that the self-incrimination privilege was not available to a corporation and therefore the *Boyd* ruling did not operate to bar a grand jury subpoena duces tecum requiring production of corporate records. The Court's reasoning stressed the different status of the individual and the corporation. The individual, it noted, "owes no duty to the State * * * to divulge his business, or to open his doors to an investigation, so far as it may tend to incriminate him." The corporation, in contrast, "is a creature of the State," and exercises its franchise subject to the "reserved right" of the State to compel its assistance in ensuring that it has not "exceeded its powers."

The Court in *Hale* also took special note of a concern repeatedly cited in subsequent entity cases—the enforcement needs of the government in regulating entities. If the government were precluded by the self-incrimination clause from compelling production of corporate records, "it would result in a failure of a large number of cases where the illegal combination was determinable only upon such papers." Not surprisingly in light of this concern, the Court, in *Wilson v. U.S.* (S.Ct.1911), rejected the claim of a corporate officer possessing subpoenaed corporate records that he could refuse to produce those records because they would personally incriminate him. The State's "reserved power of visitation," the Court noted, "would seriously be embarrassed, if not wholly defeated in its effective exercise, if guilty officers could refuse inspection of the records and papers of the corporation." As the records were those of the corporation, not personal records, and were held "subject to the corporate duty," the official could "assert no personal right * * * against any demand of the government which the corporation was bound to recognize." The subpoena in *Wilson* was directed to the corporation, but *Dreier v. U.S.* (S.Ct.1911) held that the result was the same where the subpoena was directed to a specified individual in his capacity as corporate custodian.

In *U.S. v. White* (S.Ct.1944), the Court extended the *Hale* exception to entities other than corporations. *White* held that the president of an unincorporated labor union could not invoke his personal privilege against a subpoena demanding union records. The privilege against self-incrimination, the Court noted, was "designed to prevent the use of legal process to force from the lips of the accused the evidence necessary to convict him or force him to produce and authenticate any personal documents that might incriminate him, * * * * [to] thereby avoid * * * physical torture and other less violent but equally reprehensible modes of compelling the production of incriminating evidence." These concerns did not apply to the entity, which lacked the qualities of human personality and therefore could not suffer the "immediate and potential evils of compulsory self-disclosure."

The *White* Court characterized the labor union as an organization with "a character so impersonal in scope of its membership and activities that it cannot be said to embody or represent the purely private or personal interests of its constituents, but rather to embody their common or group interests only." In *Bellis v. U.S.* (S.Ct.1974), however, the Court concluded that the entity exception remained applicable even though the entity embodied personal as well as group interests. The functional key was that the organization "be recognized as an independent entity apart from its individual members." Thus, a small law firm, organized as a partnership, was an entity for this purpose even though it "embodied[d] little more than the personal legal practice of the individual partners."

Bellis noted that "this might be a different case if it involved a small family partnership, or * * * if there were some other pre-existing relationship of confidentiality among the partners." Lower courts have viewed any such exceptions as quite narrow. Indeed, even where there is no formal partnership agreement, a structured business organization may fall within the entity exception. Thus, the entity exception was held to apply to persons who owned commercial property as tenants in common, had a separate bank account for business activities relating that to that property, and utilized an assumed name in conducting such business. *In re Grand Jury*

Proceedings (Shiffman) (6th Cir.1978). On the other hand, a husband-wife professional service firm, though organized as a partnership under the Uniform Partnership Act, was held not to constitute an entity where it had no employees and no office outside the couple's home. *In re Grand Jury Subpoena* (E.D.N.Y.1985).

§ 20.10 The Entity Agent

Because the entity has no self-incrimination privilege, and the entity agent is responding in a representative capacity in producing the documents of the entity, *U.S. v. Wilson* (see § 20.07) and a series of other early 1900s cases held that the entity agent could not invoke the agent's personal privilege even though the content of the documents were clearly incriminating to the agent. Prior to *Fisher*, the only major open issue as to production by an entity agent was where the agent's responsibility ended. The lower courts had held, with some suggestion of approval by the Supreme Court, that the agent could be required to testify for the purpose of identifying the documents. However, once this was done, the agent could exercise his personal privilege as to further questions relating to the records (e.g., how they were prepared). In an analogous situation, the Supreme Court held that an officer of a local union, having established that he no longer possessed the subpoenaed records, could then assert the privilege as to questions concerning their disposition. *Curcio v. U.S.* (S.Ct.1957). But note *U.S. v. Rylander* (S.Ct.1983) (custodial agent still carried burden of establishing that he no longer had the records, which could not be met by simply claiming the privilege).

After *Fisher* introduced the act-of-production doctrine (see § 20.01), several lower courts concluded that the entity agent should be allowed to claim the privilege as to the act of production, at least where the subpoena was directed to the particular entity official rather than to the entity itself. In *Braswell v. U.S.* (S.Ct.1980), a closely divided Supreme Court rejected that position. The *Braswell* majority concluded that *Fisher*'s adoption of the act-of-production doctrine had not altered the unavailability of the privilege to the entity agent. The Court's pre-*Fisher* rulings on the responsibility of the agent had not ignored the testimonial aspects of the act of production, but had correctly considered any such testimonial elements to be properly attributed to the entity rather to the agent acting on its behalf. Even where the subpoena was directed by name to a particular entity official having control of the records, rather than simply to the entity itself, that official was not performing "a personal act, but rather an act of the [entity]" in complying with the subpoena. The dissent argued that this position was allowing the law "to be captive to its own fictions," but the majority responded that *Fisher* itself had accepted this distinction in the course of analyzing the act-of-production rationale. Thus, the *Braswell* majority noted, "whether one concludes—as did the Court [in *Fisher*]—that a custodian's production of corporate records is deemed not to constitute testimonial self-incrimination or instead that a custodian waives the right to exercise the privilege, the lesson of *Fisher* is clear: A custodian may not resist a subpoena for corporate records on Fifth Amendment grounds." To rule otherwise, as the Court had noted in its earlier rulings, would "largely frustrate legitimate government regulation of such organizations" and have a "detrimental impact," in particular, on "the Governments efforts to prosecute 'white collar crime' * * * as the greater portion of evidence of wrongdoing by an organization or its representatives is usually found in the official records of that organization."

Braswell, however, added an evidentiary limitation not mentioned in the earlier cases rejecting self-incrimination claims by entity agents. Since the agent's act of production is an act of the entity and not the individual, the government "may make no evidentiary use of the 'individual act' against the individual." Illustrating this point, the Court noted that "in a criminal prosecution against the custodian, the Government may not introduce into evidence before the jury the fact that the subpoena was served upon and the corporation's documents were delivered by one particular individual, the custodian." The government would be limited to showing that the entity had produced the document and to using that act of the entity in establishing that the records were authentic entity records that the entity had possessed and had produced.

CHAPTER TWENTY–ONE
SEARCHES

§ 21.01 Searches vs. Subpoenas: Advantages and Disadvantages

Very often a search does not present a viable alternative to the subpoena duces tecum in obtaining business records because the constitutional prerequisites for a search are not available. Where these prerequisites arguably can be met, the subpoena duces tecum might still be preferred for several reasons. For one, the administrative costs of a subpoena are far less, as there the subpoenaed party, rather than law enforcement offers, must bear the time consuming task of assembling the documents. Second, the subpoena may be more effective in gaining all relevant documents. Since that subpoenaed party is more familiar with the records and their location, that party's good faith compliance is more likely to include all documents within the specified categories than an investigator's search for the same documents. Also, since the subpoena need not be shaped to fit the probable cause prerequisite, it can be more broadly framed, thereby further insuring that relevant documents are not overlooked.

Third, a grand jury subpoena duces tecum does not open the investigation to the public (assuming the subpoenaed party does not want to make it public) and does not reveal the grounding for the subpoena to the subpoenaed party. The search, however, typically does both. The affidavit presented to obtain the warrant is presumed to be open to the public (although the court may place the affidavit under seal on a proper showing of need). Morever, even if sealing is ordered, the owner of the seized property, on a motion challenging the seizure, will eventually see the affidavit and learn far more about the nature of the investigation than the target of a grand jury investigation who moves to quash.

Fourth, searches causes business disruptions that are deemed unfair and inappropriate where directed at a person who is merely a custodian of records and not a criminal suspect. Indeed, Congress has severely limited the permissible use of searches against third party nonsuspects under the Privacy Protection Act (42 U.S.C. § 2000 6a-20006a-12) and the DOJ guidelines mandated by that Act. Searches directed at a "disinterested third party" require an internal prosecutorial authorization, which is to be granted only if the subpoena alternative would "substantially jeopardize the availability or usefulness of the material sought." Also, further restrictions are placed on searches of the media for journalistic "work product" or searches of disinterested third party physicians, lawyers, or clergymen for records containing confidential information on their patients, clients, or parishioners.

Fifth, the remedy for conducting an unconstitutional search can be far more severe than the remedy for issuing an invalid subpoena. The subpoena is challenged prior to compliance, and if it is held invalid, the government can return with a property framed subpoena. A search is challenged after the fact, and if the search is held to be invalid because of inadequacies of the probable cause affidavit, the warrant, or the execution of the search, a successful motion to suppress is likely to follow (with certain exceptions, see § 21.04). The evidence that was seized is then permanently lost to the government for use in its case-in-chief.

On the other side, assuming a search is legally available, it offers certain advantages over the subpoena duces tecum. First, a search comes without advance notice and therefore does not offer the party in possession of the documents the opportunity to destroy, conceal, or alter the documents. Second, the search gives the government immediate access to the documents. Third, the search places an officer in a position to examine a larger body of documents in seeking to identify those specified in the warrant, and should the officer find in plain view an incriminating document (perhaps as to another crime) that the government never anticipated, he can seize that document (and perhaps use it to obtain a search warrant authorizing a broader search). Fourth, by placing investigators on the premises, the search facilitates possibly "on the spot" questioning of employees.

Fifth, the search has a certain symbolic significance. The disruptive impact of the search can convey a special sense of urgency to those involved. It also conveys to the public the message that prosecutors are adopting an aggressive stance towards white collar crime by subjecting suspects to the same procedures applied to street crimes. In this regard, the absence of the secrecy requirements that attach to a grand jury investigation may be a distinct advantage.

Finally, while an individual (though not an entity) may assert a self-incrimination to a subpoena decum (see § 20.02), that objection is not available to the subject of a search, even a search for documents. As the Supreme Court noted in *Andresen v. Maryland* (S.Ct.1976), the "records seized contai[n] statements that the subject voluntarily committed to writing," and the seizure by another does not require the subject to "say or do anything" (i.e., he is not "compelled" to be a "witness").

§ 21.02 Fourth Amendment Requirements

The Fourth Amendment to the United States Constitution provides that, "[t]he right of the people to be secure in their persons, houses, papers, and effects against unreasonable searches and seizures, shall not be violated, and no Warrants shall issue, but upon probable cause, supported by Oath or affirmation, and particularly describing the place to be searched, and the persons or things to be seized." Almost all of the searches involved in white collar cases will require a warrant. The searches here are of business premises or residences, and they are not likely to present any of the narrow exceptions to the warrant requirement that occasionally apply to the search of such buildings. Accordingly, those searches will have to meet the requirements of the second clause of the Fourth Amendment (the so-called "warrant" clause). Typically, the searches in white collar investigations will be aimed at obtaining documents. The major warrant clause stumbling blocks in obtaining a warrant for a document search are (1) establishing probable cause and (2) describing the documents to be seized with sufficient particularity.

§ 21.03 Probable Cause

In *Illinois v. Gates* (S.Ct.1983) the Supreme Court noted that "[p]robable cause is a fluid concept – turning on the assessment of probabilities in particular factual contexts—not readily, or often usefully, reduced to a neat set of legal rules." The magistrate issuing the warrant must conclude on the basis of a "practical, common-sense" analysis of the information presented that "there is a fair probability" that evidence of a crime will be found in the place to be searched. A magistrate's finding of probable cause is given deference by a reviewing court, but there are limits. "Sufficient information must be presented to the magistrate to allow that official to determine probable cause; his action cannot be a mere ratification of the bare conclusions of others."

The special difficulty presented in establishing probable cause for a search for documents lies not in establishing probable cause as to the commission of a crime, but in establishing probable cause that particular documents constitute evidence of that crime. Thus, where probable cause was based on reports of a series of fraudulent cash transactions, a court held that those illicit dealings in cash provided an obviously insufficient basis for believing that evidence of the crime was to be found in the company's bank account records. So too, the warrant was faulted because it authorized the seizure of documents that predated by several months the start of the fraudulent transactions and the supporting affidavit failed to allege any grounds for believing that the scheme reached back to that earlier date. *U.S. v. Diaz* (1st Cir.1988). On the other hand, where an organization is "permeated by fraud", that may establish probable cause to seize all of its records. *In re Grand Jury Investigation Concerning Solid State Devices* (9th Cir.1997) (also noting that this analysis did not apply where the business "routinely engaged in fraudulent practices," but also engaged in "some legitimate activity," in contrast to a "boiler shop").

§ 21.04 Particularity of Description

Particularity of description initially requires that the documents specified for seizure be limited by the probable cause grounding. But particularly also requires that the officer exercising the search can identify "with reasonable certainty" the items so specified. Document searches pose a special difficulty in this regard because simple descriptions do not sufficiently distinguish one document from another. Courts note that a more particular description is required when other objects of the same general classification are likely to be found at the place to be searched. Moreover, they note that the possibility of a mistaken seizure is of special concern where the "innocent objects" that might mistakenly be seized are documents. Thus, generic descriptions (e.g., "billings") often must be qualified by reference to content or date.

On the other hand, courts do, on occasion, sustain some very open-ended descriptions. *Andresen v. Maryland* (S.Ct.1976) sustained a warrant which authorized seizure of a long list of specific documents relating to fraud with respect to certain realty, but also added the end phrase "together with other fruits, instrumentalities, and evidence of crime at this [time] unknown". Although acknowledging that the execution of a warrant "authorizing a search and seizure of a person's papers" presents "grave dangers" ordinarily not present in searches "for physical objects whose relevance is more easily ascertainable," the Court sustained this very general end phrase under the facts of the case. The needed content of the unknown items was sufficiently established by reference to the items and subject matter specified in the first portion of the paragraph, and no more was needed in light of the character of the particular investigation. The government here was looking at a "complex real estate scheme whose existence could be proved only by piecing together many bits of evidence" and "that complexity * * * could not be used as a shield to avoid detection when the State has demonstrated probable cause to believe that evidence of crimes is in the suspect's possession."

§ 21.05 The *Leon* Exception

Ordinarily, evidence obtained through an unconstitutional search and seizure may not be used by the prosecution in its case-in-chief. *U.S. v. Leon* (S.Ct.1984), however, created an exception to that "exclusionary rule" remedy as to certain unconstitutional searches made pursuant to a warrant. *Leon* held that "the Fourth Amendment exclusionary rule should be modified so as not to bar the use in the prosecution's case-in-chief of evidence obtained by officers acting in reasonable reliance on a search warrant issued by a detached and neutral magistrate but ultimately found to be unsupported by probable cause." *Leon* reasoned that the "exclusionary rule is designed to deter police misconduct rather than to punish the error of judges," and therefore it had no functional validity where the police officer acted in reasonable reliance upon the prior judgment of the magistrate. That was true in the case before the Court, as the search warrant affidavit here "provided evidence sufficient to create disagreement among thoughtful and competent judges as to existence of probable cause," producing an "officer reliance on the magistrate determination [that] was objectively reasonable." The Court added in this regard that what was "objectively reasonable" would be determined in light of what a "reasonably well-trained officer would have known"

Leon does not exempt from the exclusionary rule all searches based on invalid warrant. The Court identified four situations where warrant flaws would still result in the application of the exclusionary rule: (1) where the officer presented knowing or reckless falsehoods in the affidavit used to obtain the warrant; (2) "where the issuing magistrate wholly abandoned his judicial rule," as illustrated by a case in which the magistrate "allowed himself to become a member * * * of the search party"; (3) where the warrant was "so facially deficient – i.e., in failing to particularize the place to be searched or the things to be seized – that the executing officers cannot reasonably presume it to be valid"; and (4) where the warrant was issued on an "affidavit so lacking in indicia of probable cause as to render official belief in its existence entirely unreasonable."

Only the third and fourth exceptions have frequently been at issue in white collar cases. In applying both exceptions, but the fourth in particular, courts emphasize that the "reasonably well trained officer" is "not expected to be a legal technician." Thus, in *Diaz* (see § 21.03), the fourth *Leon* exception was held not to apply to a warrant error of including an earlier document starting date than supported by the probable-cause affidavit. The officer in fact had probable cause to believe the scheme extended back to that date and thought incorrectly that he had set forth enough information to encompass that date in the probable-cause affidavit. Consideration must be given, the court noted, to the "special problems for investigators attempting to draft warrants * * * [in] fraud investigations." On the other hand, *Diaz* held that *Leon* did not exempt that portion of the warrant which improperly authorized seizure of bank account records. Here, there was a "complete lack of justification" for including these items (as the prior fraud cited in the affidavit included only cash transactions) and the officer could not reasonably rely on the magistrate's conclusion that probable cause extended to those records.

§ 21.06 Execution of the Warrant

Leon applies only to reasonable reliance upon an invalid warrant. Fourth Amendment violations in the execution of the warrant, valid or invalid, continue to be subject to the exclusionary rule. With respect to document searches, claims of unconstitutional execution usually relate to the seizure of documents not specified in the warrant. In some instances, the claim is that the officer erred in treating a particular document as within a particular category adequately specified in the warrant, but more often the claim relates to the seizure of a document clearly not specified in the warrant, which the government justifies under the "plain view" doctrine.

Under the plain view doctrine, if an officer, in the proper course of executing the search, comes across other matter in plain view and has probable cause to believe that matter constitutes evidence of a crime, the officer may seize that matter even though it is not among the items specified in the warrant. A critical issue in plain view cases is whether the officer was acting in the proper execution of the warrant when he came across the seized item in plain view. As applied to documents, the resolution of this issue typically depends on whether the officer had reason to inspect the document even though it turned out not to be one of the documents specified in the warrant. The Supreme Court has recognized that, in the course of identifying those documents that fit within the warrant description, officers will be required to "examine at least cursorily" many documents that they will then determine not to be within that description. *Andresen v. Maryland* (§ 21.04). These documents then will be in plain view, and if their proper examination carries the officer to the point where the content of the document establishes probable cause as to a different crime, the Fourth Amendment permits immediate seizure of the document. That was exactly what happened in *Andresen*, where the warrant authorized a search for documents relating to false pretenses in the sale of real estate lot 13T, and the officers came across (and seized) documents evidencing an identical modus operandi as to another lot in the same subdivision.

In looking for documents specified in the warrant by reference to content or type, the executing officer is not restricted by the business' apparent filing system; where documents have incriminating content, they might well not be stored in the "obvious place". As a result, officers often must examine vast quantities of intermingled records to find the specified records. Indeed, the administrative burden of this task often justifies seizing a large batch of intermingled records and removing them to a place where the sorting out process would be less intrusive. Some courts have suggested that where records are stored electronically on a computer, the need to individually examine large quantities of records is reduced because of search devices that can readily identify content and produce only documents that fit the categories specified in the warrant, but others courts consider a visual inspection of a variety of records to be as justified here as it would be for paper records.

§ 21.07 Regulatory Inspections

Regulatory inspections can uncover criminality that may ultimately lead to the charging of a criminal offense. Notwithstanding this potential, regulatory inspections even may occur during the pendency of a criminal action. In *U.S. v. Gel Spice Co. Inc.* (2d Cir. 1985), the Second Circuit stated that, "even if the FDA were pursing criminal enforcement of the Act at the time of the inspections in question, standing alone this does not imply or suggest that the inspections were conducted in bad faith."

The Fourth Amendment applies to regulatory searches. *Camara v. Municipal Court* (S.C.1967).

Such searches, however, do not require the same level of probable cause as the search conducted as part of a criminal investigation. Courts use a "balancing test" to determine whether a particular inspection is reasonable—weighing "the need to search against the invasion which the search entails"—and therefore considering such factors as the "routine nature" of the search and the value of such special techniques as area canvassing in meeting the "reasonable goals of code enforcement." *Camara*. Thus, the probable cause grounding may be held to exist, notwithstanding the lack of a particularized showing of suspicion as to the individual business, simply because the agency follows an administrative scheme, and thereby provides a set of criteria that protect against arbitrariness in the selection of the premises to be inspected.

Unlike traditional searches of business premises, regulatory inspections are often exempted from the Fourth Amendment's warrant requirement, even where there is no emergency requiring immediate action. The Supreme Court has held that a warrant ordinarily is needed for routine fire department inspections and OSHA inspections, but not for inspections of liquor licensees, licensed firearm dealers, and mining operations. *New York v. Burger* (S.C.1987) (reviewing the precedent)

Burger, which upheld warrantless searches of automobile junkyards under a state statute regulating vehicle dismantlers, offered a multi-factored analysis for determining whether a statutory scheme authorizing warrantless inspection was acceptable under the Fourth Amendment. The Court

stressed, in particular, the following considerations:
(1) The regulatory scheme is industry specific and
the industry is heavily regulated (producing a
reduced expectation of privacy); (2) a "substantial
government interest informs the regulatory scheme";
(3) warrantless inspections are "necessary to further
[the] regulatory scheme" (e.g., "frequent and
unannounced inspections" are needed); (4) the
statutory inspection scheme "provides a
constitutionally adequate substitute for a warrant"
by advising the regulated businesses "that the search
is made pursuant to law and has a properly defined
scope" and by "limit[ing] the discretion of the
inspecting officer"; and (5) the permitted inspection
is "carefully limited as to time, place, and scope."

CHAPTER TWENTY-TWO
ATTORNEY- CLIENT PRIVILEGE

§ 22.01 Grounding and Policy

The attorney-client privilege (also known as the lawyer-client privilege) is an evidentiary privilege that protects the confidentiality of certain communications between a client and an attorney. In the federal courts, the privilege is recognized pursuant to Rule 501 of the Federal Rules of Evidence. Rule 501 provides that, in proceedings relating to a federal-law cause of action (which includes the enforcement of federal criminal and regulatory law), evidentiary privileges "shall be governed by the principles of the common law as they may be interpreted by the courts of the United States [i.e., the federal courts] in light of reason and experience." The attorney-client privilege is a well established part of the federal common law of privileges, although federal courts are divided on certain aspects of the privilege that bear particularly upon the investigation of white collar crime.

The objective of the attorney-client privilege, the Supreme Court has noted, is to "encourage full and frank communications between attorneys and their clients and thereby promote broader interests in the observance of law and administration of justice." *Upjohn Company v. U.S.*, (S.Ct.1981). The assumptions underlying this objective are: (1) ensured confidentiality of communication "encourages clients to make full disclosure to their attorneys," *Upjohn*; (2) such complete disclosure is needed for attorneys to render appropriate legal advice and provide proper legal services; and (3) "the social good derived from the proper performance of the functions of lawyers acting for their clients * * * [will] outweigh the harm that may come from the suppression of the evidence in specific cases," *U.S. v. United Shoe Machinery Corp.* (D.Mass.1950).

Citing Wigmore's analysis of evidentiary privileges, federal lower court have frequently noted that, because the attorney-client privilege presents "an obstacle to the investigation of the truth," it should be "strictly confined within the narrowest possible limits consistent with the logic of its principle." A "strict" or "narrow" construction of this privilege is said to be particularly appropriate because, as Wigmore noted, "its benefits are all indirect and speculative [and] its obstruction [of the truth] is plain and concrete." However, the Supreme Court has stated that courts should not narrow a long established application of the privilege on the basis of no more than "thoughtful speculation" that the narrowing would be consistent with the underlying purpose of the privilege. See *Swidler & Berlin v. U.S.* (S.Ct.1988) (government argument for an exception to the posthumous application of the privilege where the deceased client's communications are relevant to a criminal proceeding, with the government contending that such a limited exception was not likely to diminish a client's willingness to confide in an attorney, did not make the compelling case needed to "overturn the common law rule").

§ 22.02 Basic Elements

The core protection of the privilege requires (1) a communication, (2) that was made by the client to a lawyer, (3) that was made in confidence, and (4) that was made for the purpose of obtaining professional legal advice (or services relating thereto). These requirements combine to impose a broad range of limitations upon the scope of the privilege. Sections 22.04 – 22.06 discuss the aspects of those limitations that bear particularly upon the investigation of white collar crime. Initially, however, § 22.03 explores derivative protections that take the privilege beyond the core protection of client communications.

The privilege can be lost through a variety of actions by the client (or the attorney, acting on behalf of the client). Section, 22.08 consider those actions, producing a waiver or forfeiture of the privilege that are most likely to be at issue in white collar investigations. Section 22.09 considers the crime-fraud exception which also makes the privilege inapplicable, here because of the client's improper purpose in making the communication.

Where the privilege does apply, it permits the client (or the attorney acting on behalf of the client) to refuse to disclose the protected communication notwithstanding an otherwise valid court order of disclosure (such as a grand jury or administrative subpoena). This protection extends both to documents or recordings that contain the communication, and to testimony, documents, or recordings that describe the content of the communication. Unlike the self-incrimination privilege, the attorney-client privilege cannot be replaced by a grant of immunity, and unlike the work-product doctrine, its protection cannot be overcome by a showing of compelling need for disclosure. However, there are exceptions that limit the protection afforded by the privilege. Sections 22.10 and 22.11 discuss two exceptions of particular significance in the white collar area (the "fiduciary exception" and the "government attorney" exception). Section 22.12 discusses a different type of "exception", the joint defense agreement which works to expand rather than limit the privilege.

§ 22.03　Derivative Protections

To supplement the core protection of client communications, courts recognize a derivative protection for communications of the attorney to the client, and for communications of both attorneys and clients to agents who facilitate attorney-client communications. As for protecting attorney communications to the clients, all courts insist that the attorney communication be confidential and that it relate to providing legal advice (which excludes, for example, an attorney's notice to the client of the date of a court appearance). Beyond this, however, lower courts are divided both as to whether the privilege should be narrowed by further restrictions, and as to what rationale should shape any such restrictions.

Many courts hold that an attorney communication will be protected only if it is directly responsive to a protected client communication and reveals, either explicitly or implicitly, the protected communication of the client. They impose these requirements on the ground that attorney communications should be privileged only insofar as needed to protect the continued confidentiality of the client communication to the attorney. Other courts accept this grounding for protecting attorney communications but extend that protection to all responsive attorney communications containing legal advice, reasoning that such communications will almost invariably reveal, at least by implication, the confidences of the client and that drawing of fine lines to exclude some responsive attorney communications only creates uncertainty that undercuts the privilege. Still other courts also protect all responsive legal advice from the attorney, but do so on a quite different rationale. They view the privilege as aimed at protecting an attorney-client dialogue, and therefore having a two-way application. This conception of the privilege has been extended by several courts to protect attorney communications containing legal advice that were not responsive to a specific client request and not based on any confidential communication from the client (such as a lawyer's self-initiated advice to a client regarding activity that the attorney independently observed).

Courts have long recognized that a limited class of persons other than client and lawyer may also share protected communications without a breach of confidentiality. That group consists primarily of the attorney's subordinates, such as secretaries, investigators, and paralegals, who operate under the supervision of the attorney and facilitate the attorney's rendering of legal services. Thus, the attorney may reveal to such persons the confidential communications of the client, and such persons can be used as conduits by client and attorney in conveying messages to each other. Courts generally have been willing to extend this permissible information-sharing circle to include technical experts retained by the attorney or the client, provided their function is simply to facilitate the transmission by technical interpretation of information flowing from the client to the attorney. See *U.S. v. Kovel* (2d Cir.1961) (accountant performing in such a role analogized to an interpreter). However, a retained expert's sharing of client's communication violates the confidentiality requirement where the expert's function is not so limited (e.g., where the expert provides technical advice for the client's use or furnishes to the attorney factual information not known to the client).

§ 22.04 The Communication Limitation

The attorney-client privilege protects against the compelled disclosure of the client's confidential communication, but not against the compelled disclosure of the client's knowledge of the factual information that was included in communication. Thus, while the client cannot be compelled to testify about what he told the attorney about a certain event, the client can be compelled to testify about what he knows about the event (even though that is probably what the attorney was told). Indeed, the client can even be required to disclose factual information gathered at the attorney's suggestion. See *In re Six Grand Jury Witnesses* (2d Cir.1992) (where client had prepared a cost analysis at the request of counsel, client could be asked about how the analysis was conducted and what conclusions were drawn, but not questions about sharing the analysis with others, as the answers here might refer to communications to counsel).

So too, a preexisting document (in contrast to a document prepared specifically for submission to counsel) does not become exempt from disclosure because it was part of the information conveyed to counsel. If the client no longer has the original in his possession, the document can be subpoenaed from the attorney. However, the client will not be placed in a worse position by having transferred the preexisting document in confidence to the attorney for the purpose of obtaining legal advice. If the client had a separate privilege grounding for resisting compelled disclosure while the preexisting document was in the client's possession (e.g., the privilege against self-incrimination), compelled disclosure from the attorney can be resisted under the attorney-client privilege. *Fisher v. U.S.* (S.Ct.1976).

Consistent with the confinement of the privilege to the narrowest limits that suit its objective (see § 22.01), the privilege extends only to that portion of the client's communication that is "necessary to obtained informed legal advice." *Fisher.* Accordingly, the privilege ordinarily does not apply to such matters as fee arrangements, the identity of the client, the dates of communications, and the general nature of the legal services rendered. As to some of these elements, the lack of protection is also justified by reference to the obligation of a person claiming the privilege to establish that an attorney-client relationship existed, as that entails disclosing the basic elements of the relationship. In recent years, various federal lower court rulings have pointed to exceptional circumstances under which the privilege should be extended to allow an attorney to refuse to identify a client. Those rulings have offered basically three different formulations of an "exception" to the traditional rule that the privilege does not protect "tangential information" such as client identity.

One view holds the privilege applicable where evidence known to the government establishes the criminality of an unknown client and disclosure of the client's identity therefore provides the "last link" in a chain of evidence incriminating the client. This position has been criticized as unrelated to the purposes of the attorney-client privilege (in contrast to the self-incrimination privilege), although proponents argue that it carves out the one situation in which the failure to protect client identity is most likely to keep a person from seeking legal advice. A second formulation holds the privilege applicable when the act of disclosure would implicate the client "in the very criminal activity for which legal advice was sought" and hence penalize the client for the seeking of that advice. This position also has been criticized as tied to client harm, rather the primary concern of protecting the confidentiality of the core communication of the client. The latter concern has led to the third formulation, which has the most widespread support in the lower court rulings. That formulation makes the privilege applicable when, in light of other information known about the client and the communication, identification of the client will amount to disclosing the content of the client's confidential communication to the lawyer.

The narrow coverage of all three of the above formulations is illustrated by rulings considering their application to an Internal Revenue Service requirement that businesses (including lawyers) receiving cash payments in excess of $10,000 report the name, address, and tax identification number of the payor.   In a series of cases challenging this requirement on various grounds, including application of the attorney-client privilege, courts have repeatedly held (with only one notable exception) that the circumstances of disclosure would not fit under any of three formulations. *See U.S. v. Sindel* (8th Cir.1995).   Of course, should client identity be held in this context to be protected under the privilege, it would then be necessary to determine whether Congress, in authorizing the cash-reporting requirement, overrode the privilege.   *U.S. v. Goldberger & Dubin, P.C.* (2d Cir.1991) (congressional intent should prevail).

§ 22.05 The Client Limitation

The attorney-client privilege does not protect third party communications to the client's lawyer, even where the third party speaks to the lawyer at the request of the client and conveys information which is critical to the attorney providing adequate legal advice. Where the client is an individual, third party communications and client communications are readily distinguished (although client communications will include communications from third persons who are client agents and act as a conduit or facilitator in conveying the client communication, as discussed in § 22.02). Where the client is a corporation, however, the distinction presents additional complexity since the corporation can speak only through individuals and a variety of different persons might be viewed as its agent for this purpose.   Prior to the Supreme Court's ruling in *Upjohn Co. v. U.S.* (S.Ct.1981), most lower courts had held that the privilege extended only to communications to the attorney by those corporate employees that were within the corporate "control group" (i.e., those in a position to establish corporate policy in response to counsel's advice). The Court in *Upjohn* rejected the control group test, and though "declin[ing] to lay down a broad rule or series of rules" for determining who spoke for the corporation, provided guidance that pointed to protecting the communications of a much broader spectrum of corporate employees in most instances.

Upjohn sustained the application of the privilege to various documents reflecting the content of communications made to counsel in the course of counsel's internal investigation of questionable payments by various employees to foreign officials. The communications in question went well beyond the corporate control group, but the Supreme Court concluded that precluding protection on that ground would "frustrat[e] the very purpose of the privilege by discouraging the communication of relevant information by employees to attorneys seeking to render legal advice to the client corporation." "In the corporate context," the Court noted, "it will frequently be employees beyond the control group * * * who will possess the information needed by the corporate lawyer * * * [as] middle and, indeed, lower-level employees can, by actions within the scope of their employment, embroil the corporation in serious legal difficulties." Also, "the attorney's advice will * * * frequently be more significant to non-control group members than to those who officially sanction the advice."

Turning to the specific circumstances of the communications at issue, the *Upjohn* Court cited a variety of factors which combined to support privilege protection. The Court noted that: (1) the communications were made (and sought by counsel) in order to secure legal advice; (2) the employees were directed by their corporate superiors to provide information to counsel; (3) the employees were "sufficiently aware that they were being questioned in order that the corporation could obtain legal advice"; (4) "the communications concerned matters within the scope of the employees' corporate duties"; (5) the communications provided "information that [was]not available from upper echelon management" and "was needed to supply a basis for legal advice"; and (6) the employees were informed that the communications were considered "highly confidential" and the communications subsequently "had been kept confidential by the company."

The *Upjohn* ruling leaves open the question of whether all of these factors are central to bringing a communication within the privilege. Lower courts have suggested that the employee must know that the communication is sought to assist in providing legal advice, but that knowledge can exist without the employee also being ordered to speak with counsel, as in *Upjohn*. So too, with the control group standard having been rejected, should it be necessary that the information sought from the non-control group employee not have been available from the control group? The *Upjohn* majority opinion specifically noted that the Court had no need to address the additional question of whether the privilege extended to counsel's interview of former employee (i.e., persons who had terminated their employment at the time of the interview).

Since the employee speaks to counsel only in a representative capacity, the ultimate authority over the waiver of the privilege (and disclosure of the employee's communication) belongs not to the employee, but to the client (i.e., the corporation). Where the employee is revealing matters that might expose him or her to personal liability, the employee may seek to obtain protection against a subsequent corporate decision to disclose by insisting that counsel represent the employee as an individual as well as the corporation. If the employee holds the privilege along with the corporation, the employee may be able to exercise the privilege to protect his or her communication, notwithstanding the corporation's desire to waive.

A corporate employee claiming that corporate counsel also represented the employee as an individual bears the burden of establishing that relationship. Absent a clear documentation (such as a separate billing), that task will be difficult, as the standing presumption is that corporate counsel represents only the corporation, even when the employee is the chief executive. See *In re Grand Jury Proceedings* (10th Cir.1998) (five-prong test must be met, including showing that corporate counsel was willing to disregard possible conflict arising from "communicating with the employee in the employee's individual capacity," and showing that the communication focused on the employee's rights and liabilities rather than the corporation's rights and responsibilities). Moreover, even if personal representation is established, it will give the employee control over waiver only as to that portion of the communication relating to the employee's "personal liability without regard to any corporate considerations." *In re Grand Jury Subpoenas (Jane Roe & John Doe)* (10th Cir.1998).

§ 22.06 The Legal Advice Limitation

The privilege applies only where the client is communicating with the lawyer for the purpose of obtaining "legal advice" (which includes not only a lawyer's statement of advice, but also the providing of legal services based on the lawyer's legal analysis). Thus, the privilege does not apply where the lawyer is being asked provide services typically offered by non-lawyers, such as detectives (e.g., a strictly factual investigation), political or labor consultants (e.g., election strategy), or accountants (e.g., tax return preparation). In interpreting the legal advice requirement, courts guard against allowing clients to substitute attorneys for other professional and thereby create an evidentiary privilege where none would otherwise exists (as in the case of accountants, as the federal law does not recognize an accountant-client privilege). At the same time, courts also recognize that non-legal considerations can be integral to the framing of legal advice. Thus, a lawyer communication which is "predominantly" or "primarily" legal in nature will not fall outside the privilege because it alludes to business considerations.

In determining whether a client's communication was for the purpose of obtaining legal advice, courts tend to apply greater scrutiny to communications made to in-house counsel (as opposed to outside counsel). Courts point to two factors in placing a greater burden on the claimant of the privilege in this setting. First, in-house counsel are often extensively involved in the business matters of a company (frequently holding a combined legal and executive position). Second, the proximity of in-house counsel often leads to keeping in-house counsel "informed" of every activity that may have potential legal consequences, and if the "legal advice" category is not carefully restricted to exclude such informational communications, the corporation will be able to shield against disclosure the bulk of its internal communications simply by routing those communications through the office of legal counsel. Accordingly, where a communication was to in-house counsel, the client/employer must clearly establish that the communication was aimed specifically at obtaining legal advice (typically by specifically requesting such advice).

22.07 The Confidentiality Limitation

The confidentiality requirement has two prerequisites: (1) the client must have subjectively intended that the communication be kept confidential, and (2) reasonable precautions must have been taken to ensure confidentiality. If either prerequisite is not met, the communication does not fall under the privilege even though a breach of confidentiality did not actually occur. If the prerequisites are met at the time of communication, a subsequent breach of confidentiality may result in the loss of the privilege through a waiver (see § 22.08) (although very often a court will find that the privilege did not apply in the first instance because the subsequent breach was indicative of an original intent not to keep the communication confidential).

Where a client conveys information to a lawyer for the purpose of public disclosure or disclosure to a third party (such as to a government agency), courts find that the subjective intent prerequisite is lacking. Thus, the privilege does not apply to communications containing information to be included in a prospectus, a tax return, a filing with an agency, or a letter to be conveyed to an opposing party. Although the lawyer will be using legal skills in shaping the information for disclosure, the attorney is treated as basically a "conduit" for conveying the communication to the third party.

The second prerequisite of reasonable precautions has been found to be lacking in a variety of situations, including: (1) the participation of a third person in the communication (which often occurs where the client viewed the third person as an appropriate agent, see § 22.03, but the court held otherwise); (2) the communication was made in a public place under circumstance which could readily have permitted known bystanders to overhear the communication; (3) a written communication (or a document describing an oral communication) was handled in a manner that made it readily accessible to employees who had no "need to know" of the communication (e.g., indiscriminately mingled with routine documents); and (4) a written communication was distributed to appropriate persons but without seeking in any way to ensure against further disclosure by those persons (such as identifying the document as "privileged" or "confidential").

§ 22.08 Waivers

In the context of the attorney-client privilege, courts use the term "waiver" to describe not only the traditional waiver ("the intentional relinquishment of a known right") but also actions that result in the unintended forfeiture of the privilege. Thus, a client's purposeful disclosure of a prior privileged communication to a third party typically produces a "waiver" whether or not the client intended to give up the privileged status of the communication. Indeed, where the attorney has the implied authority to act on behalf of the client, an attorney's disclosure to a third party will produce a waiver even though the client had no notice of the intended disclosure.

Purposeful disclosures producing waivers include disclosures to the public, disclosures to experts assisting the client (e.g., auditors), intercorporate disclosures to employees who have no "need to know", disclosures to opponents in the course of negotiation or litigation, disclosures to government agencies, and disclosures pursuant to a subpoena or court order where no objection is made (waiver does not occur where a court, over objection, erroneously orders disclosure). The general rule as to such waivers is that the party cannot "pick and choose" and thereby limit the waiver. A disclosure as to one aspect of a communication constitutes a waiver as to the entire communication, and, indeed, as to all other communications relating to the same subject matter. So too, a disclosure as to one party constitutes a waiver as to all parties. A minority position, stressing the dilemma forced by a corporation when its internal investigation reveals violation of federal regulations, argues for an exception to the complete waiver principle where voluntary disclosure is made to a regulatory agency. Under this exception, the waiver is limited to the regulatory agency, at least where the disclosure agreement with the agency preserves confidentiality. The majority position, however, rejects any such exception as inconsistent with the function of privilege and improperly promoting the corporation's tactical use of bargaining in dealing with different agencies.

Where disclosure was inadvertent, courts will not so readily find waiver, and when they do, are more likely to restrict the scope of the waiver. Although some courts continue to adhere to the traditional view that the client bears the risk of an inadvertent disclosure, most courts now deem critical whether reasonable safeguards were in place to preclude disclosure. Where disclosure occurred, notwithstanding such safeguards, as a consequence of theft or fraud by a third party, courts generally hold that there is no waiver. Where disclosure was due to client or attorney carelessness, notwithstanding reasonable precautions (as where the attorney accidentally included a few privileged documents, properly segregated and labeled, among a multitude produced in response to a subpoena), many courts hold there is no waiver if the carelessness was slight and counsel made a prompt attempt to rectify the error. Where reasonable precautions were not taken, the inadvertent disclosure will almost always be treated as a waiver, but that waiver is likely to be limited to the documents actually disclosed, rather than all documents relating to the same subject matter.

Courts commonly note that the lawyer-client privilege is designed only to be used defensively as a "shield" and not offensively as a "sword". Under this principle, where a client, in the capacity of witness or defendant, justifies his or her behavior by reference to advice received by counsel, the client is held to have "impliedly waived" the privilege for communications to and from counsel relating to that advice. In the corporate context, since the client is the corporation, the privilege ordinarily can be waived only by the control group (i.e., the corporate officers and directors) on behalf of the corporation. However, as discussed in *Upjohn* (see § 22.04), an even wider range of corporate employees may participate in lawyer-client communications on behalf of the corporation, so it often happens that an employee (or former employer) will later voluntary disclose what he knows about the communications, acting to serve his own interests (typically as a target of an investigation who wishes to cooperate with the government). Where such a disclosure is made against the wishes of the corporation, it ordinarily will not constitute a waiver of the corporation's privilege, and the corporation may not be compelled to disclose further privileged information sought to establish its liability.

§ 22.09 Crime-Fraud Exception

Client communications made for the very purpose of furthering an ongoing or future crime or fraud (and, perhaps, other intentional torts as well) fall outside the attorney-client privilege because they rest on a misuse of the attorney-client relationship. Typical crime-fraud scenarios are the client who seeks legal advice for the purpose of structuring a transaction so as to make undetectable an underlying crime or fraud and the client who seeks a legal service that will further the crime or fraud (e.g., preparing a deceptive legal document that might later be used in a fraud). Since clients may appropriately seek an attorney's advice concerning past wrongdoings, communications relating to past behavior will only fall within the crime-fraud exception if the client's purpose is to facilitate continuing that activity or executing a cover-up. The key is the purpose of the client, not the knowledge of the lawyer, as the exception applies whether or not the lawyer is aware of the client's purpose. It also applies whether or not that purpose was actually achieved.

A party invoking the crime-fraud exception must present a prima case as to the client's ongoing or planned criminal or fraudulent activity and also establish that the client's communications was made to further that wrongful activity. Lower courts are divided as to the quantum of proof needed for a prima facie case. Some speak of "probable cause"; some speak of evidence sufficient to "require explanation" by the opposing party; still others speak of evidence which would, if believed, establish an ongoing or future wrongdoing to the satisfaction of a reasonable trier of fact (apparently under the more-likely-than-not standard of proof). Under *U.S. v. Zolin* (S.Ct.1989), if there is a threshold showing of a "factual basis adequate to support a good faith belief by a reasonable person" that the communication itself "may reveal evidence to establish that the crime fraud exception applies," the district court has discretion to examine the communication in camera and consider its contents in determining whether the necessary quantum of proof (which the Court declined to define) has been met. In the context of grand jury settings, the government showing in support of a crime-fraud claim often may be made in camera, with the district court having further discretion to determine that the showing is sufficient without informing the opposing party (typically a client/witness or a client/intervenor) of the content of that showing. Courts support such in camera, ex parte determinations as needed to preserve grand jury secrecy (see § 16.02) and to avoid burdening the grand jury process with a hearing that could turn into a "minitrial" (See §16.05).

§ 22.10 The Fiduciary Exception

The "fiduciary exception" is not based on a forfeiture of the privilege's protection, but on a recognition that the true beneficiary of the legal advice may not be the nominal client but persons in a fiduciary relationship with that client. The prime example of such "ultimate clients" are the shareholders of the corporation. Since all corporate actions, including privileged communications, are undertaken on their behalf, shareholders have a strong claim for access to the privileged communication where they claim that it would show that management acted contrary to the fiduciary duty owed to them. The reality of shareholder litigation, however, is that actions supposedly brought on behalf of all shareholders may in fact have little shareholder support and have a grounding more strategic than substantive. If shareholder actions, such as stockholder derivative suits, automatically called for disclosure of privileged communications, that could well work to the disadvantage of shareholders in the long run by discouraging management from seeking legal advice on decisions likely to be second-guessed by dissatisfied shareholders (or, the lawyers who specialize in such actions).

Balancing these concerns, the leading ruling of *Garner v. Wolfinbarger* (5th Cir.1970) held that shareholders could gain access to privileged communications but only upon a showing of cause. In determining whether cause exists, *Garner* directed district courts to consider a variety of factors including: the number of shareholders pursuing the claim and the percentage of the shares they represent; the "bona fides of the shareholders"; the nature of the shareholder's claim (particularly whether it claims misconduct that would be criminal) and whether it is "obviously colorable"; the "apparent necessity or desirability of the shareholders having the information"; the possibility of obtaining that information from other sources; and the extent to which the communication is identified (in contrast to the shareholders "blindly fishing"). Courts have extended the "good cause" approach of *Garner* to other fiduciary situations, such as a government action against former officials of a pension fund for violation of their fiduciary responsibilities and actions by union members against union officials.

§ 22.11   The Government Attorney Exception

Although direct holdings are sparse, courts generally agree that government entities (such as regulatory agencies, executive departments, and local and state governments) can be treated as "clients" with respect to their communications with government lawyers in much the same way that corporations may be clients in their communications with in-house counsel. Thus, a government entity may exercise the attorney-client privilege in the context of civil and regulatory litigation to preclude compulsory disclosure of confidential, legal-advice communications between government officials and government lawyers. However, in the few cases to address the government's exercise of the privilege in the context of grand jury proceedings, courts have held that the privilege must give way to the grand jury's obligation to obtain all information relevant to a criminal investigation. These courts emphasize two factors that distinguish the government lawyer from the private lawyer. First, the government lawyer's foremost obligation is not to protect a wrongdoer client within the limits of the law, but to ensure compliance with the law. This obligation "to uphold the public trust" carries with it a duty to report to appropriate authorities evidence of criminal conduct on the part of government officials. Indeed, in the federal system, an executive branch attorney has a statutory obligation under 28 U.S.C. § 535(6) to "expeditiously report to the Attorney General" any information received in the attorney's employment "relating to" criminal violations by government employees.   Second, the interests of the governmental entity as a client are quite different from the interests of a private entity, for the governmental entity does not face the potential of criminal liability, and it has an obligation to the public which includes "exposing wrongdoing by public officials."

§ 22.12 Joint Defense Agreements

A joint defense agreement is designed to extend the coverage of the attorney-client privilege through a "pooling arrangement" in the disclosure of lawyer-client communications. Under such an arrangement, participant clients may share communications to their lawyers (and the lawyers responsive communications) with the lawyers for the other participants, and may communicate directly with those lawyers. Communications that otherwise would not be protected because made in the presence of, or shared with, third parties, are now privileged because each counsel for each participant has become, in effect, a co-counsel for the other participants.

The expanded coverage created by a joint defense agreement is only permissible if all participants have a "common interest" (which leads to the description of the underlying rationale as either the "common interest" or "community of interest" doctrine). While the common interest does not necessarily have to relate to litigation, the common interest most commonly established in the white collar context is a common litigation opponent (or potential opponent) involving the same subject matter. Thus, a common interest exists among persons subject to the same grand jury investigation as to the same or related transactions. Where the common interest exists, communications are protected, but only insofar as they relate to the common interest and meet the other requirements for a protected communication (e.g., are aimed at obtaining legal advice). The party asserting the privilege bears the burden of showing both that there was a common interest and that the parties intended to engage in a cooperative effort in obtaining legal assistance. While a formal joint defense agreement is not essential, it is very helpful in meeting this burden.

A participant in a joint defense arrangement may rely on the privilege to refuse to testify as to his own communications to his own attorney, his communications to the attorneys of other participants, and the responsive communications of the various attorneys. Should the participant decide to become a cooperating witness, he may waive the privilege as to his own communications, but not as to the communications of the other participants (and another participant may therefore intervene to exercise the privilege as to these communications). A complete waiver occurs only where the participants are directly involved in litigation against each other.

CHAPTER TWENTY-THREE
WORK PRODUCT PROTECTION

§ 23.01 Character and Purpose

The work product doctrine grants protection against the compelled production of certain materials developed by an attorney in anticipation of litigation. The doctrine emanates from the Supreme Court's opinion in *Hickman v. Taylor* (S.Ct.1947), holding that the "work product" of an attorney, developed in "anticipation of litigation," had a qualified exemption from pretrial discovery by the opposing party in a civil case. That exemption, the Court reasoned, would encourage lawyers to generate valuable trial preparation aids by removing the strong disincentive that would flow from those aids regularly being available to litigation opponents through pretrial discovery. An effective adversary system required "a zone of privacy in which a lawyer can prepare and develop legal theories and strategies, with an eye toward litigation, free from the intrusion of adversaries."

Courts sometimes describe work product protection as a "privilege" and sometimes describe it as an "immunity," although they acknowledge that neither characterization fits precisely. An evidentiary privilege (unless waived or otherwise lost) grants absolute protection against compelled production, while work-product protection is qualified, as it can be overcome (at least as to certain types of work product) by a sufficient showing of need. Also, an evidentiary privilege extends to all types of

387

proceedings, but it is not clear that the work product protection has that range.   See *U.S. v. Nobles* (S.Ct.1975) (White, S., concurring) (questioning whether work product protection applied as a barrier to the evidentiary use at trial of non-opinion work product).   Characterization of work product protection as an "immunity" is usually associated with its origin as an exemption from pretrial discovery (recognized in both civil and criminal cases).   However, work product protection extends beyond that limited setting.   It is available, for example, as an objection to a subpoena in the contexts most relevant to the investigation of white collar crime – grand jury and regulatory agency investigations.   Indeed, the discussion that follows focuses on those work-product issues most likely to arise in white collar investigations.

§ 23.02   Basic Elements: *Hickman* and Rule 26(b)(3)

Although *Hickman v. Taylor* (S.Ct.1947) and Rule 26(b)(3) of the Federal Rules of Civil Procedure both deal with pretrial discovery, courts look to these sources in determining the basic features of work product protection in other contexts as well. *Hickman* established three basic components of the privilege, and Rule 26(b)(3) repeated and added to those three components.

The *Hickman* Court initially provided a basic definition of work product, using as a point of reference the lawyer's function in the "proper preparation of a client's case" in "anticipation of litigation."   Such preparation demands that the lawyer "assemble information, sift what he considers to be the relevant from the irrelevant, prepare his legal theories, and plan his strategy", and that work is "reflected . . . in interviews, statements, memoranda, correspondence, briefs, mental impressions, personal beliefs, and countless other tangible and intangible ways – aptly though roughly termed . . . the 'work product of the lawyer'."

Second, *Hickman* established that, while "such materials [would not be] open to opposing counsel on mere demand," disclosure could be required where the party "who would invade that privacy [of work product materials] * * * establishes adequate reasons to justify production through a subpoena or court order." As an illustration of an adequate reason, it noted that, "where relevant and non-privileged fact remains hidden in an attorney's file and where production of these facts is essential to preparation of one's case, discovery may properly be had."

Third, *Hickman* identified one class of work product that would rarely, if ever, be subject to disclosure on a need basis. The most critical element of work product protection was ensuring that "an attorney's thoughts * * * [were] his own." Thus, work product that revealed an attorney's mental impressions, conclusions, evaluations, strategies, and theories required the greatest protection, and it would be a "rare situation", if any, in which disclosure of such work product (which came to be known as "opinion work product") would be ordered. This distinction between opinion work product and other work product has been carried forward in subsequent work product jurisprudence, with the non-opinion work product sometimes described as "fact workproduct".

Federal Rule 26(b)(3) is often described as having "substantially incorporated" the *Hickman* standards in identifying when matter otherwise discoverable under Rule 26 will require a special showing of need as a prerequisite for disclosure.   Initially, Rule 26(b)(3) describes the material in this category as "documents and tangible things * * * prepared in anticipation of litigation or for trial by or for another party or by or for that other party's representative (including the other party's attorney, consultant, surety, indemnitor, insurer, or agent)."   This provision differs from *Hickman* in two respects. First, it refers only to documents and tangible things, while the rationale of *Hickman* would certainly extend as well to requiring an attorney to testify as to work product matter (e.g., opinions) that were never recorded.   Courts have concluded, however, that such work product coverage remains under the authority of the common law protection as set forth in *Hickman*.

Second, while *Hickman* focused on the personal work product of the attorney, Rule 26(b)(3) clearly extends work product protection to materials prepared by others. This provision, as noted in *U.S. v. Nobles* (S.Ct.1975), recognizes that "attorneys often must rely on the assistance of investigators and other agents in the compilation of materials in preparation for trial."   Therefore federal courts uniformly accept as within work product protection materials developed by nonattorneys who are acting under the general supervision of the attorney.   The language of Rule 26(b)(3) extends beyond that situation and also encompasses the work of nonattorneys assisting the client in anticipation of litigation without attorney supervision.   However, a substantial line of cases reason that, where there has been no involvement of an attorney sufficient to suggest the "employment of an attorney's legal expertise," it should be presumed that the materials were not truly developed in anticipation of litigation.

Rule 26(b)(3) also sets forth a standard as to the showing needed to overcome work product protection. Discovery will be available "only upon a showing that the party seeking discovery has substantial need of the materials in the preparation of the party's case and that the party is unable without undue hardship to obtain the substantial equivalent of the materials by other means." This standard has replaced the more general "adequate reasons" standard of *Hickman*, and is applied in the context of investigatory subpoenas as well as pretrial discovery. Rule 26(b)(3) also recognizes, consistent with *Hickman*, that greater protection must be afforded "opinion" work product. It states that, "in ordering discovery * * * when the required showing has been made, the court shall protect against disclosure of the mental impressions, conclusions, opinions, or legal theories of an attorney or other representative of a party concerning the litigation."

Lower courts are divided in their reading of the Rule 26(b)(3) provision on opinion work product. One view is that it provides for absolute protection of opinion work product. The other is that such work product may be discoverable under rare circumstances, as suggested by *Hickman*, but good cause here requires a stronger showing of necessity than the "substantial-need-and-undue-hardship" standard.   See   *Upjohn   v.   U.S.*   (S.Ct.1981) (recognizing this lower courts split, but finding no need to resolve the issue). As a practical matter, in the investigation context, work product protection is only overridden as to non-opinion work product and that is not easily achieved. In the grand jury setting, the availability of alternatives often poses a stumbling block; the grand jury is not limited to consideration of evidence admissible at trial and therefore "substantial equivalents" include sources (e.g., hearsay testimony) that could not be used at trial. See *In re Grand Jury Subpoena Dated Oct. 22, 2001* (2d Cir.2002). The necessary showing is most likely made as to the transcribed statements of a witness (an item not likely to contain opinion work product) where the witness is deceased or otherwise unavailable. The need standard also may be met where the actions of the attorney are under investigation, although disclosure in such cases is more likely to be ordered under the crime-fraud exception.

§ 23.03 Anticipation of Litigation

Although *Hickman* had in mind preparation for a lawsuit, the "litigation" that must have been anticipated as a prerequisite for the creation of work product can include any form of adversary process, including an investigatory subpoena from a grand jury or an administrative agency. Where the alleged work product was created before an adversary proceeding was actually initiated (e.g., before a complaint was filed or subpoena received), it often will be less than obvious that the material, though prepared at a lawyer's direction, was prepared "in anticipation of litigation." Courts frequently require either or both of two types of proof in such situations. One type is specific evidence indicating that the purpose behind the creation of the alleged work product was to assist in potential litigation. Relevant factors here include the content of documents (e.g., whether they refer to prospective litigation) and the usual role of counsel (particularly where only in-house counsel was involved). A question frequently asked is whether the same document most likely would have been prepared apart from any concern about potential litigation.

The second type of proof often required relates to the likelihood of litigation. Courts here insist on a showing that, at the time of the creation of the alleged work product, there was an identifiable prospect of the initiation of particular litigation in the near future. Courts requiring such proof note that almost every business activity carries a potential for litigation, and the routine use of counsel's input on that potential should not be sufficient to cloak otherwise routine business documents with work product protection. The potential conflict between this approach and one that focuses on motivational evidence is illustrated by the situation in which the alleged work product was clearly motivated by the prospect of litigation likely to flow from a proposed business transaction, but that litigation was obviously contingent upon a future business decision to enter that transaction (in contrast to *Hickman's* reference to preparation for possible litigation "after a claim has arisen"). See *U.S. v. Adlman* (2d Cir.1998) (majority upholding work product claim so long as the document was prepared "because of the prospect of litigation").

The anticipation-of-litigation requirement has been the subject of particular attention in cases involving internal corporate investigations. Such investigations have an obvious business purpose (to determine if practices are inappropriate and, if so, to correct them) apart from responding to possible litigation. Also, in many industries, certain types of investigations are routine (e.g., accident reviews), and placing them all under the work-product shield is viewed as excessive. Accordingly, a party relying on the work product doctrine to protect internal investigation materials will have to establish that the investigation, even though conducted by counsel, was different in character and purpose from investigations regularly conducted by in-house counsel. This may require establishing many of the same features as were identified in *Upjohn* as bringing the employee-communications there within the attorney-client privilege (see § 22.05). Indeed, *Upjohn* concluded that internal investigation materials at issue there (which went beyond the employee interview reports) were protected work product.

Even if an internal investigative report is work product, some aspects of the investigation will not be protected. The work product protects documents prepared under the direction of counsel and the thoughts of counsel, but that does not preclude discovering from the persons interviewed by counsel the very same information that may have been given to counsel. Indeed, quite often, the identity of the persons interviewed must be disclosed. So too, preexisting documents examined as part of the investigation and left in the possession of counsel are not protected as work product, although the work product doctrine ordinarily protects against requiring disclosure of the attorney's selection and compilation of existing documents, as that reveals potential litigation strategy.

§ 23.04 Waiver

As in the case of the attorney-client privilege (see § 22.08), a voluntary disclosure of work product materials to a third party may constitute a waiver. Here, however, the focus of the protection is not on preserving the confidentiality of the lawyer-client relationship, but protecting the adversarial process by precluding forced sharing with an adversary. Accordingly, a voluntary disclosure constitutes a waiver only where the disclosure is to an adversary or to some other third party under circumstances that substantially increase the possibility that the adversary will gain access to the materials. Thus, there is no need for a special rule (compare § 22.12) to avoid waiver where work product is disclosed to a third party with a common interest (e.g., another investigative target), since such a person also seeks to prevent disclosure to the adversary.

So too, in light of the function of work product protection, courts do not treat the inadvertent disclosure, even to an adversary, as an automatic waiver. Rather, courts here follow the recent trend in the treatment of inadvertent disclosures of lawyer-client material, focusing on whether reasonable security precautions were in place (see § 22.08).

The lawyer-client privilege model also applies to certain other aspects of work-product waiver. In general, a purposeful waiver as to one adversary constitutes a waiver as to all, although here too, a minority position would recognize an exception as to disclosures to government agencies (see § 22.08). Implicit waivers here also are recognized where the client seeks to make affirmative testimonial use of work product. Thus, *U.S. v. Nobles* (S.Ct.1975) held that where a party's investigator testified as to his recollection of work party interviews, the opposing party was entitled to the work product documents recounting that interview.

§ 23.05   Crime-Fraud

For largely the same reasons as apply to the lawyer-client privilege (see § 22.09), a crime-fraud exception also applies to work product protection. It applies to the client's use of the lawyer client relationship for the same wrongful purposes, and requires a similar relationship of the material at issue to that wrongful purpose (i.e., the work product material must relate to that aspect of the lawyer's performance that would further the client's wrongful purpose).   Standards of proof also follow the standards developed in applying the crime-fraud exception to attorney-client material.

One major distinction separates the work-product exception for crime-fraud from the lawyer-client exception. Since the work product protection serves the interest of the attorney apart from the client, where the client has been involved in the ongoing or future crime or fraud, the "innocent attorney" still has a separate interest in not revealing his mental processes. Accordingly, client fraud eliminates the problem of non-opinion work product, but the attorney remains free to insist upon protection of opinion work product. *In re Special September 1978*

(Grand Jury (II) (7th Cir.1980).

PART FOUR
PUNISHMENT
CHAPTER TWENTY–FOUR
SANCTIONS

§ 24.01 Introduction

An indeterminate sentencing system was the norm in the United States federal criminal system for nearly the past one hundred years. Although a judge had the outside restrictions of the maximum sentence specified in the statutory offense, coupled with basic Eighth Amendment prohibitions against cruel and unusual punishment, an enormous latitude was afforded to a judge in deciding a convicted defendant's term of imprisonment, fine, or imposition of probation. Discretion was also given to parole officers in making their parole determinations.

This indeterminate sentencing system was premised upon a goal of rehabilitation. By giving broad discretion to the court and parole officer, they were able "to make their respective sentencing and release decisions upon their own assessments of the offender's amenability to rehabilitation." *Mistretta v. U.S.* (1989).

This "outmoded rehabilitation model" was designated a failure by a 1983 Senate Report. The report noted two significant consequences of the indeterminate sentencing model: judicial disparity in sentences and uncertainty in time to be served by a defendant. *Mistretta v. U.S.*. To correct these perceived problems, Congress passed the Sentencing Reform Act of 1984.

This Act created a Sentencing Commission charged with the duty of establishing determinative sentencing guidelines. The guidelines mandate the imposition of sentences within set ranges as computed via a grid system that considers the defendant's offense level in conjunction with the offender's criminal history. Although the guidelines are not advisory, they also do not endorse a strict determinative sentencing system with no judicial discretion.

On November 1, 1991, the United States Sentencing Commission adopted guidelines for sentencing organizations. These guidelines provide fines, probation, and in some instances restitution. The sentencing guidelines for organizations permit reductions for self-reporting and for effective programs to prevent and detect violations.

In addition to sentences mandated pursuant to federal sentencing guidelines, white collar criminals often are subject to collateral proceedings in the civil arena. Some white collar offenders have faced a loss of license or exclusion from participating in government contracts. For example, lawyers have found their convictions used as a basis for suspension and disbarment from the legal profession. Convicted defense contractors have in some cases been precluded from obtaining future government contracts.

§ 24.02 Federal Sentencing Commission

The Sentencing Reform Act of 1984 creates a United States Sentencing Commission. This Commission "is established as an independent commission in the judicial branch of the United States ..." (28 U.S.C. § 991(a)). The Commission is composed of seven voting members appointed by the President, "with the advice and consent of the Senate," and two nonvoting ex-officio members. The Attorney General, or a designee of the Attorney General, is a non-voting ex-officio member of the Commission. Not more than three of the members of the Commission can be federal judges, and not more than four members of the Commission may be from the same political party. (28 U.S.C. § 991). The Sentencing Reform Act of 1984 directs the Commission to devise sentencing guidelines for the imposition of criminal sentences in federal court. (28 U.S.C. § 994). The Act also abolishes the Parole Commission.

Seven factors are set forth as considerations in imposing a sentence. These factors include, "the nature and circumstances of the offense and the history and characteristics of the defendant, ... any pertinent policy statement issued by the Sentencing Commission ..., and the need to avoid unwarranted sentence disparities among defendants with similar records who have been found guilty of similar conduct." (18 U.S.C. § 3553(a)). A court is instructed that a sentence shall be sufficient "but not greater than necessary to comply with the [following] purposes, ... the need for the sentence imposed (A) to reflect the seriousness of the offense, to promote respect for the law, and to provide just punishment for the offense; (B) to afford adequate deterrence to criminal conduct; (C) to protect the public from further crimes of the defendant; and (D) to provide the defendant with needed educational or vocational training, medical care, or other correctional treatment in the most effective manner."

Congressional legislation instructs the Commission to "insure that the guidelines reflect the inappropriateness of imposing a sentence to a term of imprisonment for the purpose of rehabilitating the defendant ..." (28 U.S.C. § 994(k)). The Commission is also instructed that the guidelines should reflect sentences other than imprisonment when the defendant is a first offender engaging in non-violent and non-serious offenses. Consideration for imprisonment should, however, be given when the offender engages in a crime of violence that results in serious bodily injury. (28 U.S.C. § 994(j)).

The Sentencing Commission is an ongoing body charged with the duty to periodically "review and revise" the guidelines. (28 U.S.C. § 994(o)). In some cases Congress will direct the activity of the Commission. For example, in the Sarbanes Oxley Act of 2004, Congress requested the Commission to "review and amend" the sentencing laws related to fraud and obstruction of justice to reflect the new penalties added by the Act.

The Commission is authorized to promulgate and submit to Congress amendments to the guidelines. "Such an amendment or modification shall be accompanied by a statement of the reasons therefor and shall take effect on a date specified by the Commission, which shall be no earlier than 180 days after being so submitted and no later than the first day of November of the calendar year in which the amendment or modification is submitted, except to the extent that the effective date is revised or the amendment is otherwise modified or disapproved by Act of Congress." (28 U.S.C. § 994(p)). Sentences are calculated by reference to the guidelines in effect at the time of the sentencing, but where the guidelines applicable at the time of the commission of the crime were more lenient, defendant may challenge application of the current guidelines on ex post facto grounds.

§ 24.03 Federal Sentencing Guidelines

The Sentencing Guidelines commence with a policy statement that includes an explanation of the methodology used in formulating the guidelines. This policy statement notes the extensive study and use of existing empirical data in formulating the guidelines. It states that the guidelines are intended "toward the achievement of a more honest, uniform, equitable, proportional, and therefore effective sentencing system." (Chapter One, Part A, Guidelines).

The policy statement preceding the actual guidelines explains the Commission's struggle with deciding if a real offense or charge offense sentencing system was more appropriate. A real offense system looks to the actual conduct engaged in by the defendant, without regard to the charges brought. A charge offense system examines the conduct that forms the elements of the offense upon which the defendant is convicted. The Commission's guidelines compromises these two positions by commencing with a charge offense system, in initially determining the base level offense, and modifying this result to consider some of the actual conduct. For example, the defendant's role in the offense and quantitative amounts involved in the offense are used to adjust the base level.

Section 1B1.1 of the guidelines provides a general overview of how to use the guidelines. It offers a step-by-step approach to determining a defendant's sentence. Section 1B1.3 of the guidelines describes the relevant conduct that a court may consider in determining the applicable guideline range. This includes "all acts and omissions ... that occurred during the commission of the offense of conviction, in preparation for that offense, or in the course of attempting to avoid detection or responsibility for that offense," and "all acts or omissions" similarly defined as to other offenses that "were part of the same course of conduct or common scheme or plan as the offense of conviction." In interpreting the "other offense" portion of this definition, the Supreme Court in *U.S. v. Watts* (S.Ct.1997) held that "a jury's verdict of acquittal does not prevent the sentencing court from considering conduct underlying the acquitted charge, so long as that conduct has been proved by a preponderance of the evidence."

In computing a defendant's sentence under the sentencing guidelines, a grid is used. On the horizontal axis there are 43 offense levels. On the vertical axis there are six criminal history categories.

Computation of a sentence can be commenced by determination of the offense level. One starts by taking the conviction and matching it to the base offense levels as specified in the guidelines. For example, the crime of mail fraud (18 U.S.C. § 1341) is located in 2B1.1 of the guidelines and carries a base offense level of six or seven "if (A) the defendant was convicted of an offense referenced to this guideline; and (B) that offense of conviction has a statutory maximum term of imprisonment of 20 years or more." If the mail fraud pertains to a public official and involves the deprivation of the intangible right to honest services (18 U.S.C. § 1346) then the guideline is located in 2C1.7 and commences with a base level of ten.

Within each guideline are adjustment factors that reflect the "real offense" as measured by all "relevant conduct.". For example, in the fraud guideline found in 2B1.1, adjustments are made for the amount of loss involved. Thus, to the base level of six or seven, there is an increase in level by adding twelve when the loss is more than two hundred thousand dollars. "[L]oss is the greater of actual loss or intended loss," with definitions of these items provided in the Commentary.

Chapter three of the guidelines provides general adjustment factors used in determining the offense level (also with reference to all relevant conduct). The first three factors considered are victim-related adjustments, role in the offense adjustments, and obstructive conduct. For example, where the "defendant knew or should have known that a victim of the offense was a vulnerable victim," the guidelines authorize an increase by two levels. (3A1.1).

An aggravating role in the offense, as specified in the guidelines, can increase the offense level. (3B1.1). Likewise, a mitigating role serves to decrease the offense level. (3B1.2). "If the defendant abused a position of public or private trust, or used a special skill, in a manner that significantly facilitated the commission or concealment of the offense," there is an increase by two levels. (3B1.3). An increase by two levels is also provided when a defendant "willfully obstructed or impeded, or attempted to obstruct or impede, the administration of justice during the course of the investigation, prosecution, or sentencing of the instant offense of conviction," (3C1.1) or "recklessly created a substantial risk of death or serious bodily injury to another person in the course of fleeing from a law enforcement officer." (3C1.2).

The Supreme Court recently held that it is constitutional for a court to enhance a defendant's sentence "if the court finds the defendant committed perjury at trial." This obstruction of justice enhancement, pursuant to 3C1.1, was found not to infringe on the defendant's constitutional right to testify. *U.S. v. Dunnigan* (S.Ct.1993).

Also contained in chapter three of the guidelines is the method for applying multiple counts in factoring the base level. Base levels applicable to each count are not added together. Rather, the most serious count is examined and relevant-conduct increases in this level of offense are provided to reflect the increase in harm. Closely related counts are grouped together. (3D1.1). Thus, when a prosecutor uses separate charges for "conduct involving substantially the same harm," the counts will be grouped together for purposes of determining the base level. (3D1.2).

A final adjustment provided in chapter three of the guidelines offers a defendant a reduction for an acceptance of responsibility. "If the defendant clearly demonstrates acceptance of responsibility for his offense," the guidelines authorize a reduction by two levels. Additionally a defendant is permitted a one level decrease when the offense level is sixteen or greater prior to the initial two level decrease for acceptance of responsibility and the government files a motion stating that the "defendant has assisted authorities in the investigation or prosecution of his own misconduct by timely notifying authorities of his intention to enter a plea of guilty, thereby permitting the government to avoid preparing for trial and permitting the court to allocate its resources efficiently." (3E1.1).

The number ascertained after taking the initial base level and factoring in the applicable adjustments reflects the number on the vertical axis. It is next necessary to determine the numerical value of the defendant's criminal history. Chapter four of the guidelines pertains to a defendant's criminal history with points added in circumstances like when a defendant has a prior sentence of imprisonment. The greater the criminal history, the greater the points attributed to the defendant.

The point on the grid at which the offense level of a defendant meets the defendant's criminal history level is the sentencing range for that defendant. It defines the period of time of a defendant's sentence. For example, an offense level of 19 with a criminal history category II results in a sentencing range of 33 to 41 months.

Below a certain point on the grid, a court has the option for alternatives to prison. Chapter five of the sentencing guidelines specifies the rules for probation, supervised release, restitution, fines, assessments, forfeitures, and costs of prosecution.

Sentencing options, such as community confinement or home detention, are also described in this chapter.

Once the grid point total is calculated, a departure—i.e., a sentence above or below that prescribed in the grid—may be considered. A judge is precluded from departing from the sentencing range on the grid unless there is a basis for departure under subsection K of chapter five. Noteworthy in subsection K is the permissibility of departure upon a motion of the government stating that defendant provided substantial assistance to authorities. (5K1.1). Only upon the filing of a 5K1.1 motion by the prosecutor may a court reduce a sentence below a statutory minimum. A sentencing judge is not bound, however, to accept a government motion for departure premised upon substantial assistance. *U.S. v. Mariano* (1st Cir.1993).

The Supreme Court considered a defendant's right to challenge the failure of a prosecutor to file a 5K1.1 motion requesting the district court reduce a sentence for substantial assistance to the government. The Court viewed the discretion normally accorded to prosecutors in decisions as applicable to the decision of a prosecutor on whether to file a substantial assistance motion under 5K1.1. Thus, claims that the defendant provided substantial assistance which the government refused to recognize, or generalized claims of the prosecutor acting on improper motive in refusing to file a 5K1.1 motion, will not merit a remedy for the defendant. The Court did state, however, that "a defendant would be entitled to relief if a prosecutor refused to file a substantial-assistance motion say, because of the defendant's race or religion." *Wade v. U.S.*

(S.Ct.1992).

In *U.S. v. Alegria* (1st Cir. 1999), the First Circuit reviewed whether prosecutors violated a plea agreement when defendant cooperated and was not provided with a 5K1.1 substantial assistance motion, a motion that would have allowed for a downward departure below the mandates of the guidelines. Although the court held that "the government must perform in good faith the discretionary obligations that it affirmatively undertakes in a plea agreement," no showing of bad faith was demonstrated in this case. In *Alegria*, the court stated that "[t]he government's good faith is only a burden of production, not of persuasion. As long as the government satisfies this modest burden, the trial court need go no further unless the defendant makes a substantial threshold showing that the government acted in bad faith."

Absent a government motion, departure from the guidelines is also permissible when "there exists an aggravating or mitigating circumstance of a kind, or to a degree, not adequately taken into consideration by the Sentencing Commission in formulating the guidelines that should result in a sentence different from that described." (18 U.S.C. § 3553(b)). Certain factors are considered encouraged while others are considered discouraged bases for departure. (5K2.0 et. seq.) In deciding whether to depart from the guidelines, courts need to consider the following four questions: "(1)What features of this case, potentially, take it outside the Guidelines' 'heartland' and make of it a special, or unusual, case? (2) Has the Commission forbidden departures based on those features? (3) If not, has the Commission encouraged departures based on those features? (4) If not, has the Commission discouraged departures based on those features?" *Koon v. U.S.* (S.Ct.1996) (*citing U.S. v. Rivera* (1st Cir.1993)).

Forbidden factors (e.g., race or socio-economic status) cannot be used as a basis for departure. Encouraged factors (e.g., diminished capacity) can be used as a basis for departure if the applicable guidelines have not taken the factor into account. If the factor is a discouraged factor (e.g., family responsibilities), or an encouraged factor taken into account by a guideline, the court should depart only when "the factor is present to an exceptional degree or in some other way makes the case different from the ordinary case where the factor is present." Factors that are omitted from the guidelines can be a basis for departure if the court determines that the case is outside the "heartland" "after considering the 'structure and theory of both relevant individual guidelines and the Guidelines taken as a whole.'" *Koon v. U.S.* (S.Ct.1996)

Court departures were limited in 2003 when Congress passed the Prosecutorial Remedies and Other Tools to End the Exploitation of Children Today Act of 2003 (PROTECT ACT). Where "substantial deference" was previously given to the district court's departure decision, the Feeney Amendment of the PROTECT ACT "now requires *de novo* review in certain situations while continuing to require that appellate courts 'give due deference to the district court's application of the guidelines to the facts' in all other situations." *U.S. v. Alfaro* (9th Cir. 2003).

Section 5G1.1 provides that if Congress has specified a statutory minimum or maximum sentence for the applicable crime, then that minimum or maximum sentence authorized by Congress shall control over the guideline range. When a defendant provides substantial assistance, the government has the option of filing a motion pursuant to 18 U.S.C. § 3553(e) requesting the court depart below the statutory minimum. The Supreme Court has held that a government motion pursuant to 5K1.1 does not authorize a court to depart below the statutory minimum absent a specific government request pursuant to 18 U.S.C. § 3553(e). *Melendez v. U.S.* (S.Ct.1996).

In addition to providing the methodology for determining a sentence, the guidelines also provide procedural structure to the plea agreement and sentencing process. For example, the commentary to the guidelines provides that "[t]he Commission believes that use of a preponderance of the evidence standard is appropriate to meet due process requirements and policy concerns in resolving disputes regarding application of the guidelines to the facts of a case." (6A1.3, Commentary).

A substantial number of the appellate criminal decisions issued in the past few years have included arguments concerning the sentencing guidelines (e.g., different methods of determining "loss" in a fraud case). In examining these cases, it is evident that ambiguities in the guidelines have resulted in substantial litigation. Differing interpretations among the circuits have also complicated this area. In some instances, however, the Sentencing Commission has amended guidelines to clarify and

foreclose the continual litigation of these issues. For
example, a recent amendment provides a new
definition for the term "loss" that resolves circuit
disputes on how to compute a fraud loss.

The sentencing guidelines have been criticized by
many judges and defense attorneys. Complaints often
focus on the lack of flexibility given to judges under
the guidelines, as well as the complexity of the
process. In *U.S. v. Harrington* (D.C.Cir.1991),
Circuit Judge Harry T. Edwards stated in a
concurring opinion that "[W]e also have come to
understand that the Guidelines do not, by any
stretch of the imagination, ensure uniformity in
sentencing." Prosecutorial discretion in charging, the
plea bargaining process, and the characterizations
placed upon the defendant by the probation officer
are three ways that serve to circumvent the
uniformity.

§ 24.04 Constitutionality of the Guidelines

The federal sentencing guidelines were initially
met with many cases contesting their
constitutionality. Lower courts resolving these issues
ruled inconsistently with some finding the guidelines
valid and others holding them unconstitutional. In
1988 the Supreme Court accepted on certiorari the
case of *Mistretta v. U.S.*, to consider the
constitutionality of the guidelines as promulgated by
the United States Sentencing Commission. In
granting the petition for certiorari the Court noted
the " 'imperative public importance' of the issue" and
the "disarray among the Federal District Courts."

The *Mistretta* case, in upholding the guidelines,
resolved two key constitutional attacks on the

guidelines. The first argument questioned the propriety of delegating the promulgation of guidelines for every federal offense to an independent sentencing commission. The second argument questioned the constitutionality of the Act in light of the separation of powers doctrine.

Justice Blackmun, writing the opinion for the majority, found Congress' delegation of authority to the Sentencing Commission to be "sufficiently specific and detailed to meet constitutional requirements." Although the Court admitted that the Commission was given significant discretion, it noted that "[d]eveloping proportionate penalties for hundreds of different crimes by a virtually limitless array of offenders is precisely the sort of intricate, labor-intensive task for which delegation to an expert body is especially appropriate."

The Court also rejected Mistretta's claim of a violation of separation of powers. Examined by the Court was the effect of the Sentencing Commission being placed in the judicial branch, having federal judges serve on the Commission, and the giving of the power to appoint and remove members of the Commission to the President. The Court found the Act's placement of the Commission within the judicial branch justified "since substantive judgment in the field of sentencing has been and remains appropriate to the Judicial Branch, and the methodology of rulemaking has been and remains appropriate to that Branch."

The Court also validated the Act's placement of federal judges on the Sentencing Commission. The Court held that the judges were not serving pursuant to their authority as Article III judges, but rather in an administrative capacity resulting from their Presidential appointment. The Court stated that, "the Constitution, at least as a *per se* matter, does not forbid judges from wearing two hats; it merely forbids them from wearing both hats at the same time." The mixed nature of the Commission did not violate the Constitution, since the Sentencing "Commission is not a court and exercises no judicial power ... the Act does not vest Article III power in nonjudges or require Article III judges to share their power with nonjudges."

Mistretta also claimed that by having the President appoint and remove the members of the Commission, the Judicial Branch was being prevented from performing its constitutional functions. The Court found that the appointment power of the President would not corrupt the integrity of the Judiciary. Likewise the removal power, limited to good cause, would pose no risk of preventing "the Judicial branch from performing its constitutionally assigned function of fairly adjudicating cases and controversies."

Mistretta has not foreclosed defendants from questioning the constitutionality of the guidelines. In light of *Mistretta,* however, it is less common to see constitutional arguments centered on a violation of separation of powers. Many of the arguments are now premised upon alleged violations of a defendant's due process rights. For example, the Eleventh Circuit, in the case of *U.S. v. Hernandez* (11th Cir.1991), rejected defendant's claim that the guidelines violated her due process rights under the fifth amendment by granting to prosecutors, as opposed to judges, the ability to determine a sentence when they move or fail to move for departures under the guidelines.

§ 24.05 Criminal and Civil Fines

Statutory provisions set forth the factors a court should consider in imposing a fine. (18 U.S.C. § 3572) For example, a court should consider "the defendant's income, earning capacity, and financial resources," as well as the burden of the fine on the defendant and others associated with the defendant. 18 U.S.C. § 3571 specifies the maximum fines that can be imposed against individuals and organizations. For example, in determining an individual's maximum fine permitted upon conviction of a felony, one looks to not more than the greatest of the "amount specified in the law setting forth the offense," a fine based on gain or loss as computed under the statute, or an amount not to exceed $250,000.

Civil proceedings brought by the government, after completion of a criminal action, can raise issues of collateral estoppel when the issue being litigated in the civil proceeding has previously been litigated in the criminal action. Parallel civil and criminal actions by the government also raise questions of double jeopardy. In *U.S. v. Halper* (S.Ct.1989), the Supreme Court accepted for review a case involving a civil action brought by the government that was premised upon the same conduct upon which the defendant had been criminally punished. The Supreme Court in reviewing this matter held that, "under the Double Jeopardy Clause a defendant who already has been punished in a criminal prosecution may not be subjected to an additional civil sanction to the extent that the second sanction may not fairly be characterized as remedial, but only as a deterrent or retribution." The Court in *Halper* remanded the case to permit the government the opportunity to show that "the District Court's assessment of its injuries was erroneous."

In *U.S. v. Ursery* (S.Ct.1996), the Supreme Court held that civil forfeitures do not constitute "punishment" for purposes of the Double Jeopardy Clause without regard to whether the forfeiture is disproportionate to the harm suffered by the government. Civil forfeitures, the Court noted, serve a unique nonpunitive function of disgorgement. The fact that they may be limited by the Eighth Amendment prohibition against excessiveness does not mean that they also are so "punitive" as to constitute "punishment."

In 1997, the Supreme Court went even further and completely disavowed *Halper.* In *Hudson v. U.S.* (S.Ct. 1997) the "Government administratively imposed monetary penalties and occupational debarment on petitioners for violation of federal banking statutes, and later criminally indicted them, for essentially the same conduct" The Court stated "that the Double Jeopardy Clause of the Fifth Amendment is not a bar to the later criminal prosecution because the administrative proceedings were civil, not criminal."

§ 24.06 Sentencing Guidelines for Organizations

Federal sentencing guidelines for organizations became effective on November 1, 1991. These guidelines provide the rules applicable for computing fines against organizations. These rules are applicable only to organizations. Thus, individual agents of an organization that are convicted for criminal conduct, are sentenced under the general federal sentencing guidelines for individuals. Not all offenses are subject to the fines provisions of the organization guidelines. For example, environmental offenses are omitted.

An overview of the guidelines is provided in Part A. (8A1.2). Part B of the guidelines provides the sentencing requirements and options relating to restitution, remedial orders, and community service. For example, "community service may be ordered as a condition of probation where such community service is reasonably designed to repair the harm caused by the offense." (8B1.3).

Part C describes the considerations for determining a fine. When the organization operated for primarily a criminal purpose, or primarily by criminal means, the guidelines state that the fine should be sufficient to divest the organization of all its net assets. (8C1.1). Organizations that are not criminal in nature, that have committed offenses listed in the organization guidelines are subject to fines as computed under these rules. Inability to pay, however, can eliminate or reduce a fine. (8C2.2).

In computing the fine, one commences by taking the offense level as listed in the guidelines for individuals and adjusting that figure as designated in the applicable guideline for individuals (see § 24.03). Multiple counts use the combined offense level as designated in the individual guidelines. (8C2.3). The base fine is then calculated by taking the amount corresponding to the offense level on a table located in the organization guidelines. (8C2.4(d)). If, however, the pecuniary gain to the organization from the offense, or the "pecuniary loss from the offense caused by the organization, to the extent the loss was caused intentionally, knowingly, or recklessly," is greater, that figure becomes the base fine. If the calculation of the pecuniary gain or loss will unduly complicate the process, then that amount should not be used in computing the fine. Further, if special instructions exist in the individual guidelines that reflect consideration of organizational fines, that special instruction should be applied.

The organization's culpability score is next determined by starting with a level of five points and adding or subtracting points based upon actions that reflect upon the organization's culpability. The level of authority and size of the organization can increase the culpability score. Points are also added when the organization is involved in or tolerates criminal activity, has a history of criminal activity, violates a judicial order, or obstructs justice. In contrast, points are subtracted when the organization has an effective program to prevent and detect violations or self-reports, cooperates, or accepts responsibility for the criminal conduct. (8C2.5). These latter guidelines provide increased incentives for an organization to plead guilty and cooperate with the government.

The Commentary to 8A1.2 notes that "[a]n effective program to prevent and detect violations of law means a program that has been reasonably designed, implemented, and enforced so that it generally will be effective in preventing and detecting criminal conduct." A failure to prevent criminal conduct "by itself, does not mean that a program was not effective." The "hallmark" of an effective program is the exercise of "due diligence." The guidelines commentary provide seven steps that should be taken by an organization for "due diligence." (8A 1.2, Commentary, Application Note 3(k)). The "[e]ntry of a plea of guilty prior to the commencement of trial combined with truthful admission of involvement in the offense and related conduct ordinarily will constitute significant acceptance of responsibility.... unless outweighed by conduct of the organization that is inconsistent with such acceptance of responsibility." (8C2.5, Commentary, Application Note 13). Civil corporate law provides added incentives to the Board of Directors of a corporation for making sure that an effective program is in place. *In re Caremark International Inc. Derivative Litigation* (Ct. Chancery Del. 1996).

The ascertained culpability score corresponds to minimum and maximum multipliers found in a table in the organization guidelines. (8C2.6). To determine the applicable fine range, one multiplies the previously determined base fine by the minimum multiplier and the base fine by the maximum multiplier. This provides the minimum and maximum guideline range. The judge imposing the fine then has ten factors to consider in determining where within the range the actual assessed fine should be. These factors include, "the need for the sentence to reflect the seriousness of the offense, promote respect for the law, provide just punishment, afford adequate deterrence, and protect the public from further crimes of the organization." The judge should consider the vulnerability of the victim, as well as the collateral civil consequences of a conviction. In addition to the ten specified factors for consideration by the court in determining the fine within the range, the guidelines also permit the court to "consider the relative importance of any factor used to determine the range." (8C2.8).

The organization guidelines contain a disgorgement provision that instructs a court to add to the fine "any gain to the organization from the offense that has not and will not be paid as restitution or by way of other remedial measures." (8C2.9). As with the individual guidelines, the organization guidelines also provide for upward and downward departures. For example, upward departures may be warranted when there is a death or bodily injury, or foreseeable risk of death or bodily injury. (8C4.2). Other examples of instances that may warrant an upward departure are threats to the market, national security, or environment. Similarly, upward departures can be given if the mandatory program to prevent and detect violations of law was implemented in response to a court order. (8C4.10). Upon a motion of the government alleging substantial assistance to authorities, a court may depart downwards from the guidelines. (8C4.1).

The guidelines set forth situations in which probation is to be given, (8D1.1), and the applicable terms, (8D1.2), and conditions of the probation. (8D1.3). Recommended conditions of probation are also specified. (8D1.4). The guidelines also account for violations of conditions of probation, (8D1.5), special assessments statutorily placed on organizations, (8E1.1), forfeiture, (8E1.2), and assessment of costs. (8E1.3).

§ 24.07 Licenses and Program Exclusion

Professional licenses are usually issued by individual states. These jurisdictions often adopt rules for the acquisition and maintenance of the license. For example, in most states a lawyer must pass a bar examination and character and fitness review for admission into the bar. When the attorney later violates the provisions set forth in the ethical mandates of that state, the attorney is subjected to bar disciplinary action. This discipline can include punishments such as a reprimand, suspension, or disbarment.

Conviction of a felony offense usually has severe implications on a professional license. The American Bar Association Model Rules of Professional Conduct, explicitly state that it is professional misconduct for a lawyer to "commit a criminal act that reflects adversely on the lawyer's honesty, trustworthiness or fitness as a lawyer in other respects." (Rule 8.4 (b)). In the Comments to this Rule, it is noted that illegal conduct "such as offenses involving fraud and the offense of willful failure to file an income tax return," reflect adversely on one's fitness to practice law. Thus, white collar offenses committed by attorneys may subject the attorney to disciplinary action by the bar, court, or the state agency charged with the enforcement of the disciplinary rules.

Discipline for felony convictions is not limited to attorneys. Many states provide for disciplinary action in other professional codes. For example, in Georgia a doctor "convicted of a felony in state or any other state, ...," may be subject to discipline. According to the Georgia statute, conviction is not limited to a finding by a judge or jury of guilt or the defendant entering a guilty plea. Rather, it includes a plea of nolo contendere in a criminal proceeding. Ga.Code Ann. § 43–34–37 (1992).

Those practicing before the Securities Exchange Commission (SEC) have been disciplined, including temporary or permanent suspension to practice before the Commission, when they have violated a provision of federal securities law. In *Touche Ross & Co. v. Securities and Exchange Commission* (2d Cir.1979), the right of the SEC to conduct administrative proceedings against an accounting firm, for the purpose of determining whether the accountants should be censured or suspended from practicing before the Commission, was questioned. The administrative proceeding in the *Touche Ross* case was commenced to determine whether the accountants had "engaged in unethical, unprofessional or fraudulent conduct in their audits" of the financial statements of two companies. The accounting firm brought this action to obtain an injunction stopping the SEC's administrative proceeding against them. The District Court granted the SEC's motion dismissing the complaint.

In affirming the right of the SEC to proceed administratively, the Second Circuit in *Touche Ross* noted that rules permitting these actions had existed for over forty years and had been the basis for disciplinary actions against professionals such as accountants and attorneys. The court noted that "Rule 2(e) thus represents an attempt by the SEC essentially to protect the integrity of its processes. If incompetent or unethical accountants should be permitted to certify financial statements, the reliability of the disclosure process would be impaired." The court found that the accounting firm would be required to exhaust its administrative remedies before the Commission prior to bringing a civil action in court.

In addition to discipline relating to a license, or discipline with respect to a right to practice before an agency, criminality can exclude an individual or company from continuing to participate in a government program. This has had significant ramifications for defense contractors convicted for fraud. Government regulation "specifically permits an agency to debar a contractor if it has been convicted of, or is subject to a civil judgment for, *inter alia*, fraud in connection with obtaining a government contract, a violation of the antitrust laws, or bribery, or for '[a]ny other cause of so serious or compelling a nature that it affects the present responsibility of a Government contractor ...'"*Robinson v. Cheney* (D.C.Cir.1989).

Health care providers may suffer collateral consequences when they engage in criminal acts. Specifically there is the possibility of exclusion from Medicare and Medicaid programs. "In 1977, Congress enacted the Medicare–Medicaid Antifraud and Abuse Amendments requiring the Secretary to suspend any physician or 'other individual practitioner' convicted 'of a criminal offense related to such physician's or practitioner's involvement' in the Medicare and Medicaid programs." *Greene v. Sullivan* (E.D.Tenn.1990).

An attorney representing an individual charged with a white collar offense needs to be particularly aware of the collateral consequences to the individual. Considerations such as civil suits, license suspensions, program debarment, and benefit exclusions, may impact the course taken in the litigation.

INDEX

References are to Pages

425

CORRUPTION
See Public Corruption

CRIME FRAUD EXCEPTION
See Attorney–Client Privilege; Work Product Doctrine

CURRENCY REPORTING CRIMES

DEAD CORPORATIONS
See Corporate Criminal Liability

Substantial Assistance, 407-408

SHERMAN ACT
See Conspiracy; Corporate Criminal Liability

STAYING OF PROCEEDINGS
See Parallel Proceedings

STRICT LIABILITY
Corporate criminal liability, 25-16
Environmental crimes, 210

STRUCTURING TRANSACTIONS
See Bank Secrecy Act

SUBPOENA
See Administrative Agency Investigations; Grand Jury Investigations

SUMMONS ENFORCEMENT
See Administrative Agency Investigations

TAX OFFENSES
Generally, 166-181
Advice of counsel, 172-173
Badges of fraud, 175
Bank deposit method, 176-177
Bankruptcy, 198
Cash expenditures method, 176-177
Conspiracy, 167
Delivering a fraudulent return, 166
Department of Justice Guidelines, 168
Direct proof, 175-176
Disclosure of information, 167
Elements, 174, 177, 178
Evasion, 166, 174-175
Extortion, 167
Failure to collect tax, 166
Failure to file return, 166, 177-178
Failure to obey summons, 167